Is This Any Way to Run a Democratic Election?

To my son, Captain Jared Wayne, US Army

May you and your generation keep the flame of American democracy burning brightly for all of us.

FIFTH EDITION

Is This Any Way to Run a Democratic Election?

Stephen J. Wayne

Georgetown University

Los Angeles | London | New Delhi
Singapore | Washington DC

Los Angeles | London | New Delhi
Singapore | Washington DC

FOR INFORMATION:

CQ Press

An Imprint of SAGE Publications, Inc.

2455 Teller Road

Thousand Oaks, California 91320

E-mail: order@sagepub.com

SAGE Publications Ltd.

1 Oliver's Yard

55 City Road

London EC1Y 1SP

United Kingdom

SAGE Publications India Pvt. Ltd.

B 1/I 1 Mohan Cooperative Industrial Area

Mathura Road, New Delhi 110 044

India

SAGE Publications Asia-Pacific Pte. Ltd.

3 Church Street

#10-04 Samsung Hub

Singapore 049483

Printed in the United States of America

Library of Congress Cataloging-in-Publication Data

Wayne, Stephen J.

Is this any way to run a democratic election? / Stephen J. Wayne, Georgetown University. — Fifth edition.

pages cm.
Includes bibliographical references and index.

ISBN 978-1-4522-0565-6 (pbk. : alk. paper) —
ISBN 978-1-4833-0193-8 (web pdf)

1. Elections—United States. 2. Political campaigns—United States. I. Title.

JK1967.W38 2013
324.973—dc23   2013007620

This book is printed on acid-free paper.

Acquisitions Editor: Charisse Kiino

Editorial Assistant: Davia Grant

Production Editor: Stephanie Palermini

Copy Editor: Kate Macomber Stern

Typesetter: C&M Digitals (P) Ltd.

Proofreader: Joyce Li

Indexer: Sylvia Coates

Cover Designer: Auburn Associates Inc.

Marketing Manager: Erica DeLuca

Permissions Editor: Jennifer Barron

Certified Chain of Custody
Promoting Sustainable Forestry
www.sfiprogram.org
SFI-01268

SFI label applies to text stock

13 14 15 16 17 10 9 8 7 6 5 4 3 2 1

CONTENTS

FIGURES, TABLES, AND BOXES

Figures

Tables

Boxes

We are a nation of critics, self-critics. As we laud our democratic system, we also complain about it. The election process in particular has been the source of much lament and critical commentary, especially in the aftermath of the controversial presidential election of 2000.

WHAT'S WRONG WITH AMERICAN ELECTORAL POLITICS?

A lot, say its critics. Their complaints are legion. The election cycle is too long, too complex, and too costly. The system is controlled by and for the few, the special interests, not the public's interest. Election laws are biased in favor of those who enacted them—the major parties and their candidates—and sometimes they have been implemented in a partisan and discriminatory manner. Money drives the process, and wealthy contributors exercise disproportionate influence over the candidates, parties, and campaigns, and on what follows from this election activity—public policy making. The news media are more interested in reporting who's ahead and their strategies for winning than in discussing substantive policy issues and their consequences for the country. Politicians are not to be trusted; they will say and do almost anything to get elected, and once elected, they are beholden to their large contributors and the special-interest groups who aided their campaigns. Moreover, incumbents have stacked the deck in favor of their own renomination and reelection, thereby undercutting two of the basic goals of a democratic electoral process—to keep public officials responsive to the people and to hold them accountable for their policy decisions and actions.

And if these allegations were not enough, there is the charge that election returns today do not result in winners who are compatible with one another, who are willing to compromise on the major policy issues, and who put the public's interest ahead of their own political and private interests. Nor does the outcome of the vote easily translate into a governing agenda and a majority coalition for achieving it, much less a functional government. All of these charges have produced negative perceptions of the electoral process today and undoubtedly have contributed to public cynicism, apathy, and mistrust of politicians and the politics in which they engage. Something is very wrong with American electoral politics, or so its critics allege.

Are these charges correct? Is the current way the best way to run a democratic election? Have we drifted from the ideals and goals of the American political tradition? If so, how and when did we do so, and what, if anything, can be done about it? If not, why are there so many persistent complaints, and why do so many people not vote?

Concerned citizens should be debating these issues. This book is intended to help them do so. My aim is to explore critical and controversial issues that confront our political system today, and to do so in a reader-friendly way. *Is This Any Way to Run a Democratic Election?* examines American democracy in theory and practice, notes where and why practices deviate from theory, and then considers reforms to close the gap.

THE ORGANIZATION AND FEATURES OF THE BOOK

The book's first chapter discusses democratic theory in general and the democratic electoral process in particular. The next five chapters (chapters 2–6) examine key aspects of electoral politics: suffrage and turnout, representation, money, the news media, and political parties. Each of these aspects shapes an election, affects its outcome, and has consequences for governing. From the environment in which elections occur, the last three chapters (chapters 7–9) turn to the process itself: the nomination and general election, and their collective and individual impact on governing.

Each chapter of the book includes features intended to pique a reader's interest in electoral issues and foster critical thinking and participation. Every chapter begins with "Did you know that . . . ," an opening feature that presents interesting and sometimes disturbing facts about democratic election practices, processes, and outcomes that may not be widely known. After a discussion of the electoral dilemmas and ways to overcome them, each chapter concludes with a short summary, followed by a critical thinking section, "Now It's Your Turn." Included in this section are Discussion Questions, Topics for Debate, research-oriented Exercises that encourage use of the Internet, and a listing of Internet Resources and Selected Readings.

WHAT'S NEW ABOUT THE FIFTH EDITION?

The election of 2012 marked the reelection of American's first African American president but also the continuation of divided government. It revealed voting patterns evident in previous elections but also significant demographic changes within the electorate. Turnout was high, particularly among minority voters, to which a very effective get-out-the-vote campaign contributed. The campaign also reaffirmed the advantage of incumbency, not only for the president but for most members of Congress.

Only one party had a competitive nomination process, a process that lasted for about 8 months, from the summer of 2011 until early April 2012. The general election campaign began after that and continued until election day, the first Tuesday following the first Monday in November. In 2012, more people made more contributions to the candidates and their parties than ever before.

More money was raised and spent, about $6 billion on the federal elections, although money was not the principal factor in determining the outcome of most of the contests.

The means by which the candidates communicated their campaigns to voters continued to change, with the Internet becoming an even more important source of election news and communications; more information was more accessible to more people, but there is little evidence that voters became more knowledgeable as a result. Mass marketing of political advertising continued, but personal messaging and microtargeting increased and seemed to be more effective in turning out less likely voters. The election outcome reflected the country's deep partisan divide, with a Republican majority in the House of Representatives and a Democratic majority in the Senate. It also portrayed the citizenry's increasing multiculturalism. Women, racial and ethnic minorities, and young voters provided a substantial portion of the Democratic vote, creating a dilemma for the Republicans—how to enlarge their base and appeal to the groups who voted Democratic without alienating their conservative supporters. For the Democrats the problem continues to be how to maintain unity with such a diverse electoral coalition. And for everyone, the problem is governance, addressing the long-term, divisive economic and social issues in a highly polarized political environment.

Are American elections democratic? Do they contribute to the governing problem? The fifth edition reexamines these questions in the light of recent elections and their implications for governance. *Is this any way to run a democratic election?*—you decide.

ACKNOWLEDGMENTS

I would like to thank the people who worked on this edition at CQ Press: Charisse Kiino, publisher, and Davia Grant, editorial assistant. I would also like to thank Kate Macomber Stern for her careful, comprehensive, and literary copyediting. Kate certainly improved the readability of this book. The reviewers of the fourth edition, Mandi Bailey, Christina Greer, Todd Schaefer, and James Sheffield, made thoughtful and helpful comments, and I thank them as well for all their help. I benefited immensely from these and other suggestions I received. I trust this edition of the book did as well.

Stephen J. Wayne
April 2013

chapter 1

Democratic Elections
What's the Problem?

Did you know that . . .

- a majority of the voting-age population does not vote in most elections in the United States?
- Bill Clinton and George W. Bush, when first elected president, each received the votes of only about one quarter of those eligible to vote; in his sizable electoral victory, Barack Obama received the votes of 33 percent of those eligible and 30 percent of voting-age adults in 2008 and 29.6 percent and 27 percent, respectively, in 2012?
- most members of Congress have no effective opposition in running for renomination, and some have no opponents in the general election?
- since 1964, more than 90 percent of members of the House of Representatives and 80 percent of the Senate have been reelected?
- no third-party presidential candidate has received any electoral votes since 1972?
- there were more ballots discarded or undercounted in New York City and Chicago in the 2000 election than there were disputed ballots in the controversial Florida presidential vote that year?
- about $5 billion was spent on federal elections in the 2007–2008 election cycle and more than $6 billion in 2011–2012?
- information about how elections are conducted in the United States is so fragmentary that the government does not know how many people are turned away at the polls, how long people stand in lines waiting to vote, how many ballots are voided or simply not counted, and how many voting machines malfunction?
- it took more than seven months in 2008 for officials and the courts to determine the winner of the election in Minnesota for a seat in the U.S. Senate?
- the average length of time that presidential candidates appeared on the evening news shows of the major broadcast networks in the last three elections was about seven seconds?
- candidate advertising in recent federal elections has been much more negative than postive?

- more than \$200 million was spent on advertising during the 2008 Democratic and Republican nomination processes, with the Democrats spending more than twice as much. In 2012, the Romney campaign was the big Republican spender, spending more than his opponents combined?
- only about one-third of the people can name the member of Congress who represents them during nonelectoral periods?

Is this any way to run a democratic election?

These facts suggest that something is terribly wrong with our electoral process. They raise serious questions about how democratic the American political system really is. They also point to the major problems within that system: low voter turnout; fraudulent, error-prone, and discriminatory voting practices; uneven and inadequate administration of elections by state and local officials; high costs and unequal resources for candidates running for office; short, compartmentalized, and negative media coverage; and contradictory, often inconclusive results. Let's take a look at some examples of these problems.

CONTEMPORARY ELECTION ISSUES

Low Voter Turnout

People fight for the right to vote when they don't have it. Americans certainly did. In 1776, British colonists, protesting taxation without representation in Parliament, declared their independence with a rhetorical flourish that underscored the people's right to alter or abolish a government that wasn't fulfilling the purpose for which it was intended.

Now, more than two centuries later, in a country that prides itself on its long and successful political tradition and on its fundamental democratic values, a majority of the electorate does not vote on a regular basis. Why do so few people vote? Does it have to do with how candidates run for office, how and when elections are conducted, or whether the public perceives that elections really matter—whether they make a difference in people's lives or in the country's future?

Congress considers low turnout to be a problem, a sign that the democracy is not as vigorous as it could or should be. During the last several decades, it has enacted legislation to encourage more people to vote. At the end of the 1970s, an amendment to the Federal Election Campaign Act (FECA) was passed to permit political parties to raise and spend unlimited amounts of money on building their grassroots base and getting out the vote, yet turnout continued to decline.

During the 1980s, amendments were added to the act to broaden its applicability and facilitate minority participation in the electoral process, yet the turnout of most population groups continued to decline.

In 1993 a "motor voter" bill, designed to make it easier for people in all fifty states to register to vote, was enacted, yet the percentage of the adult population reporting that it registered decreased in the years following the passage of the law.

In 2002, Congress enacted the Help America Vote Act, which provides money to states to computerize their voter registration lists, buy more accurate voting machines, and allows for provisional voting for people who claim that they registered but whose names do not appear on the lists of eligible voters in the precinct in which they live and vote. Millions of new voters have been registered since the enactment of the 2002 legislation. In 2002, 74.7 percent of the voting-age population was registered to vote; by 2010, that figure had climbed to 78.7 percent, 186.9 million voters.[1] As the percentages indicate, the increase in new voters has exceeded the growth of the voting-age population.

Turnout has been increasing among the voting-age population as well, although not as rapidly as voter registration, according to turnout expert Michael McDonald, a political science professor at George Mason University. Table 1 notes the figures since the beginning of the twenty-first century.

The bad news is that still more than four out of ten people eligible to vote do not do so in presidential elections and six out of ten in the midterm elections.[2]

The issue of nonvoting raises serious questions about the vibrancy of America's civic culture and the health of its democratic political institutions.

Is this a product of flawed democracy

TABLE 1.1   **Turnout in Federal Elections in the Twenty-First Century (Based on the Voting-Age Population)**

Year	Percent of Voting-Age Population (VAP)
2000	50.0
2002	33.3
2004	55.4
2006	37.1
2008	56.9
2010	37.8
2012	53.6

Source: Michael McDonald, "United States Elections Project: Voter Turnout." http://elections.gmu.edu/Turnout_2012G.htm

underrepresentation

With so many people not voting, do elections reflect the judgment of all the people or of a small and unrepresentative proportion of them? Similarly, to whom are elected officials more responsive—the entire population or the people who elected them? Do elections with low participation rates still provide an agenda for government and legitimacy for its actions? If they do not, then what does?

Fraudulent, Error-Prone, and Discriminatory Voting Practices

The Florida voting controversy in the 2000 election in which the official results were disputed highlighted many of the voting problems that have plagued the U.S. electoral system since its creation. The Constitution charges the states with the conduct of federal elections. The states set most of the rules for registration, ballot access, and absentee voting; they determine the period during which voting occurs, the procedures for exercising a vote, and the manner in which votes are to be tabulated and reported. Local electoral districts within the states often designate the polling places, run the election, and provide the ballots or machines for voting. As a consequence of the decentralization of election administration, there is considerable variation in voting procedures among the states and even within them.

Political parties indirectly affect the vote by the influence they exert on elected and appointed state officials. In fact, for most of the nation's first one hundred years, the major parties actually ran the elections. They rallied their supporters, got them to the polls, and made sure they voted "correctly" by designing and distributing color-coded ballots on which only the names of their candidates appeared. They also had poll watchers observing how people voted.

Allegations of fraudulent practices, including voting by noncitizens and the deceased, casting multiple ballots in the same election, and under- and over-counting of the votes were rampant. The adoption of the secret ballot and the administration of elections by state officials were responses to these unfair, underhanded, and undemocratic election practices. The development of machines to tabulate the vote was another. But problems persisted because most state legislatures still enacted election laws and drafted legislative districts to benefit those in power.

Registration and residence requirements have been used to limit the size of the electorate. Geographic representation in one of the two legislative bodies (prior to the 1960s) gave rural areas a disproportionate advantage. In some states, the laws were administered in a discriminatory and haphazard fashion, making it more difficult for some people, particularly minorities, to vote.

Not until the 1960s did the Supreme Court and Congress address some of these issues.[3] The Court ruled that population and population alone had to be the criterion by which representation was determined: one person–one vote. The Voting Rights Act of 1965 was intended to end discriminatory practices

quite late in our history

and effectively extend suffrage to all eligible citizens. Registration requirements were eased, voting hours were extended, absentee voting opportunities were expanded, and for a time, money for party-building activities was exempted from federal contribution limits.

These laws and judicial decisions went a long way toward extending the franchise, encouraging turnout, and ending some of the practices which undercut the democratic character of U.S. elections. But they did not eliminate all of those practices. Nor did they improve the actual conduct of elections. After the 2000 election controversy in Florida, the U.S. Commission on Civil Rights issued a report concluding that African Americans in that state were much more likely than white voters to be turned away from the polls.[4] Researchers at the Massachusetts Institute of Technology (MIT) and the California Institute of Technology (CalTech) deduced that between four million and six million votes for president in the 2000 election were not counted, some because of registration foul-ups, some because of voter confusion and error, and some because of faulty equipment.[5] In close elections, these undercounted votes could have made a difference and even changed the final outcome.

Problems remain today. Registration foul-ups, inadequate parking, long lines to vote, insufficient numbers of poll workers, machine and computer malfunctions, and poor ballot designs continue to hamper the act of voting. Can an election be considered democratic if citizens have to overcome these hurdles in order to vote? Can the results be regarded as legitimate if the votes of a sizable proportion of a state's population, enough to have changed the outcome of the election, are not correctly counted? Can the election be said to represent the will of the people if the ballots are confusing to many voters, and if some of the votes were not properly cast and thus voided? A lot of people do not think so. Six months after the Supreme Court's decision that effectively determined George W. Bush's victory in Florida and thus in the Electoral College, 26 percent of the American people indicated that they still did not regard him as the legitimate president.[6]

High Costs and Unequal Resources

Campaign finance is another issue and has been one for the last four decades. The federal election campaign finance system has broken down. From 1992 through 2002, both major parties used a loophole in the law to solicit large contributions from wealthy donors and spent hundreds of millions of dollars on behalf of their candidates for federal office.

The Bipartisan Campaign Reform Act (BCRA), enacted in 2002, was designed to end this practice, but it has not done so. Although the act prohibits national parties from accepting contributions that exceed federal limits, it has not stopped their supporters from creating nonparty groups that solicit and spend contributions not subject to the federal limits. The Supreme Court upheld these practices in its *Citizens United* decision.[7] The Court ruled that corporations and, by implication, labor unions could spend unlimited amounts of money to advocate their interests in political campaigns. What followed this decision was the creation of Super PACs, most with patriotic and democratic-sounding names, that provided an organizational mechanism by which sizable contributions could be made and spent on political activities that furthered the interests of certain groups and individuals and the candidates who supported them.[8] In the 2011–2012 election cycle, Super PACs reported independent expenditures of over $631 million while other nonparty groups spent an additional $400 million, amounts well in excess of what these groups spent in previous elections.[9]

In addition to these supplementary campaigns, each party has used its access to and the facilities of its officeholders as inducements and rewards for obtaining large donations, the maximum amount allowed by law. Private telephone numbers of cabinet secretaries and congressional committee heads have been made available to top contributors. As president, Bill Clinton held numerous coffee hours in the White House to encourage people to give money to the Democratic Party. He rewarded those who gave the most with trips on Air Force One, trade missions with the commerce secretary, and sleepovers in the Lincoln bedroom. Not to be outdone by his Democratic predecessors, George W. Bush's vice president, Dick Cheney, lavishly entertained the most generous GOP contributors at a gala at his official residence in April 2001. Although the practice of using government facilities finally ended during the George W. Bush administration, elected officials still solicit funds and reward contributors with access, appointments, and social invitations, practices that are not consistent with the operation of democratic government.

Even without the illegal solicitations and legal circumvention of the campaign finance legislation, the amount of money required to mount an effective campaign for federal office has become astronomical, a consequence in large part of mass media advertising. Moreover, the advertising itself has distorted rather than enhanced political debate.

Is too much money being raised for and spent on election campaigns? Do those who contribute represent a cross section of Americans or do they overrepresent the most prosperous individuals and groups in society? What do contributors, especially those who give the maximum amount to a candidate, get for their money? The answer is access, influence, political appointments, and frequently the policy outcomes they desire; at least that is what the public believes.

The resources issue also affects how elections are conducted. The failure of states to allocate sufficient funds for election administration can affect the accuracy of their registration lists, accessibility of voting places, wait time at the polls, difficulty in completing ballots, and slower and less reliable tabulation of the results, all of which influences turnout and can affect the outcome of elections.

Compartmentalized and Negative Media Coverage

Closely related to the issue of money is that of news coverage. For better or worse, the mass media have become the principal vehicle through which candidates for national office communicate to voters. Political parties have become less effective intermediaries than they used to be. Reliance on the news media would not be so bad if the goals of the media were similar to those of the parties, candidates, and country, but they are not.

Although the news media are not oblivious to the need to educate the public, they also are interested in making money—the more, the better. Profit from advertising is based on the size of the audience. To enhance the size, many news media outlets present the news that they believe would be most interesting to the most people most of the time. In campaigns, the most newsworthy items tend to be the dramatic ones—the horse race, with all its color and drama; the unexpected occurrences; the verbal and tactical mistakes; and the confrontations as well as the human dimensions of a candidate's personal character and family. These subjects engage readers, viewers, and listeners but do not necessarily educate, energize, or motivate them to participate in campaigns and vote. In fact, press compartmentalization, negativism, and spin are often blamed for low turnout and for the public's cynical attitude toward candidates, parties, and the political system.[10] The multiplication of news sources, the speed of communications, and the proliferation of niche journalism also affect the amount of information to which the public has access, its accuracy, and its relevancy for campaigns and governance.

How to square the interests of largely private media with the needs of an informed and involved electorate is no easy task, nor one that Congress wishes to tackle. Not only must First Amendment protections for the press be considered, but the desires of the public for the news it wants, not necessarily the news it needs, also must be weighed in the balance.

Contradictory, Often Inconclusive Results

Another problem, less obvious but equally dangerous for a democratic political system, is that elections may not contribute to governing but actually make it more difficult. Candidates make promises, political parties present platforms, and groups promote issues. But in a heterogeneous society, policy priorities and issue stands are likely to be diverse and even inconsistent with one another. Elections in the United States reflect this diversity far better than they mirror a popular consensus. They regularly produce mixed and incompatible results with unclear meanings and undefined mandates. Parties often share power, making the institutional divisions that much greater and more difficult to overcome. In an age of political polarization, reinforced by ideology, these divisions have become more pronounced, political rhetoric has become more strident, civility among elected officials has declined, and compromises on major policy issues have been made much more difficult.

Each of these problems—turnout, voting, money, and governing—points to shortcomings in the democratic electoral process in the United States, gaps between theory and practice. One goal of this book is to examine those gaps; another is to discuss ways they could be narrowed or, perhaps, eliminated. Finally, the book aims to stimulate thinking about democracy in general and democratic elections in particular.

To answer the central question—Is this any way to run a democratic election?—this chapter next examines the nature of democracy and some of the ways in which a democratic political system may be structured. The discussion then turns to the role of elections in a democracy and the criteria that elections must meet to be considered democratic. Finally, the chapter concludes with a look at the inevitable tensions within a democratic electoral system between political liberty and citizen equality, between majority rule and minority rights, and between a free press and an informed electorate.

THE NATURE OF DEMOCRACY

A **democracy** is, simply put, a government of the people; it connotes sovereignty. Initially used in ancient Greece, where such a system was first practiced, the term itself comes from the Greek words *demos,* meaning "people," and *kratos,* meaning "rule." In a democracy, the people rule.[11]

But which people? Everyone? Everyone who is a citizen? Every citizen older than eighteen years of age? Every eighteen-year-old citizen who is literate and mentally competent? Every eighteen-year-old, literate, mentally competent citizen who has knowledge of the issues and can apply that knowledge to make an intelligent judgment? The list of qualifications could go on and on. Naturally, an informed electorate is desirable, but the more people excluded because they lack certain characteristics, qualifications, or credentials the less likely the electorate will reflect the general population. So can't make standards

And how do the people rule? By themselves? By selecting others and holding them accountable? By agreeing to a set of rules and procedures by which some are selected to perform certain public tasks, such as teaching school, maintaining law and order, or protecting the country's security? too high

There is no single right answer to these questions. There are many types of democracies, distinguished by *who* and *how:* by who makes the decisions and by how power is distributed.[12]

Who Makes Public Policy Decisions?
on a bigger scale this can get crazy

When the people themselves make public policy decisions, the democracy is said to be a **direct democracy.** A New England town meeting in which all residents participate on matters of local interest, such as where to build a new town hall or whether to recycle disposable waste, is an example of direct democracy at work. A state ballot initiative on which voters indicate their preferences on a range of issues, such as legalized gambling, abortion, same-sex marriage, proof of legal status for noncitizens, or benefits for illegal immigrants or new residents, is another example of direct democracy. When George W. Bush, as a managing partner of the Texas Rangers, helped convince voters of Arlington, Texas, to support a special tax to pay for two-thirds of the cost of a new baseball stadium, he was engaging in direct democracy, as were residents of Colorado and Washington in 2012 when they voted to decriminalize the use of marijuana. In a direct democracy there is true collective decision making. Obviously, in a country as large and diverse as the United States, such a system in which all citizens had the opportunity to vote on most major policy issues would be impractical and undesirable for the nation as a whole.[13] There would be too many people with limited information and understanding of the issues participating in too many public policy decisions. As a consequence, most democracies are by necessity representative democracies, in which people choose others to represent them in government, to formulate and implement public policy in a deliberative manner, and sometimes even to adjudicate it in accordance with a country's constitution and laws.[14]

[handwritten margin notes: "chaotic" ; "implying some are better suited/informed to lead"]

A basic goal of representative government is to be responsive to the needs and interests of the people who elected that government. How can these needs and interests be identified? One way is through elections. Although elections aren't the only means by which public views find expression and can influence public policy—other ways include public opinion polls, focus groups, direct correspondence, civic initiatives, and public advocacy campaigns—elections are the most decisive and popular method for doing so. They also tend to be the fairest way in which public choice can be exercised That's why elections are such a critical component of a democratic political system. They are a mechanism through which the citizenry expresses its desires and by which it can evaluate the qualifications of candidates for office and the performance of those in office who seek reelection. Elections link government to the governed.

How Is Power Distributed?

Another way to categorize democracies is according to how they distribute power. In a **popular, or plebiscitary, democracy,** the people exercise considerable influence over the selection of government officials and the policies they pursue. Such a system provides opportunities for the populace to initiate policy issues and vote on them directly as well as to elect candidates and, if necessary, to remove them from office. Ballot access is easy, there are few impediments to voting, and the people have the last word.

In a **pluralistic democracy,** a wide variety of groups—from political parties to nonparty groups with economic interests (such as business, labor, and the professions) to those motivated by social and political (ideological and issue-oriented) beliefs—compete for influence. They do so in accordance with their own interests and beliefs, using their own resources to gain and maintain public support. James Madison argued in *The Federalist,* No. 10, that such factions in society were inevitable and that one of the merits of the Constitution that was being debated for ratification was that it made it difficult for any one faction to dominate the government.[15]

A third model is an **elitist democracy,** in which power is concentrated in fewer hands than in a pluralistic system. There is more hierarchy, and more discretion is exercised by those in power. However, to maintain its democratic character, the system requires that there be competition between elites in elections and in governing. Popular control is maintained through an election process in which elites in power are judged retrospectively by their past performance and prospectively by the policy promises they make and the leadership images they create.

In all three systems, government officials remain accountable to those who elected them. Whatever the form of democratic government, it rests directly or indirectly on popular consent. Elections anchor government to its popular base. Without elections, a democratic political system cannot exist.

ELECTIONS AND DEMOCRACY

Elections tie citizens to their government. They provide a mechanism by which the people can choose those government officials—legislators, top executives, and, in some cases, judges—who make, implement, and adjudicate public policy. Elections are also a means by which the public can hold these officials accountable for their actions and keep them responsive to the public's needs, interests, and desires.

To make decisions on who makes public policy and to evaluate how well they do so, voters need information about the beliefs, positions, and proposals of the candidates and their parties. The mass media are a conduit for such information. Without a free press reporting the election news, the electorate would either have to gather and analyze its own information or be dependent on those with a vested interest in doing so—candidates, parties, and interest groups. Naturally, those with an interest in the election outcome would be inclined to release information that puts them and their interests in the best possible light. The public needs alternative sources which are credible and objective; diverse and independent news media are most likely to meet such informational goals, but a government-controlled press or one that is influenced by a small group of individuals or corporations is not.

In choosing the people who will run the government, elections provide direction to that government. They establish the agenda—the promises and policy positions of the winners—which guides public officials after the election, and they help build coalitions that facilitate governing.

Elections also confer legitimacy on government and what it does. By giving citizens an opportunity to select public officials and influence their policy agendas, elections contribute to the ongoing support for the policy decisions and administrative actions that follow. Whether people agree with a particular

=/TRUST

policy or not, they are more likely to accept it as valid and lawful if they perceive that those who made it were selected in a fair and honest way and make their decisions according to an established set of rules and procedures. They also will be more likely to accept the policy if they know that they will have other opportunities down the road to express their opinions, participate in a political campaign, and vote for the candidates of their choice. Similarly, people will respect and abide by the decisions of elected officials, even approving their performance in office when they do not like them personally, as long as they consider their election to be legitimate. Take President Bill Clinton, for example. His job approval exceeded his personal favorability throughout his second term, and especially after his affair with White House intern Monica Lewinsky became public.[16]

Criteria for Democratic Elections

For elections to be consistent with the basic tenets of a democratic political system, they must be "free, fair, and frequent."[17] The principle of inclusiveness should apply. Adult citizens must be eligible to vote, have the opportunity to do so, and must be able to exercise their right freely without fear or coercion.[18] The votes must be weighted equally in determining the winner. The results of the election must be accepted as official and binding for a limited period of time, after which another election must occur. Without the guarantee of a future election, it would be difficult to hold those in office accountable for their actions.

Let's explore these essential criteria: political equality, universal suffrage, meaningful choice, and the free flow of information about the candidates, issues, and their parties.[19] **Political equality** is essential. It is a basic building block for a democracy. There can be no classes or ranks no individuals or groups whose positions elevate them and their votes to a higher status. As Thomas Jefferson put it in the Declaration of Independence, "All men are created equal."[20] If everyone is equal, then all should have the opportunity to exercise an equal voice in the running of the political system. At the very least, this means that the principle of one person–one vote must apply to all elections unless otherwise specified by the Constitution. It also means that all votes count equally, that no individual, group, region, or jurisdiction should gain extra representation or exercise extra influence. Translated into election terminology, equality requires **universal suffrage,** the right of adult citizens to be able to vote.

one man one vote essential

Unless all adult citizens have an opportunity to participate in the electoral process, the election results cannot be said to reflect the views of the entire country. The exclusion of any group of citizens because of any characteristics other than those directly related to their capacity to exercise an informed and intelligent vote (such as having sufficient mental capacity to make an intelligent voting decision) naturally weakens the representative nature of the system. The more people excluded, for whatever reason, the less the government can be said to rest on the consent of the governed.

less representation

The right to vote is considered a civic responsibility. There are a few democracies that require its citizens to perform this responsibility or suffer a penalty, such as a fine, if they do not. Most democracies, however, do not require voting. They operate on the principle that people should have the right not to vote, if they so desire, if they do not like the choices they have, do not care who wins, or do not believe the outcome of the election will not affect them in any meaningful way. Then, there are those who forget to vote or are unable to do so for reasons of health, work, travel, or family obligations.[21] The bottom line, however, is that citizens must have the right and opportunity to vote and must be able to do so freely.

They must also have a **meaningful choice.** Contestation is important. If there were only one candidate for an office or if all the candidates had equal qualifications and voiced essentially the same views, then there would be grounds for claiming that the voters did not have a meaningful choice.

To choose is to select from among diverse alternatives, but how diverse should they be? A choice among candidates who differ widely in their beliefs, particularly if the views of some of them are extreme, may amount to no real choice at all for most people. If the major parties were to agree on the same candidate and the only other candidate were unknown to most voters, the choice for most voters would not be meaningful. In other words, the choices should lie within the broad parameters of public acceptability, yet be distinctive enough for voters to distinguish between candidates and assess them on the basis of their own values, attitudes, and opinions.

Related to making a meaningful choice is the **free flow of information and ideas.** At the very least, there should be alternative sources of information, not just from the candidates, the parties, the government, or a dominant group that controls the news media. Unless there is ample information and discussion within the public arena, people will have difficulty understanding the issues, much less determining which candidates are most qualified and merit support.

A free press that provides this information is essential. Few, if any, subjects, issues, or questions should be off limits. Few, if any, arguments should be precluded, no matter how unpopular they may be. That is why the allegation of a candidate being unpatriotic, if that candidate expresses opposition to government policy, undercuts the very fabric of a democratic electoral process. The objective must be the creation of an environment in which voters can make informed judgments based on an enlightened understanding of the issues.[22] That objective can only be accomplished in a society in which free and broad expression is encouraged and protected.

Democratic Electoral Systems

The number of people elected, the way winners are determined, and the size and shape of electoral districts may vary within the country as well as among countries. In the United States, the United Kingdom, and some other democratic nations, public officials are elected on the basis of **plurality rule in single-member districts.** Simply put, this means that the candidate who receives the most votes for a particular office within an electoral district wins. Unless rules specify otherwise, the winner need not receive a majority of the vote; a simple plurality is usually sufficient. If there is a majority requirement, however, and no candidate receives more than half the votes in the initial balloting, there is usually a runoff election between the top two vote getters in the first round of voting.[23]

The U.S. Supreme Court has ruled that all legislative districts must be equal in population to ensure that the one person–one vote principle prevails. The exceptions are the Senate, in which each state, regardless of its population, has two senators, and the Electoral College, in which each state is entitled to electors equal in number to its congressional delegation.[24]

The main advantage of a plurality voting system is that it is simple and direct. The winner is easily and usually quickly determined, and the elected representative is accountable to the entire district. Responsibility, in other words, can be pinpointed.

The principal disadvantage of such a voting system is that those in the minority are less likely to be represented by a candidate of their choice. Their views and interests may not be adequately considered when public policy decisions are made. Moreover, plurality voting tends to enlarge the advantage of the majority if that majority is equally dispersed across the entire electoral area.[25] What happens is that those in the majority tend to vote for candidates who have similar demographic and attitudinal characteristics. Overcoming this voting behavior requires that minorities constitute a large proportion of the voters within the electoral district, at least 40 percent according to David Epstein and Sharyn O'Halloran.[26]

To improve minority representation in Congress, the U.S. Department of Justice, citing the 1982 Voting Rights Act and several Supreme Court decisions, pressured states to create legislative districts in which minority groups, such as African Americans and Hispanics, constitute a majority of the voters. However, the Supreme Court subsequently declared that race could not be the *primary* factor for determining the boundaries of these districts, once again putting minority groups at a disadvantage in the U.S. system of plurality voting in single-member districts.

There is another way, however, to achieve broader representation: Institute a system of **proportional voting,** in which the winners are determined in proportion to the vote that they or their party receives. In some democratic countries, such as Canada and Israel, parties run slates of candidates in districts. Similarly, in the presidential nomination process in the United States, there may be proportional voting. Democratic Party rules have required it throughout the nomination period since 1972; beginning in 2012, Republican Party rules prescribe it for all contests held before April 1st of the year of the election and permit it after that in accordance with state law.

The principal advantage of proportional voting is that it provides a fairer and more accurate representation of minorities in the government. A disadvantage is that majoritarian sentiment is more difficult to discern. Such sentiment, often referred to as political or policy consensus, must be constructed after the election by those who have been elected rather than by the electorate in the votes they have cast.

Proportional voting also increases the likelihood of a multiparty government, in which coalitions among competing parties may be necessary to achieve an operating majority. Multiparty coalitions, however, are apt to be more fragile and less able to agree on public policy than a government controlled by a single party. Moreover, it is more difficult to assign credit or blame for what the government does in the case of a multiparty coalition than with a single party.

In a plurality system, coalition building occurs primarily within the major parties, not between them. Each of the parties tries to reach a broad cross section of the electorate. In doing so, they have to balance diverse and often conflicting interests. Thus, the major parties in a plurality system are apt to be more heterogeneous and, conversely, in a proportional voting system, more homogeneous.

As the plurality-proportional voting dichotomy suggests, election procedures and rules are not neutral. They benefit some at the expense of others. These clashes of interests create ongoing tensions within a democratic electoral process. They are what politics is all about, temporarily resolving tension on an issue by issue basis.

TENSIONS WITHIN A DEMOCRATIC ELECTORAL SYSTEM

The problem of obtaining a fair election outcome underlies the natural tensions in a democratic political system between political liberty and equality, between majority rule and minority rights, and between a free press and an informed electorate.

Liberty versus Equality

If a democracy is based on the consent of the governed, then the ability to give that consent and, if need be, to take it away is essential. That's why political liberty is so important. It is the freedom to decide for oneself and act on the basis of that decision. Take that freedom away, and a democratic political system cannot exist.

In the electoral process, liberty requires the right to vote as one chooses, not to vote if one chooses, and in either case, to make the voting decision freely and without duress. It is the right to exercise personal choice within the framework of the political system. Accessible voting places, guidance in voting, and casting a secret ballot help protect that right.

Freedom to provide financial and other support to the candidate of one's choice, however, can undermine the equity principle. A conflict is created when certain people have more resources at their disposal than others to use in campaigns. Should individuals and groups be free to spend as much money as they want to promote their ideas, beliefs, and candidates, or should spending be limited to ensure that every citizen has a more equal opportunity to affect the outcome of the vote?

Proponents of unlimited expenditures cite the constitutional protection of free speech and the right of people to spend their money as they see fit. Opponents argue that elected officials are more likely to be responsive to large donors and big spenders than to average citizens. Moreover, they claim that the advantage of the wealthy extends past the election to governing and to the public policy that government makes.[27]

A related issue pertains to participation itself, to personally getting involved. For a variety of reasons, those with a higher income and more education participate at a higher rate than do those with less income and education.[28] Their higher rate of participation magnifies their influence on the election results and on the decisions made by elected public officials.

↑ income
↑ participation
↑ influence on election

There are many forms of participation, from the simple act of voting, to working for a candidate (ringing doorbells, handing out literature, sending e-mail or text messaging, coordinating events, and the like), to contributing money to a candidate's campaign and spending money to promote one's own views, which may or may not coincide with those of a particular candidate. Placing no restrictions on these activities allows those with the interest, time, resources, and will to do more, and, as a result, to potentially exercise greater influence. At what point should a line be drawn between voluntary actions of citizens in the electoral process, which should be encouraged, and the activities that give an unfair advantage to those with superior resources at their disposal?

Majority Rule versus Minority Rights

Plurality voting decisions seem to be a pretty straightforward criterion for a democratic society. If every vote is equal, the candidates who received the most votes should win. The problem, as we have already noted, is that plurality voting systems overrepresent the majority, whereas proportional systems give more representation to minorities.

Many factors affect the majority–minority relationship: the ways the boundaries of electoral districts are drawn and the number of people elected within them, how the ballot is organized, whether candidates are listed by office or by party, and even where, when, and for how long voting occurs. If registration is difficult, voting places few and not easily accessible, the hours for voting too short, or the ballot too complicated and confusing, then turnout will be lower; those in power will more likely remain in power; and those who benefit under the current arrangement will continue to do so.

Voting conditions bad = lower voter turnout, power remains

Representation of groups within the society also can be affected by ballot access. In 1992 and 1996, Ross Perot's Reform Party spent millions of dollars and used hundreds of volunteers and paid workers just to obtain the necessary signatures just to get on the ballot in all fifty states. The Reform and Green Parties did this as well, albeit much less successfully, in recent presidential elections. But for the Republican and Democratic candidates, ballot access is automatic. They have a built-in advantage. Is that fair?

The majority–minority issue extends to government as well. Should majority rule be restricted so that minorities are better protected when public policy decisions are made? James Madison thought so. Fearing that the "tyranny of the majority" could deny minorities their basic rights, he argued successfully for a divided government that separates institutions representing differing constituencies so that no single group could easily dominate. But in the process, Madison and his colleagues at the Constitutional Convention created a system that has enabled powerful minorities to exercise a tyranny of their own, preventing change and thereby thwarting the desires of the majority or plurality in violation of a basic precept of democratic theory.

A Free Press versus an Informed Electorate

The framers of the Bill of Rights believed that a free press was essential. In a government based on the consent of the governed, those in office must be held accountable for their decisions and actions. Similarly, the qualifications, promises, and positions of candidates for elective office must be evaluated by the electorate.

The public cannot assess candidates running for office or the performance of those in office unless they have the necessary information to do so. The problem is that most sources for such information—the candidates, their parties, interest groups, policy-oriented think tanks, even government officials—have a stake in the outcome that affects the information they present and how they present it. Although information from stakeholders in the election is still valuable, it must be evaluated with the interests of the source in mind.

Here's where a free press comes in. For some of the same reasons that we select others to represent us in government, we also depend on others to inform us about politics and government, to help us sort out what's going on and make informed judgments. That's the role of the news media—to be a watchdog, to provide the information they believe we need to know or would be interested in knowing. Anticipating that the press will perform this role is itself an incentive for those running for office not to lie, although they are still prone to exaggerate their claims. It is also a motivation for those holding office to stay attuned to public opinion and not to behave in a manner that would draw unfavorable attention and admonishment.

A free press is unfettered but not necessarily neutral. News reporters describe the campaign as they see it. Naturally, their perceptions are influenced by their own political beliefs, their journalistic needs, and their personal feelings about the candidates and issues. To the extent that many in the news media share

more frivolous, could be biased

similar political and professional orientations, their reporting of the campaign reflects a pack mentality, a collective reading and interpretation of events.[29] This journalistic outlook colors the public's understanding and its evaluation of the candidates and parties. It gives the electorate a jaundiced view that highlights the dramatic and human elements of the campaign, usually at the expense of a detailed debate over substantive issues.

What can be done about the media's orientation and perceived bias? Restricting press coverage is not only impractical but also violates the First Amendment's protection of freedom of the press. Relying on the candidates to monitor the coverage they receive seems equally impractical given their vested interest in favorable coverage. Nor can the government take on a supervisory role over political communication in a campaign, especially in light of the number of incumbents who seek reelection. How, then, can citizens obtain the information they need, particularly as it relates to policy issues and their impact on society—information that many consider essential for voters to make an informed judgment based on an enlightened understanding of the issues?

How can citizens be informed

SUMMARY: DEMOCRATIC ELECTION DILEMMAS IN A NUTSHELL

In theory, a representative democracy is a government of the people, by some of them, and for all of them. It is connected to the people through elections of the people's representatives. One democratic dilemma is how to provide citizens with equal opportunities to affect the electoral and governmental processes without reducing their freedom to pursue their own interests and utilize their own resources as they see fit. Another dilemma is how to provide electoral mechanisms that are efficient and representative, effective and accountable, dynamic and deliberative—a tall order, to be sure!

To meet these criteria, citizens must be accorded universal suffrage and equal voting power. They must be free to vote, given the opportunity to do so, have a meaningful choice, and be able to obtain timely information about the parties, candidates, and issues that is sufficient to make informed judgments when they vote.

In practice, contemporary elections fall short of meeting these criteria. There is universal suffrage in theory, but large-scale nonvoting in practice. There are many choices of candidates and some of policy initiatives as well, but a lot of people still complain that their choices are unsatisfactory because they are too narrow, too broad, or all distasteful.

All votes count equally, but all groups do not benefit equally from current electoral procedures and practices. Ethnic and racial minorities, in particular, seem to be disproportionately disadvantaged by plurality voting in single-member districts. Wealthy people have the advantage that their superior resources provide. Finally, the United States has a free press but, in the view of many in the electorate, neither an objective nor a responsible one. Complaints that the media are too powerful, too judgmental, and too negative are regularly reported in

power to the wealthy

survey and anecdotal research.[30] That much of the electorate is underinformed and underinvolved has been attributed in large part to the press's penchant for reporting the most entertaining news, as well as to inefficient and ineffective grassroots operations by party and nonparty groups and personal attacks by the candidates and their campaigns against one another. But from the perspective of the mass media, driven by audience size, a very competitive news environment, and conventions of contemporary journalism, interesting and exciting news is what the public wants, so they provide it.

The disjunctions between democratic theory and practice arise from many sources: the manner in which the electorate can and does participate in elections; the ways in which elections are structured and conducted, and the manner in which representatives are chosen; the structure of the party system and the candidate orientation of electoral politics; laws governing financial contributions and expenditures; press coverage, particularly its emphasis on the contest, its orientation toward personal character issues, and its general negativity; the parties' methods for selecting their nominees; the ways campaigns are run, appeals communicated, and images created; and finally, incompatible outcomes, unclear meanings, and vacuous mandates.

Now It's Your Turn

Discussion Questions

1. How nearly universal must suffrage be for the popular will to be asserted?

2. Can elections be structured to reflect both majority sentiment and minority views at the same time?

3. What current electoral issues pit individual liberty against political equality?

4. To what extent is the democratic goal of an informed electorate that makes enlightened voting possible, and to what extent is it necessary?

5. Can the news media serve the informational needs of the electorate and the profit motives of media owners simultaneously?

6. What are the most serious problems that threaten the democratic character of the American electoral system?

Topics for Debate

Challenge or defend the following statements:

1. It is possible to have political liberty and citizen equality simultaneously.

2. If the majority always rules, then the rights and interests of the minority are always going to be threatened.

3. A press that is both free and fair is a contradiction in terms.

4. To make sure that voters can make informed judgments, they should be required to know the principal candidates and their major issue positions before being allowed to vote.

5. A democratic government cannot exist without a democratic electoral process.

6. Literacy should be a qualification for voting.

Exercises

1. How democratic is the constitutionally prescribed electoral process?

   a. Answer this question by first examining what the Constitution requires and allows for national elections, noting its democratic and undemocratic features.

   b. To the best of your knowledge, have the nondemocratic features of American elections been changed by amendment, law, or practice? If so, how and why; if not, why not?

   c. Is the electoral system becoming more or less democratic today, and are the changes that have occurred in the electoral process good or bad for the country as a whole? Give examples to support your view.

   d. What aspects of the last presidential election reflect positively or negatively on the democratic character of the U.S. electoral system? Do you anticipate that the same positive or negative aspects will be apparent in the next election?

2. Advocates of democracy have urged that the electoral system be made as democratic as possible to achieve the ideal of a government of, by, and for the people. Others are reluctant to change a system that has worked so well for so long and has become so large a part of America's political tradition. What do you think? Would democracy be better served if the system were changed, or would it actually impede the functioning of the electoral and governing systems? Might too much democracy be a bad thing? If you had to choose between liberty and equality or between majority rule and minority rights, how would you choose and why?

INTERNET RESOURCES

The Internet is a rich source of information on campaigns and elections. Here are some of the best generic sources for all kinds of information. Most of them contain links to the news media, public interest groups, ongoing political campaigns, polling organizations, and appropriate government agencies.

Media Sites on Politics and Elections

- CNN: www.cnn.com
- C-SPAN: www.cspan.org
- FOX: www.foxnews.com
- Los Angeles Times: www.latimes.com
- National Public Radio: www.npr.org
- New York Times: www.nytimes.com
- Politico: www.politico.com
- Real Clear Politics: www.realclearpolitics.com
- Washington Post: www.washingtonpost.com

Government Sites on the Electoral System

- Census Bureau: www.census.gov/compendia/statab/

  Publishes the yearly *Statistical Abstract*, which contains information on registration, turnout, and voting results in recent federal elections.

- Election Assistance Commission: www.eac.gov

  Established by the Help America Vote Act, the commission provides information on how to register and vote, state and federal election laws, and surveys of who registers and who votes.

- Federal Election Commission: www.fec.gov

  Provides easily accessible data on campaign finance activities filed by candidates and compiled in tabular form by analysts at the FEC.

- Library of Congress: http://thomas.loc.gov

  Provides access to Congress, its committees, members, legislative process, rules, and schedules, as well as reports on campaigns and elections.

- National Archives and Records Administration: www.archives.gov/federal-register/electoral-college/

  Contains official statistics about past presidential elections, the Electoral College, election laws, and presidential documents.

- White House: www.whitehouse.gov

  Contains not only information on presidential and vice presidential activities, speeches, press releases, and official business, but also links to all other parts of the government.

SELECTED READINGS

American Political Science Association Task Force on Inequality and American Democracy. "American Democracy in an Age of Rising Inequality." *Perspectives on Politics* 2 (December 2004): 651–666.

Barber, Benjamin R. *A Passion for Democracy*. Princeton, NJ: Princeton University Press, 1998.

Bartels, Larry M. *Unequal Democracy: The Political Economy of the New Gilded Age*. Princeton, NJ: Princeton University Press, 2008.

Cain, Bruce, Russell Dalton, and Susan Scarrow. *New Forms of Democracy? The Reform and Transformation of Democratic Institutions*. Princeton, NJ: Princeton University Press, 2003.

Dahl, Robert A. *Democracy and Its Critics*. New Haven, CT: Yale University Press, 1989.

—. *How Democratic Is the American Constitution?* New Haven, CT: Yale University Press, 2001.

—. *A Preface to Democratic Theory*. Chicago, IL: University of Chicago Press, 1956.

Diamond, Larry. *Developing Democracy*. Baltimore, MD: Johns Hopkins University Press, 1999.

Downs, Anthony. *An Economic Theory of Democracy*. New York, NY: Harper and Row, 1957.

Dowding, Keith, Robert E. Goodin, and Carole Pateman, eds. *Justice and Democracy*. Cambridge, England: Cambridge University Press, 2004.

Dryzek, John. *Discursive Democracy*. Cambridge, England: Cambridge University Press, 1990.

Dryzek, John, and Patrick Dunleavy. *Theories of the Democratic State*. London, England: Palgrave/Macmillan, 2009.

Held, David. *Models of Democracy*. Stanford, CA: Stanford University Press, 2006.

Hirst, Paul. *Representative Democracy and Its Limits*. Oxford, England: Polity Press, 1990.

Schlozman, Kay Lehman, Sidney Verba, and Henry E. Brady. "Weapon of the Strong? Participatory Inequality and the Internet." *Perspectives on Politics* 8 (June 2010): 487–509.

Schmitter, Philippe, and Terry Karl. "What Democracy Is . . . and Is Not." *Journal of Democracy* 2 (Fall 1991): 75–88.

Shapiro, Ian. *The State of Democratic Theory*. Princeton, NJ: Princeton University Press, 2003.

Stout, Jeffrey. *Democracy and Tradition*. Princeton, NJ: Princeton University Press, 2004.

Tilly, Charles. *Democracy*. Cambridge, England: Cambridge University Press, 2007.

Thompson, Dennis. *Just Elections: Creating a Fair Electoral Process in the United States*. Chicago, IL: University of Chicago Press, 2002.

Tocqueville, Alexis de. *Democracy in America*. New York, NY: HarperCollins, 1988.

Warren, Mark, ed. *Democracy and Trust*. New York, NY: Cambridge University Press, 1999.

—. "Voting with Your Feet: Exit-Based Empowerment in Democratic Theory." *American Political Science Review* 105 (November 2011): 683–701.

Welch, Susan. "The Impact of At-Large Elections on the Representation of Blacks and Hispanics." *Journal of Politics* 52 (1990): 1050–1076.

NOTES

1. "The Impact of the National Voter Registration Act of 1993 on the Administration of Elections for Federal Office, 2009–2010," Election Assistance Commission, June 30, 2011. http://www .eac.gov/assets/1/Documents/2010%20NVRA%20Report.pdf.

2. Michael McDonald, "Voter Turnout," http://elections.gmu.edu/voter_turnout.htm.

3. In the past, the Court had stayed out of controversies over legislative districting, contending that these involved political issues and were therefore nonjusticiable—that is, they were not subject to review by the Court (judicial review).

4. U.S. Commission on Civil Rights, "Voting Irregularities in Florida during the 2000 Presidential Election," June 2001, http://www.usccr.gov/pubs/vote2000/report/main.htm. Florida state officials and Republican members of the commission criticized the conclusions of the report, asserting there was no evidence that the disproportionate disfranchisement of African American voters resulted from discriminatory behavior of state and county election officials.

5. Massachusetts Institute of Technology and California Institute of Technology, "Voting: What Is and What Could Be," July 17, 2001. Caltech/MIT Voting Technology Project http://www .vote.caltech.edu/content/voting-what-what-could-be

6. Gallup Poll, "Seven out of 10 Americans Accept Bush as Legitimate President," July 17, 2001, http://www.gallup.com/poll/4687/Seven-Americans-Accept-Bush-Legitimate-President.aspx

7. *Citizens United* v. *FEC* 558 U.S.08–250 (2010).

8. The Super PACs were required to report the names of contributors of $200 or more to the Federal Election Commission, but since the contributors were numerous, the identities and interests of the big contributors did not become well known to the general public unless and until the news media mounted a sustained focus on them.

9. In 2004, nonparty groups raised and spent more than $440 million, using this money to fund surrogate campaigns on behalf of their respective parties and candidates; in 2008, they raised and spent about to $260 million. Center for Responsive Politics, "SuperPACs." http://www .opensecrets.org/pacs/superpacs.php?cycle=2012. Center for Responsive Politics, "Outside Spending." www.opensecrets.org/outsidespending/

10. For example, see Stephen Ansolabehere and Shanto Iyengar, *Going Negative: How Political Advertisements Shrink and Polarize the Electorate* (New York: Free Press, 1995); and Thomas E. Patterson, *Out of Order* (New York: Knopf, 1993).

11. For a good basic discussion of democracy, see Robert A. Dahl, *On Democracy* (New Haven, CT: Yale University Press, 1998). Dahl has written extensively on this subject, and two of his other well-known works on democratic theory are *A Preface to Democratic Theory* (Chicago, IL: University of Chicago Press, 1956) and *Democracy and Its Critics* (New Haven, CT: Yale University Press, 1989).

12. An excellent discussion of types of democratic systems appears in David Held, *Models of Democracy* (Stanford, CA: Stanford University Press, 2006).

13. Former Alaska senator Mike Gravel, one of the Democrats running for the party's 2008 presidential nomination, proposed a national ballot initiative in which voters would cast votes on major policy issues. Gravel's proposal and candidacy received little media attention and public support, however.

14. In many of the southern states, judges are elected in partisan or nonpartisan elections. In other states, they are appointed by the governor, legislature, or special commission, in some cases later subject to an up or down vote by the electorate. At the federal level, judges are nominated

by the president and appointed with the advice and consent of the Senate. Federal judges serve during good behavior for life.

15. James Madison, *The Federalist,* No. 10.

16. Gallup Poll, "Presidential Approval Ratings—Bill Clinton," 1993–2001, www.gallup.com/poll/116584/Presidential-Approval-Ratings-Bill-Clinton.aspx.

17. Robert Dahl, "What Political Institutions Does Large-Scale Democracy Require?" *Political Science Quarterly* 120 (Summer 2005): 188.

18. The cost of conducting elections (maintaining registration lists, printing ballots and buying machinery for other methods of voting, tabulating the results, and overseeing the conduct of the election) is borne primarily by the states. In the past some states enacted a poll tax ostensibly to pay for these costs, although the taxes were also used to prevent poor people from voting. In 1937, the Supreme Court ruled that poll taxes did not violate the Fourteenth and Fifteenth Amendments to the Constitution, a decision that sparked a campaign to get the states and Congress to abolish poll taxes. The campaign had considerable success, and by 1960, five states in the South retained these taxes. The enactment of the Twenty-fourth Amendment, which was ratified in 1964, banned poll taxes in federal elections. Two years later the Supreme Court decided that the Fourteenth Amendment's equal protection clause also forbid them in state elections.

19. For a classic discussion of the fundamental principles of democracy, see James W. Prothro and Charles M. Grigg, "Fundamental Principles of Democracy," *Journal of Politics* 22 (May 1960): 276–294.

20. President Obama restated Jefferson's words in his 2009 inaugural address: "The time has come to reaffirm our enduring spirit; to choose our better history; to carry forward that precious gift, that noble idea passed on from generation to generation: the God-given promise that all are equal, all are free, and all deserve a chance to pursue their full measure of happiness." Barack Obama, "President Barack Obama's Inaugural Address," January 20, 2009, www.white house .gov/blog/inaugural-address

21. For a discussion of the democratic right not to vote and purposive nonparticipation, see Mark E. Warren, "Voting with Your Feet: Exit-based Empowerment in Democratic Theory," *American Political Science Review* 105 (November 2011): 683–701.

22. Dahl, "What Political Institutions," 196.

23. Several southern states, including Louisiana and Georgia, require runoffs if the winning candidate does not receive more than half the total vote.

24. The exception is the District of Columbia, which has no voting representation in Congress but was given three electoral votes by the Twenty-third Amendment to the Constitution. The number of electoral votes was determined on the basis of what the District's representation would have been if it had been a state at the time of the ratification of the amendment in 1961.

25. Dahl, *On Democracy,* 132–134.

26. David Epstein and Sharyn O'Halloran, "Measuring the Electoral and Policy Impact of Majority-Minority Voting Districts," *American Journal of Political Science* 43 (April 1999): 367–395. A more recent study by Zoltan L. Hajnal found that African Americans are more likely than other groups to cast votes for losing candidates; see "Who Loses in American Democracy? A Count of Votes Demonstrates the Limited Representation of African Americans," *American Political Science Review* 103 (February 2009): 37–57.

27. Sidney Verba, Kay Lehman Schlozman, and Henry E. Brady, *Voice and Equality: Civic Voluntarism in American Politics* (Cambridge, MA: Harvard University Press, 1995), 512.

28. Ibid., 511–533.

29. S. Robert Lichter, Stanley Rothman, and Linda S. Lichter claim in their book *The Media Elite* (Bethesda, MD: Adler and Adler, 1986) that most national correspondents are liberal in ideology and Democratic in political allegiance.

30. *Striking the Balance: Audience Interests, Business Pressures, and Journalists' Values* (Washington, DC: Pew Research Center for the People and the Press, 1999); Pew Research Center for the People and the Press, "Big Doubts about News Media's Values: Public Votes for Continuity and Change in 2000," February 25, 1999; and Pew Research Center for the People and the Press, "High Marks for the Campaign, a High Bar for Obama," November 13, 2008.

Popular Base of American Electoral Politics

Did you know that . . .

- fewer than one-fifth of adults living in the United States were eligible to vote in the first election held under the Constitution?
- by 1800, about one-third of those eligible actually voted—practically all of them adult white males?
- Congress almost refused to allow Wyoming to enter the Union in 1890 because its state constitution allowed women to vote?
- the United States has a lower rate of voting than do most European democracies?
- despite the fact that most Americans believe that voting is a civic responsibility, 15 percent report that they vote only part of the time, seldom, or not at all?
- about one quarter of the eligible U. S. population is not registered to vote?
- at the beginning of the twentieth century, three out of four eligible voters cast ballots in the presidential election; at the beginning of the twenty-first century, only a little more two out of four did so?
- Hispanics, until recently, the fastest-growing group in the population, turn out at lower rates than do most other minority groups?
- election day is not and never has been a U.S. national holiday?
- about one-third of the voters in the last two presidential elections said they cast their ballots before election day?
- the people who do vote are disproportionately better educated, have higher incomes, and are older than those who don't vote?
- nonvoters are less informed, less partisan, and less trustful of government than are voters?

Is this any way to run a democratic election?

[handwritten: universal suffrage]

To be democratic, an electoral system must allow all adult citizens to vote and to have their votes count equally.[1] Most proponents of democratic elections also believe that such a system also should encourage people to vote and facilitate their doing so. To what extent do U.S. elections meet these democratic goals? To what extent do they achieve participatory democracy in theory and in practice?

This chapter will answer these two questions that underlie the popular foundation of American democracy. It begins with a historic overview of suffrage and turnout and then turns to the reasons why people do not vote, the factors that influence those who do, and the difference turnout makes for a democratic political process, for the parties and their candidates, and for public policy outcomes. Proposals for increasing voter turnout are then assessed in light of contemporary trends in the American electoral system.

SUFFRAGE IN AMERICAN ELECTIONS

A participatory democracy was not what the framers had in mind when they drafted the Constitution. Most of the delegates who attended the Philadelphia convention neither desired nor encouraged large-scale public involvement in politics. The relatively low level of education most people had at the time, poor communications within and between the newly independent states, and the distrust that pervaded relations among the people of the thirteen states led the delegates at the Constitutional Convention to design a government that would be responsive to various segments of the society but not necessarily to the popular mood of the moment.

[handwritten: lack of representation]

Who should vote was a contentious issue in 1787. Not wanting to derail the Constitution's ratification by imposing conditions on suffrage to which some states might object, the framers decided not to decide who should be allowed to vote. They left the matter to the individual states, subject to any restrictions Congress might later establish. *[handwritten: which made it a slippery slope]*

Expanding the Right to Vote

[handwritten: not universal]

Initially, most state constitutions limited suffrage to white male citizens twenty-one years of age and older who owned property and were Christians. Gradually, these restrictions on voting were eliminated. By the 1830s, most states had removed religion and property ownership as conditions for suffrage, thereby enfranchising about 80 percent of adult white males.[2]

In some northern states, African American males also were allowed to vote. The vast concentration of African Americans were in the South, however, and not until after the Civil War were they granted suffrage. The Fifteenth Amendment, ratified in 1870, removed race and color as qualifications for voting. In theory, it enfranchised all African American males who were citizens.

In practice, only those who lived in the North and in the border states could easily vote. A series of institutional devices, such as poll taxes, literacy tests, and restrictive primaries in which only Caucasians could participate (so-called white primaries), effectively combined with social pressure to prevent African Americans in the South from voting for another hundred years.[3]

Women, too, were denied the right to vote. Wyoming was the first territory to grant women equal voting rights with men in 1869, and it was the first state to do so after being admitted to the Union in 1890. In fact, Congress tried to compel Wyoming to rescind women's suffrage as a condition for entering the Union, but the Wyoming legislature refused, declaring, "We will remain out of the Union 100 years rather than come in without the women."[4] Congress relented. Only a few other states, primarily in the West, followed Wyoming's lead. By 1904, only four states permitted women to vote.[5]

The almost exclusive authority that states exercised to determine eligibility began to break down after the Civil War. During the next hundred years, Congress essentially nationalized the right to vote. A series of constitutional amendments and statutes limited the states' power to restrict suffrage. First, the Fifteenth Amendment (1871) prevented states from discriminating against otherwise eligible citizens on the basis of race, color, or previous condition of servitude. The Seventeenth Amendment (1913) required all states to elect their senators by popular vote. The Nineteenth Amendment (1920) prohibited gender from being used as a qualification for voting, and the Twenty-fourth Amendment (1964) precluded states from denying the vote for federal officials to residents who failed to pay a poll tax or any other tax.[6] The most recent constitutional restriction on the states, the Twenty-sixth Amendment (1971), forbade them from setting an age older than eighteen years as a condition for voting.

These constitutional strictures have been supplemented by laws that also have limited state discretion on suffrage. The 1964 Civil Rights Act prevented a literacy test from being required for any citizen with a sixth-grade education from an accredited school in the United States or its territories. The 1965 Voting Rights Act authorized the federal government to send examiners to register voters in any legislative district in which 50 percent or more of the eligible adult population was not registered to vote.[7] Amendments to this law further precluded states from imposing a residence requirement of more than thirty days for voting in any presidential election. The 1993 motor-voter bill requires states to make registration material available at their motor vehicle and social services offices, as well as at military recruitment centers, thereby enabling residents to register at these offices or by mail when they apply for or renew their driver's license, receive state health or welfare benefits, or enlist in the armed services. The law also created an Election Assistance Commission that currently makes a National Mail Voter Registration Form available on its Web site (www.eac.gov) for downloading. The site indicates the addresses to which the form should be sent in all fifty states and the District of Columbia.

towards ideal

Together, these constitutional amendments and statutes have established nearly universal suffrage, a policy that most Americans support. Prior to the enactment of the Twenty-sixth Amendment, 70 percent of the population favored lowering the voting age to eighteen.[8] Since 1944, a large majority of Americans have favored eliminating the Electoral College and using a direct popular vote to select the president.[9]

Limiting the Right to Vote

The only state restrictions that remain in place are those which prevent otherwise qualified citizens from voting because they are or have been in jail or a mental institution. The jail and felony restrictions disfranchise 5.85 million Americans, about 2.5 percent of the voting age population.[10] Of this number about 1.4 million are African American males, or approximately 13 percent of all African American men. In states that permanently disfranchise felons, that percentage rises to about 25 percent.[11] To help remedy this problem, the National Commission on Federal Election Reform has recommended that voting rights be restored to convicted felons who have served their time in jail.[12] About half the states that prohibited felons and ex-felons from voting prior to 2000 have since changed their laws return suffrage rights to people who have served their sentences (and in some cases, completed their probation periods); eleven states continue to disfranchise felons and those who have been dishonorably discharged from the military on a temporary or permanent basis.[13]

Since the 2000 election, there also have been allegations that minority voters, especially those who live in low-income areas, are much more likely than others to be prevented from voting or to have their votes voided for not completing the ballot properly. A report by the U.S. Commission on Civil Rights—following the controversial 2000 Florida election—condemned officials of that state for their unequal treatment of African American voters. The commission noted that 54 percent of the disqualified ballots were cast by African Americans, a group that constituted only 11 percent of Florida's electorate at the time.[14] Another study, this one prepared for Democrats on the House Governmental Reform Committee, found that in the country as a whole, 4 percent of all ballots cast in low-income districts were not counted, compared with 1.2 percent in higher-income districts.[15] Whether the differential in disqualified votes is a consequence of discriminatory behavior by state election officials, better voting machines and shorter lines in more affluent areas, or simply more errors made by less-educated voters remains a subject of considerable controversy. Voting irregularities and fraudulent voting practices have also been alleged in recent elections. During the 2008 election, Republicans charged that an organization supporting Barack Obama, the Association of Community Organizations for Reform Now (ACORN), fraudulently registered voters. Although the Obama campaign paid $800,000 to that group to help get out the vote in that election,

is it really discriminatory or is it simply circumstance / societal problem

his campaign organization denied involvement in any illegal registrations and attributed them to overzealous workers for ACORN.[16] The organization subsequently announced its closing.

Eliminating voter fraud has been a justification for some states to enact legislation that requires citizens to present government-issued, photo identification in order to vote. The laws, enacted by Republican-controlled state legislatures and approved by Republican governors, were challenged by Democrats that believed that they were intended to reduce turnout disproportionately among people with low incomes and low education levels, racial and ethnic minorities, and the young, groups that tend to vote Democratic. However, the Supreme Court upheld this requirement in the case *Crawford v. Marion Election Board* 533 U.S.181 (2008). Fifteen states require a photo-ID in order to vote.[17] Others require some identification, such as a utility or bank statement, to confirm residence.

that's fair, you need it for must things

Although universal suffrage has been established in the United States, the costs of voting are not uniform among the population. They may be higher for single parents, higher for parents with young children, higher for the elderly and infirm, and higher for low-wage earners who work two or more jobs to make ends meet or people who are paid on an hourly basis. They also may be higher for those who have to travel greater distances to vote. Generally speaking, people who fall into the "high-cost" category tend to be those with lower incomes. This fact introduces an economic bias into the voting electorate.

economic bias, not discrimination

Some people may lack the skills to read the ballot and comprehend the differences among candidates and their parties; they may not be able to cope with the registration requirements, understand ballot initiatives, or know how to cast their ballots properly. Punching out the chad in Florida was a problem in 2000 that led to many untabulated and voided vote cards. People with physical disabilities may have difficulty getting to the polls, especially if the elections are held in facilities inaccessible to the handicapped. Obtaining absentee ballots can also be a problem in states that still require proof of out-of-state business or disabled status before issuing such a ballot.

VARIATIONS IN VOTER TURNOUT

right to, or not to vote

Even though suffrage has been extended to most American citizens, many of them do not exercise their right much of the time (see Figure 2.1). In the 1996 presidential election, a majority of the adult population (51 percent) did *not* vote; in 2000, a bare majority voted. Turnouts in 2004 and 2008 were higher. In 2004, turnout was 55.4 percent of the voting-age population (VAP) and 60.7 percent of the voting-eligible population (VEP), which excludes noncitizens, incarcerated individuals, ex-felons, and others precluded by state law from voting; in 2008, VAP went up to 56.9 percent and VEP to 62.3; in 2012, it was 53.6 percent VAP and 58.7 percent VEP.[18]

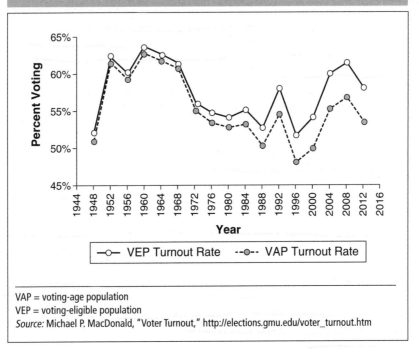

FIGURE 2.1   **Presidential Turnout Rates 1948–2012**

VAP = voting-age population
VEP = voting-eligible population
Source: Michael P. MacDonald, "Voter Turnout," http://elections.gmu.edu/voter_turnout.htm

Types of Elections

people don't care as much

In nonpresidential years, the proportion of the population voting is even lower, usually in the range of 30 to 40 percent for congressional elections, and much lower than that in off-year elections for state and local officials. In 2006, the percentage for the VAP was 37.1 and for the VEP was 41.3; in 2010 the percentages were 37.8 and 41.6, respectively.[19] Put another way, about 60 percent of eligible voters failed to vote in these elections.

Turnout in primaries is less than in the general election. In 2004, turnout in the primaries averaged 15 percent of the voting-age population, although it was higher in the more competitive states that held their contests before the presidential nominees had been effectively determined.[20] In 2008, with two competitive presidential nominations occurring, turnout increased, as approximately 59 million people voted (42.2 percent of registered voters, 32.5 percent of eligible voters, and 26.8 percent of the voting-age population);[21] in 2012, with only a competitive Republican nomination, turnout declined to 26 million in the presidential primaries (17.8 million for the Republicans and 8.3 million for the Democrats). In only one state, New Hampshire, did turnout exceed 25 percent; it was 31.1 percent.[22]

Historical Trends

Voter turnout in the United States has fluctuated considerably. After 1800, the development of the party system provided the incentive and organizational mechanism to expand the proportion of the population who voted. Turnout rose, ranging from 25 to 50 percent of those eligible between 1800 and 1828, with the higher rates in elections in which the parties were most competitive. But the competition didn't last long. One of the parties, the Federalists, ran its last presidential candidate in 1816 and effectively disintegrated after that. With the advent of one-party dominance, turnout began to decline.

By the mid-1820s, however, factions within the Democratic-Republican Party led to a more competitive political environment and, ultimately, to the reemergence of a two-party system. As that system evolved, the parties tried to get more people involved and out to vote; they succeeded by popularizing election campaigns.[23] Beginning in the 1840s, rallies, oratory, and parades brought out the faithful and the curious alike, thereby contributing to higher turnout.[24]

The new partisan activism continued in nonelectoral periods as well. Patronage jobs, political influence, and even a little monetary aid were given to loyal supporters, who were expected to return the favor on election day. This expectation was reinforced by the parties' oversight of the voting process. Precinct captains got out the voters, the parties printed their own color-coded ballots that contained only the names of their candidates, and poll watchers recorded who voted and how they voted.[25]

As a consequence of these activities, turnout soared; in some elections in the second half of the nineteenth century, more than 80 percent of eligible voters reportedly cast ballots. However, corruption and fraudulent voting practices were also rampant. Multiple voting, ballot stuffing, vote tampering, and irregularities in tallying the vote led states to print their own ballots and monitor election activities more closely. In addition, registration procedures were instituted to ensure that only those who were eligible could vote.

Although these reforms were designed to protect the integrity of the electoral process, they also made the act of voting more difficult. People had to register first, sometimes well in advance of the election, and do so at places and times designated by the states. Some states also enacted poll taxes to pay for the cost of the election. These taxes were particularly onerous for low-income voters.

That wasn't the worst of it, however. The taxes and literacy tests were implemented in a discriminatory manner by election officials, primarily in the South. They became barriers to prevent African Americans, as well as many poor whites, from voting.

Decreasing competition between the political parties in the South following the Civil War also contributed to lower turnout. The South became a one-party region, dominated by the Democrats. Because the winner of that party's nomination was a prohibitive favorite to win the general election, there was less incentive for southerners to vote. The Republicans also gained sufficient strength to dominate in the Northeast, with much the same depressing effect on turnout.

On top of all this, both parties seemed determined to establish as many safe congressional seats as possible for their candidates. The adoption of the seniority rule in selecting the chairs of standing committees in Congress provided added incentive for state parties to protect their congressional incumbents who had risen to positions of power by "creative" districting that effectively secured their seats.

Although a reform movement at the end of the nineteenth century gave more power to rank-and-file voters through the introduction of presidential primaries in many of the states, it did not increase the rate of turnout. By the end of World War I, this reform movement had all but dissipated, and states reverted to nomination procedures that facilitated control by party leaders. With the exception of the 1928 presidential election, turnout throughout the 1920s was less than 50 percent of those eligible to vote.

The realignment of political parties in the 1930s, and especially the appeal of Franklin D. Roosevelt's Democratic Party to people on the lower rungs of the socioeconomic scale (blue-collar workers, poor farmers, and racial and ethnic minorities), reenergized the electorate, contributing to a larger proportion of the population voting, especially in presidential elections, for the next thirty years. Turnout, however, did not return to the levels it reached during the second half of the nineteenth century.

By the end of the 1960s, it was again on the decline. The civil rights movement and the Vietnam War created divisions within the majority party, the Democrats, marking the beginning of a trend of less intense partisan allegiances among supporters of that party. Technological advances in communication, particularly the advent of television campaigning, increased the candidate-centeredness of elections, weakened party organizations, and led to a decline in partisan loyalties. Television, however, proved to be a less effective way to mobilize voters than personal contact by party workers and volunteers.

The decreasing turnout levels ended at the close of the twentieth century. Since then, partisan parity during much of this period has resulted in closer elections; party identification has strengthened; partisan voting patterns have emerged; and the parties, using new communication technologies to reach more people and target more messages more directly to voters, have placed greater emphasis on grassroots organizing and turnout campaigns. Voter registration has become easier (only one state, North Dakota, does not require voter registration), absentee ballots are more readily available, and early voting periods have been established, although since the 2008 election some states have reduced the hours for early voting, citing tight budgets as their rationale.[26] Nonetheless, these factors have contributed to the increase in the proportion of the electorate voting in the twenty-first century.

INFLUENCES ON VOTING

More people claim they vote than actually do.[27] They do so because most citizens consider voting a civic responsibility. According to national surveys conducted by the Pew Research Center for the People and the Press, almost 90 percent of those surveyed agreed with the statement, "I feel it is my duty as a citizen to always vote."[28] Approximately two-thirds of Americans say that they feel guilty when they do not do so.[29] So most people say they always or nearly always vote.

Why People Do Not Vote: Excuses Real and Concocted

Despite the widespread belief that voting is an important responsibility of citizenship, a substantial portion of the population does not vote. Many lack the motivation to do so. Today, a majority of people still subscribe to the proposition that "most elected officials do not really care about what people like me think."[30] They don't see what difference it makes to them who wins the election. Nor do they see their votes mattering all that much, although in Florida in the 2000 presidential election, in the 2004 governor's election in the state of Washington, in the 2008 Minnesota contest for U.S. senator, and in several of the congressional midterm elections in recent years, a small number of votes could have changed the outcome.

People are cynical, and they distrust politicians.[31] They most often cite candidate dishonesty and untruthfulness, a lack of pertinent information, and negative campaigning as reasons for not voting.[32] However, when negativity is examined within the context of other factors, such as the level of mistrust people bring to the election, it seems to be a less important influence on nonvoting.[33] Much depends on how campaign news and ads are viewed and by whom. For example, if the negativity seems appropriate, such as opposition to a salient issue, it actually may increase turnout. But if the negativity seems excessive or inappropriate, such as mudslinging or harsh and vindictive personal ads, it can adversely affect turnout and even boomerang against the candidate who uses such tactics.[34]

People give a myriad of other reasons or excuses for not voting. Some say that they are too busy trying to earn a living, raise a family, or meet other day-to-day responsibilities. And perhaps they are. Some people may be conflicted, unable to decide among competing candidates, parties, and policy alternatives. Their decision not to vote may be a considered judgment, a protest about the candidates, the parties, or their public policy positions: the candidates may not seem appealing, qualified, or sufficiently different from one another. They may take positions with which people strongly disagree. The issues may not seem relevant to people in the conduct of their everyday lives.

Other reasons for not voting have to do with election rules and procedures, particularly registration requirements. Despite enactment of the motor-voter law, some people still find registration difficult or inconvenient and either fail to register or to do so on time. Others are prevented from voting because their registrations are not properly recorded; they come to the wrong precinct to vote; or their registration is challenged when they get to the polls. The Voting Technology study conducted by MIT and CalTech, mentioned in Chapter 1, estimated that three million people were not able to cast valid ballots in 2000 because of registration mishaps of one type or another. This number is in addition to the four to six million individuals whose votes were not counted.[35] Today, according to the Pew Center on the States, about one quarter of the population is not registered to vote.[36]

One of the principal reasons for the relatively large number of unregistered voters (over 50 million) is that people move from one voting precinct to another within and between states. Another is that many states have not spent sufficient funds to computerize their registration records. To help rectify these problems, Congress enacted the Help America Vote Act in 2002 to provide for provisional voting when registration disputes occur. A person claiming to be registered but whose name does not appear on the precinct voting list may cast a provisional ballot that will be accepted if the registration issue is resolved in the voter's favor.

Rules and procedures, designed to maintain the integrity of a democratic voting system, place burdens on potential voters. As previously mentioned, finding the time, getting to the polls, understanding the intricacies of the ballot, and even knowing how to vote—which lever to push, hole to punch, box to check, or, more recently, how to negotiate a touch-screen computer—all are factors that discourage some people from voting or disqualify others whose votes were cast improperly.

The controversy over the "butterfly" ballot in Palm Beach County, Florida, in the 2000 election is a case in point. Under Florida's election law at that time, individual counties were responsible for the design of the ballots, monitoring of elections, and tabulation of votes. In Palm Beach County, a Democratic election official designed an easy-to-read ballot on which the names of all the candidates appeared on a single punch card. To fit everything on one side of the card, the ballot contained two columns of names (one column on each edge of the ballot) but only one column of "chads," the perforated holes that voters were supposed to punch out (see Figure 2.2) (down the center of the ballot). Some voters were confused and punched the chads for the wrong candidates; other voters punched two chads, automatically voiding their ballots. Additionally, some voters did not punch out the chads completely, leaving them dimpled or hanging. The voting machines undercounted ballots with chads that were not completely removed.[37]

Finally, the competitiveness of the election and the campaigns of the candidates also affect turnout. More competitive elections attract a larger vote for obvious reasons. They are also more likely to generate better-funded and more vigorous campaigns, which should result in higher turnout of voters.

FIGURE 2.2   Presidential Election Ballot Used in Palm Beach County, Florida in 2000

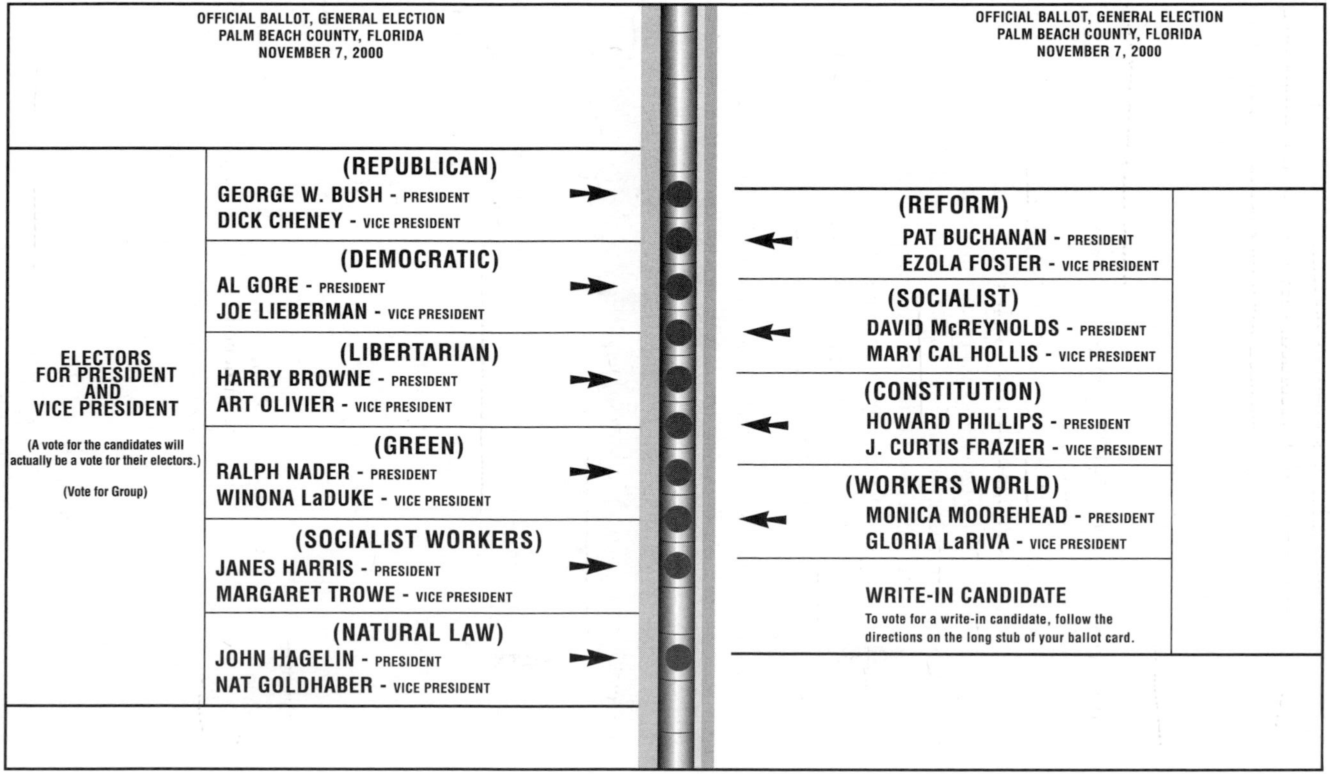

OFFICIAL BALLOT, GENERAL ELECTION
PALM BEACH COUNTY, FLORIDA
NOVEMBER 7, 2000

ELECTORS
FOR PRESIDENT
AND
VICE PRESIDENT

(A vote for the candidates will
actually be a vote for their electors.)

(Vote for Group)

(REPUBLICAN)
GEORGE W. BUSH - PRESIDENT
DICK CHENEY - VICE PRESIDENT

(DEMOCRATIC)
AL GORE - PRESIDENT
JOE LIEBERMAN - VICE PRESIDENT

(LIBERTARIAN)
HARRY BROWNE - PRESIDENT
ART OLIVIER - VICE PRESIDENT

(GREEN)
RALPH NADER - PRESIDENT
WINONA LaDUKE - VICE PRESIDENT

(SOCIALIST WORKERS)
JANES HARRIS - PRESIDENT
MARGARET TROWE - VICE PRESIDENT

(NATURAL LAW)
JOHN HAGELIN - PRESIDENT
NAT GOLDHABER - VICE PRESIDENT

OFFICIAL BALLOT, GENERAL ELECTION
PALM BEACH COUNTY, FLORIDA
NOVEMBER 7, 2000

(REFORM)
PAT BUCHANAN - PRESIDENT
EZOLA FOSTER - VICE PRESIDENT

(SOCIALIST)
DAVID McREYNOLDS - PRESIDENT
MARY CAL HOLLIS - VICE PRESIDENT

(CONSTITUTION)
HOWARD PHILLIPS - PRESIDENT
J. CURTIS FRAZIER - VICE PRESIDENT

(WORKERS WORLD)
MONICA MOOREHEAD - PRESIDENT
GLORIA LaRIVA - VICE PRESIDENT

WRITE-IN CANDIDATE
To vote for a write-in candidate, follow the
directions on the long stub of your ballot card.

Source: The *Washington Post*, October 23, 2001, www.thewashingtonpost.com.

In presidential elections, the battleground states that both presidential campaigns target have higher turnout levels than do states which do not receive as much candidate attention (see Table 2.1).[38]

candidate attention = ↑ turnout

Why People Do Vote

Political Attitudes. Personal feelings and beliefs are important in motivating people to vote. Interest in the election, concern over the outcome, and feelings of civic responsibility are factors that affect how regularly people vote. Naturally, those who feel more strongly about the election and have more interest in it are more likely to participate in the campaign and vote than those who do not have these feelings or interest. *INTEREST*

PARTY AFFILIATION Identification with a political party is another motivation for voting. The more intense a person's partisan affiliation, the more likely that person will be to vote. From the late 1960s through the 1980s, partisan attitudes weakened while the proportion of the population claiming to be independent increased. These factors contributed to declining turnout during this period. *MY VOTE MATTERS*

Political efficacy, the belief that one's vote really matters, declined during this period, which also reduced voting, according to three political scientists, Paul R. Abramson, John H. Aldrich, and David W. Rhode, who study voting

TABLE 2.1	**Voter Turnout in the Battleground States, 2008–2012 (percentages)**	
		Percentage
Battleground State	2008	2012
Colorado	71.6	71.1
Florida	68.0	63.6
Iowa	69.7	70.2
Nevada	57.2	57.2
New Hampshire	72.5	70.9
North Carolina	66.1	66.1
Ohio	67.8	65.2
Pennsylvania	64.2	59.4
Virginia	67.6	66.9
Wisconsin	72.7	72.5
U.S. average	62.2	58.7

Note: Figures based on the total number of ballots cast by eligible voters.

Source: Michael P. McDonald, "General Election Turnout Rates," http://elections.gmu.edu/Turnout_2008G.html; http://elections.gmu.edu/Turnout_ 2012G.html.

behavior.[39] People became more cynical and less trusting of government and those who ran it. Many felt that government was less sensitive to their needs, run for special interests by politicians who would say and do practically anything to get elected and reelected. The perception that public officials were more interested in serving their own needs than those of their constituents fueled the belief that it just didn't matter all that much who won.[40]

Political efficacy has remained low, but in 2008, it was less related to participation than was partisan identification except for voters who considered themselves independents.[41]

Social and Economic Factors. Several social and economic variables, such as education, income, and age, also correlate with turnout as well as with one another. Of these factors, education is the most important. The greater a person's education, the more likely it is that person will vote.[42] Higher learning develops the cognitive skills necessary to process information and to make informed judgments. It provides the skills to maneuver through the intricacies of the electoral process: meeting the registration requirements, obtaining an absentee ballot, and understanding the ballot and how to mark it correctly.[43]

Education also affects personal success. It increases a person's stake in the system, interest in an election, and concern over the outcome. Because the lesson that voting is a civic responsibility is usually learned in the classroom, schooling can contribute to a more highly developed sense of civic responsibility.[44]

Education, income level, and occupational status tend to correlate with one another. College-educated people have better connections, more skills, and greater knowledge; as a consequence, they have more opportunities to earn more money than those who lack these resources. They also have a greater stake in their community, hence a greater desire to choose the officials that make and implement public policy.

Individuals with higher incomes and more professional jobs also have higher rates of voter turnout. Income differentials are even more evident in other forms of electoral activity, such as volunteering to help a campaign and, especially, contributing money. Naturally, the large donors tend to be the most affluent citizens.

Age is another factor that contributes to voting. Older citizens turn out in higher numbers than those who are younger. They may do so because they have more interest in the election, more concern over the outcome and how it might affect them, and, in some cases, more time to become involved. In addition, older people tend to have greater economic interests and community ties, two other reasons for participating. For many of them, too, voting is a habit developed over the years.

With education and income levels rising since the end of World War II, one would have expected turnout to increase during most of this period. It did not do so, however. Between the 1960s and the 1990s, turnout declined. Most scholars believe that the decline would have been more severe had not education and income levels risen.[45]

What then explains the decline in turnout during this period? A growing number of political scientists see rising inequality as a principal culprit. The gap among income groups in the United States has widened, not only between the rich and poor, but also between the rich and the middle class.[46] The disparity in incomes has contributed to living patterns segregated on the basis of income in which residents of the wealthier communities have more incentives to vote—more education, more political awareness, and more civic responsibility—while those who live in the poorest communities have fewer incentives to do so.[47]

The differences in participation among groups along economic and social lines have also been affected by organizational change. Special-interest groups, structured on the basis of industries, professions, and beliefs, have proliferated while mass-mobilization groups, such as labor unions, have declined. According to Joe Soss and Lawrence R. Jacobs, these social changes have encouraged political parties and their nominees to focus their turnout efforts among the people who would be most likely to vote, thereby enlarging the participation gap between the advantaged and disadvantaged.[48] The gap has been evident in recent elections. Turnout percentages increase as income levels get higher.

Situational Variables. The electoral environment also contributes to or detracts from voting. In addition to the level of competition between the parties and their nominees, the state of the economy, the saliency of issues, and the political climate all affect turnout and voting behavior. The more people are upset with the current state of affairs, the more likely they are to vote. Bad economic conditions tend to bring out more people than do good conditions. Similarly, issues that directly affect significant portions of the population are more likely to generate turnout than those which are theoretical or not of immediate concern. Naturally, the attractiveness of the candidates, the scope and impact of their appeals, the excitement of the campaign, coverage by the news media, and personal and social networking are also factors, individually and collectively, which can result in a larger proportion of the population voting.

In 2004, concern with international and domestic terrorism combined with social issues—such as same-sex marriage—motivated more people to vote. The Republican campaign highlighted these issues to mobilize a larger-than-usual vote. In 2008, broad dissatisfaction with the George W. Bush administration over the war in Iraq, the abrogation of civil liberties, the sharp rise in the costs of energy, and, especially, mushrooming economic problems—declining property values; increasing mortgage foreclosures; the credit crisis; the failure of major investments firms, banks, and a major insurer; and increasing unemployment—all led to a higher turnout.

Contributing also was the resonance and hopefulness of Barack Obama's campaign message, "Yes, we can"; the effective use of the Internet by his campaign operatives to raise money, gain volunteers, get out voters; the expanded efforts of his campaign in the normally red (Republican) states; and the excitement that his candidacy generated for Democrats and independents, particularly for younger voters and racial and ethnic minorites; all these elements worked to stimulate a larger vote. In 2012, high voting turnout by minorities, especially Hispanics, combined with an effective get-out-the-vote campaign by Obama to keep turnout near its 2008 levels.

CONSEQUENCES OF NOT VOTING

Does it matter that so many of those eligible to vote do not do so? Most observers believe that it does, even though they concede that the outcome of most elections and the policies of newly elected officials might be the same even if a greater number of nonvoters participated. Postelection surveys of voters and nonvoters show little difference in their candidate selections, policy preferences, and political attitudes.[49] Their findings suggest after elections nonvoters say that they support the winning candidates in roughly the same proportion as do voters.[50] Moreover, the policy positions of voters and nonvoters also seem to be similar, but there is no way of knowing whether nonvoter preferences would be confirmed if nonvoters actually voted. A hypothetical proposition cannot be tested empirically, so we do not know whether the results of the election would change.

There is evidence, however, that turnout has significant partisan implications. Since Republicans in general are more likely to possess certain demographic characteristics that contribute to greater turnout—higher income, more education, and an older age—and all things being equal, they are more likely voters than Democrats and have, for the most part, since 1948, according to the post-election surveys conducted by the American National Election Studies.[51] That Republicans usually constitute a larger number of likely voters led the Romney campaign to conclude on the eve of the 2012 election that they would win when their polls showed them ahead among this group. However, the Obama campaign successfully expanded the electorate by getting more of those less likely to participate to do so. The larger-than-usual turnout among less likely voters increased the Democrats' share of the total vote.[52] The same logic would apply to the partisan minority within a district. If partisan intensity contributes to the decision to vote, then it would follow that a larger-than-usual turnout would include more people with less strongly held partisan views or no partisan views at all. In either case, the odds are that the partisan majority within the electoral district would be adversely affected.[53]

Incumbency is a third variable that is affected by turnout. Grievances against elected officials energize the electorate more than does contentment or apathy. Anger is a strong motivator for political participation. That is why an unfavorable environment, such as a bad economy, hurts incumbents more than a favorable environment helps them. Moreover, the greater the unpopularity of incumbents, the more likely they will face quality challengers also adversely impacting on their reelection.[54]

Turnout also has significant implications for a democratic electoral process. It weakens the link between citizens and their elected representatives. It also enlarges the representational gap between the general public and the electorate.

Unequal Representation and Turnout

The demographic differences between voters and nonvoters have produced an electorate that is not representative of the general population. It has also resulted in class bias in voting as well as in other aspects of electoral activity, such as contributing money to the candidates and parties, attending rallies, and volunteering time.

Those who are most disadvantaged, who have the least education and the lowest incomes, and who need a change in conditions the most, actually participate the least in the electoral process. Those who are the most advantaged by having high incomes and more education and who benefit from existing conditions and presumably from public policy as it stands, vote more regularly. These trends in who votes work to reinforce, even to perpetuate, the status quo and have contributed to unequal representation in government.

The tendency of higher-income, well-connected, older Americans to get more involved in politics and to vote more often has naturally encouraged candidates seeking office to address those voters' issues, be they taxes, health care costs, or the security of pension plans, rather than issues in which the poor and the young might have more interest and concern, such as obtaining health care coverage, the availability of government subsidies for housing, or overcrowding in prisons. If issues are geared to those who vote, then it follows that elected officials are more likely to make policy decisions that reflect the interests and desires of those who elected them rather than people who voted against them or stood on the sidelines.

Research by prominent political scientists provides empirical evidence that political activity enhances representation.[55] In other words, those who are more active and tend to vote more regularly tend to reap the benefits of their participation in the political process. They select like-minded individuals, communicate their beliefs and desires to them, and use the threat to defeat them in the next election to persuade their representatives to support their interests.[56] It is more likely that the policy issues of these activists will be addressed, and probably in a manner that works to their economic and social self-interest.

Having the will and resources to affect political activity allows the advantaged to maintain and even extend their advantage. The American Political Science Association's Task Force on Inequality and American Democracy put it this way:

The privileged participate more than others and are increasingly well organized to press their demands on government. Public officials, in turn, are much more responsive to the privileged than to average citizens and the least affluent. Citizens with lower or moderate incomes speak with a whisper that is lost on the ears of inattentive government officials, while the advantaged roar with a clarity and consistency that policymakers readily hear and routinely follow. The scourge of overt discrimination against African-Americans and women has been replaced by a more subtle but potent threat—the growing concentration of the country's wealth and income in the hands of the few.[57]

In short, economic inequality extends political inequality, which in turn is reflected in public policy decisions. It is a vicious cycle, one that is difficult to break. To do so would require that the disadvantaged organize and increase their level of participation and that the advantaged share more equitably the benefits they receive.

In addition to income gaps, turnout differentials among political parties and ethnic, racial, and gender groups also affect their representation throughout the political system in elections, governance, and public policy. The turnout advantage that Republicans enjoy has given the GOP greater legislative representation than their proportion of the population would merit. Similarly, greater turnout by men than women until 2004 reinforced their electoral success. Although more women voted than men in 2004 and 2008, the percentage of women elected to office has increased only marginally. The election of 2008 was the first in which the turnout of whites and blacks was the same.[58] In contrast, Hispanics, one of the largest and most rapidly growing ethnic groups in America, constitute about 16 percent of the population but were only 7 percent of 2010 electorate, one percent more than in the previous midterm election.[59] Hispanic turnout increased in 2012 to 10 percent of the electorate according to the large exit poll conducted for major news organizations by Edison Research (see Table 9.2).

Increased Difficulties Governing

In addition to representational issues, variations in turnout can produce other problems for a democratic electoral process. Low turnout can make the meaning of the election less clear, the claim of a public mandate more problematic, and the task of fulfilling campaign pledges and promises more difficult. It also can have a negative impact on building and maintaining a majority coalition for governing. If fewer people vote, the proportion of the population who will be initially supportive of the newly elected government will be smaller, and those in elective positions may find it more difficult to gain support for their policies and legitimacy for their actions.

Low turnout can also become a policy issue. One of the cornerstones of U.S. foreign policy since the end of World War II has been the promotion of and support for democratic values, institutions, and processes around the world. The failure of so many Americans to vote undercuts the credibility of that policy goal. Compare voter turnout in the United States with turnouts in other democratic countries, as shown in Table 2.2.

Some scholars actually see benefit in having a significant proportion of the electorate not voting on a regular basis. They claim that lack of interest and inactivity enhances the quality of those who participate, mutes political conflict, promotes social stability, and implicitly provides support for public policy decisions by not challenging those decisions or holding policymakers accountable.[60] In this sense, apathy can be viewed as satisfaction with existing conditions; otherwise, it is argued, people would be more likely to protest in the streets and at the ballot box. Those who support this position point to the fact that bad times and discontent normally bring out a larger vote than do good times and public contentment.[61]

Most democratic theorists, however, do not subscribe to the belief that apathy is a positive social trait. Rather, they see it as an illness, a symptom of discontent within the political system by a significant segment of the population.[62]

POSSIBLE SOLUTIONS TO THE NONVOTING PROBLEM

Change the Electoral System

Although they are not required to do so, most states have established single-member legislative districts in which the candidate with the most votes wins. A few states require the winner to receive a majority of the total vote; in most states, however, a plurality is sufficient.

A winner-take-all voting system is easy to understand, consistent with the one person-one vote principle, and fair so long as all adult citizens have the right to vote. But such a system does not necessarily encourage voting *unless the election is competitive;* and most elections in the United States are not. If the winner takes all, the losers and the people who voted for them get nothing. Thus, for those in the minority, whose views are not likely to prevail and whose candidates are not likely to win, what is the incentive to vote?

Being a good citizen and fulfilling a civic responsibility are not sufficient motivation for a significant proportion of the eligible population to vote. Having influence on election outcomes and on the resulting governance and public policy are motivation, however.[63] Thus, one way to encourage more people to vote is to make elections more competitive; another is to change the system itself so that more people vote for the winners.

Elections are not competitive for two major reasons: one relates to the drafting of the districts and the other to the candidates running for office. The party in power drafts legislative districts in such a way as to maximize its competitive advantage, a practice is known as gerrymandering.[64] Thus, most districts are drawn in such a way as to favor one or the other of the major parties, hardly an incentive for opponents of that party to get out and vote.

TABLE 2.2 International Voter Turnout in Selected Countries

Country	Year	Type of election	Turnout of Voting-Age Population voters (percentage)	Registration required to be on voting lists: yes (Y) or no (N); Voting: voluntary (V) or compulsory (C)	Rest day (R) or workday (W)
Argentina	2011	Presidential	77.4	Y / C	R
Australia	2010	Parliamentary	81.2	Y / C	R
Austria	2010	Presidential	49.1	Y / V	R
Belgium	2010	Parliamentary	93.3	Y / C	R
Brazil	2010	Parliamentary/Presidential	80.6/77.2	Y / C	R
Canada	2011	Parliamentary	53.8	N / V	W
Chile	2010	Presidential	59.1	Y / C	R
Czech Rep.	2010	Parliamentary	78.5	Y / C	W
Egypt	2012	Parliamentary/Presidential	55.0/50.0	Y / C	W
Finland	2011	Parliamentary	70.1	Y / V	B*
France	2012	Presidential	71.2	Y / V	R
Germany	2009	Parliamentary	64.6	Y / V	R
Greece	2012	Parliamentary	69.4	Y / C	R
India	2009	Parliamentary	56.5	Y / V	B*
Iran	2009	Presidential	75.5	N / V	R
Iraq	2010	Parliamentary	64.0	N / V	W
Ireland	2011	Parliamentary	63.8	N / V	W
Israel	2013	Parliamentary	67.8	Y / V	W

(continued on next page)

TABLE 2.2 **International Voter Turnout in Selected Countries** (*continued*)

Country	Year	Type of election	Turnout of Voting-Age Population voters (percentage)	Registration required to be on voting lists: yes (Y) or no (N); Voting: voluntary (V) or compulsory (C)	Rest day (R) or workday (W)
Japan	2012	Parliamentary	59.3	Y / V	R
Korea, Rep. of	2012	Parliamentary/Presidential	54.3/75.8	Y / V	
Mexico	2012	Parliamentary/Presidential	63.7/64.6	Y / C	R
Poland	2011	Parliamentary	48.5	Y / V	R
Romania	2009	Presidential	59.2	Y / V	R
Russia	2011	Parliamentary	60.1	Y / V	R
South Africa	2009	Parliamentary	56.6	N / V	R
South Korea	2012	Parliamentary	56.4	Y / V	R
Spain	2011	Parliamentary	63.3	Y / V	W
Switzerland	2011	Parliamentary	40.0	Y / V	R
United Kingdom	2010	Parliamentary	65.8	Y / V	R
United States	2010	Legislative	41.6	N / V	W
	2012	Presidential	53.4	N / V	W

B* = Election conducted over more than one day.

Sources: International Foundation for Electoral Systems, "Electionguide.org: Voter Turnout," www.electionguide.org; Michael M. MacDonald, "2010 and 2012 General Election Turnout Rates," United States Elections Project, George Mason University, http://elections.gmu.edu/Turnout_2010G.html; http://elections.gmu.edu/Turnout_2012G. html; International Institute for Democracy and Electoral Assistance, "Voter Turnout," www.idea.int/vt/index.cfm.

A second factor that discourages turnout is the advantage that incumbents have when they run for reelection. Their name recognition, fund-raising abilities, services, and other tangible benefits they can provide constituents plus experienced office staff and campaign operatives help them gain renomination and reelection by sizable margins. These margins discourage quality challengers.

Reversing these noncompetitive aspects of elections would require those in power to reduce or eliminate their political advantage, an action that they are unlikely to undertake voluntarily. In the interests of promoting more democratic elections, a few states have established nonpartisan legislative or judicial commissions to redraw their electoral districts to maximize competition.[65] A few more have tried to limit the advantage of incumbency by enacting more equitable campaign finance laws and by establishing term limits. Both of these legal and constitutional reforms have engendered considerable political opposition within the states as well as legal challenges, however. The Supreme Court has held that limiting congressional terms by statute violates the Constitution because it adds an additional qualification to the three constitutional qualifications that currently exist for holding national office.[66]

The alternative is to change the electoral structure itself from single-member to multimember districts, and change the system by which the results are tabulated from winner-take-all to proportional voting. Such a change would increase the incentives for more candidates to run and more parties to compete. It would give voters more choices in the election, likely provide them with more responsive public officials after the election, and thus enable more people to influence government and public policy. All of these factors should encourage more people to vote.

But power within the political and governmental systems would also be more dispersed; majority coalitions would become more difficult to build and maintain; as a consequence, the government would be less stable, public policy less innovative, and accountability more difficult to pinpoint. These changes would also run counter to the American political tradition, one that has received considerable support over the years. Opposition to changing the way Americans select their president has prevented a modification of the Electoral College despite the election of three nonplurality winners, the controversial vote in Florida in 2000, and numerous other problems (see Chapter 3).

Lower the Costs of Voting

What can be done about the problem of nonvoting? Describing the problem—the reasons people give for not voting—and the factors that influence turnout is easier than solving it. Congress has dealt with the issue by enacting two laws. The first, the National Voter Registration Act of 1993 (also called the motor-voter bill), designed to make registration easier, more accessible, and less time-consuming, has done so although not as much as the Congress hoped.[67] (See Table 2.3.) The second, the Help America Vote Act of 2002, was intended

TABLE 2.3	**Registration History since the Enactment of the "Motor Voter" Law**

Year	Voting Age Population (VAP) (in millions)	Registered Voters (in millions)	Registered Percentage of VAP
2012	240.9	*	*
2010	237.4	186.9	78.7
2008	233.1	190.5	81.7
2006	225.7	172.8	76.6
2004	220.4	176.2	79.9
2002	215.1	160.7	74.7
2000	209.8	162.5	77.4
1998	201.3	154.0	76.5
1996	196.8	150.4	76.4
1994	193.0	134.1	69.5
1992	189.5		

* Not Available

Source: "Election Administration and Vote Survey: Registration History," Election Assistance Commission, June 30, 2011. www.eac.gov/assets/1/Documents/2010%20NRA%FINAL%20REPORT.pdf

to improve the accuracy of registration lists and vote tabulation methods as well as provide better oversight of the decisions state and local electoral officials make on election day. The intent of the law was avoiding election controversies, thereby boosting the legitimacy of elections among various population groups that may have perceived discrimination, and maximizing voter turnout. Although turnout has improved, many problems still remain.

Professor Heather Gerken, an election expert at Yale Law School, describes the electoral system in the United States as "clunky at best and dysfunctional at worst." Ballots are discarded. Poll workers are poorly trained. Registration lists work badly. Lines can be too long. Machines malfunction. Partisan officials change the rules of the game to help themselves and hurt their enemies. Election administrators cannot agree on what constitutes a best practice, or even whether there is any such thing. Authority is decentralized, so it's hard to know who's to blame when a problem occurs. Most experts agree that the election system chronically underfunded, often poorly run, and sometimes administered in a partisan fashion.[68]

Aware of the difficulties of enacting more legislation at state and federal levels to better fund elections, train election officials, and reduce partisan influence, Gerken suggests that states and localities calculate how democratic their election systems actually are with the use of a democracy index. That index would be based on three criteria: voter registration (the extent to which every eligible voter who wants to register can do so), voting (the extent to which every registered voter who wants to cast a vote can do so), and vote tabulation (the accurate counting of every ballot that is properly cast). Gerken believes that the system needs to be convenient for citizens and that it needs to have votes tabulated in a timely and accurate manner.[69]

Implementing a democracy index would not require additional national legislation, although it might require greater funding, both public and private, to collect the data necessary for election officials to calculate their democracy score. Gerken is counting on the competitive instincts of states and local election officials and the people they represent; she sees bragging power and pride in being more democratic than other states and communities as the primary motivating factor that will improve the conduct of elections and involve the general public in those efforts.

The Pew Center of the States has followed through on Gerken's suggestion. In 2013, the Pew Center released a comprehensive, interactive Performance Index which measures how well states are administering their elections based on 17 criteria that include absentee and provisional voting, military overseas ballots, registration procedures, tabulation accuracy, and wait times.[70] (You can determine how well your state is doing by accessing the Pew site at www.pew states.org/research/data-visualizations/measuring-state-election-performance.)

President Obama has also recognized problems. In his 2013 State of the Union address, he stated that a 102-year-old Florida resident (who was in the audience) had to wait in line over 3 hours to vote. The president proposed a national, bipartisan commission on election reform to examine wait time and other voting issues.

What else can be done by Congress and the states to reduce the personal costs of voting, costs measured in time, effort, and perhaps lost wages? One way to make it easier for people to find the time to vote is to hold elections on days that are not workdays for most people—for example, on a holiday or a Sunday. The United States is one of the few democracies that still conduct elections on a workday (see Table 2.3). Although employers are required by law to give their employees time to vote, and not penalize them financially for doing so, some people still find it difficult to take the time off to vote.

Making election day a holiday would make it easier for more people to vote; however, there would be opposition to such a proposal. Some businesses would lose money by being closed or forced to pay employees extra for working on a holiday. Schools would be closed, thereby increasing the burden on single parents. And some people employed in essential or recreational services, such as police, fire, hospital, or even restaurant employees, would still have to work.

A second and somewhat less costly alternative would be to combine election day (held on the Tuesday following the first Monday in November) and Veterans Day (November 11), a proposal made by the Federal Election Commission in 2001. However, veterans groups might object to partisan politics replacing the raison d'être for a federal holiday that memorializes those who fought and died in defense of their country.

Instead of being held on a federal holiday, elections could be held on a Sunday, as they are in many European countries. But Sunday elections would compete with religious services, recreational activities, and family events.[71] Besides, many people work on Sundays or are otherwise engaged (especially during the professional football season). Under the circumstances, it is not clear whether turnout would increase all that much if elections were held on a Sunday or whether the American people would support such a change. Turnout could conceivably decrease.

As we have already noted, some states have extended the time people have for voting, although in recent years some have also cut back on their extended period, citing budget constraints as the primary reason.[72] Most keep their voting places open for at least twelve hours; some allow their citizens to vote up to twenty-one days before the election. Others permit "no-fault" absentee ballots, so people can vote by mail without having to certify that they will be out of the state at the time of the election. Oregon has gone even further. In 1998, voters in that state approved a ballot initiative that requires voting by mail ballot. Voting over the Internet also may be a possibility in the not-so-distant future if the security and integrity of the voting system can be protected.[73]

Increase the Costs of Not Voting

The most far-reaching and controversial proposal for increasing the proportion of the population who votes is simply to require voting as an obligation of citizenship and fine those who fail to do so. After all, there are other citizen obligations mandated by law that have penalties for noncompliance, obligations such as reporting for selective service, paying income taxes, and serving on juries. Should voting be treated any differently from these other civic responsibilities? For several democratic countries, the answer is no. Australia, Argentina, Belgium, Brazil, and more recently South Africa, have mandatory voting systems, and their turnouts are naturally higher than countries which do not make voting compulsory. (See Table 2.2.)

Requiring all citizens to vote would convert equality in theory to near-equality in practice. Moreover, it would reduce the distinction between the electorate and the population. Government officials would have to be more responsive to the entire adult population rather than to just a portion of their electoral constituency. With mandatory voting, the poor, less educated, less informed, and less partisan would be better represented than they are today.

But mandatory voting also could result in less informed and perhaps less intelligent electoral decisions. It could reduce the quality of the electorate's judgment. Besides, there would undoubtedly be strong opposition to such a proposal. Some argue that mandatory voting would prevent people from protesting the choices they have by boycotting the election. Others claim that mandatory voting is undemocratic, that a democracy which prides itself on personal liberty should allow its citizens to decide whether or not they wish to vote.

Enhance the Incentives for Voting

With individual choice a value and voting a basic right, those interested in expanding participation have suggested other ways to encourage more people to participate in elections. These include engaging in media campaigns in which prominent citizens urge others to get involved; better civic education in schools and communities, in which the responsibilities of citizenship are stressed; and bipartisan informational campaigns by parties and nonpartisan groups that would tell people why they should get out and vote. These so-called bipartisan efforts have themselves become controversial, however, because they have been used by political parties and nonparty groups to further their own political agendas and circumvent campaign finance regulations.

More effective grassroots organizing seems to have gotten more people to vote, but such an expenditure of time, money, and effort by the political parties cannot be legislated by Congress or the states. More competitive elections also should improve turnout, but the parties have little motivation for decreasing their number of safe seats. Holding fewer elections might boost turnout as well, but such a proposal would require longer terms of office, a proposition that a cynical and distrustful public is unlikely to support. Gaining better representation for those in the minority in electoral districts might encourage more people to vote, but achieving this representation would probably involve a fundamental change in the electoral system from single-member districts and plurality voting to multi-member districts and proportional voting. Such a proposal is unlikely to be supported by a majority of the American people.

Other ideas include shortening the election cycle, limiting negative campaigning, instituting voluntary codes of conduct for candidates, and providing more and better information about the candidates and their positions. But such changes might run up against the First Amendment protections of freedom of speech and of the press, and they are thus not likely to be legislated by Congress or upheld by the federal judiciary.

The bottom line is citizens' beliefs about politics and government need to conform to their actual behavior if voter turnout is going to be significantly increased. There's no easy way to accomplish this objective. Periodic scandals involving people in government, campaign finance issues, and the concentration of presidential campaigns in a relatively few contested states have contributed to public cynicism and mistrust of politicians. In short, nonvoting remains an attitudinal problem, one that is not likely to go away soon.

Getting people to the polls is only part of the problem; getting them to vote properly and getting officials to count those votes accurately is another one. Voting procedures need to be simplified, and the tabulation of votes needs to be improved.[74] Suggestions include eliminating confusing ballot designs, replacing aging voting machines and punch cards with optical scan equipment and computers, allowing voters who accidentally spoil their ballots or make mistakes to correct them, and having enough election officials on hand to explain how to vote to those who have difficulty doing so.

SUMMARY: SUFFRAGE AND TURNOUT DILEMMAS IN A NUTSHELL

The U.S. electoral system wasn't designed to be a participatory democracy, but it has been evolving toward one. In theory, there is universal suffrage; in practice, most people do not vote regularly. In theory, every adult citizen has an equal opportunity to participate; in practice, those with greater resources are in a better position to do so. In fact, educational and economic advantages are both motivations for and consequences of voting. In theory, elected officials are supposed to be responsive to all the people; in practice, they tend to be more accessible and responsive to those who elected them, and even if that were not the case, the public perceives it to be, and that perception creates an appearance of inequality.

Although low turnout is thought to be undesirable in and for a democratic political system, the remedies lawmakers have proposed and instituted to deal with the problem have not worked nearly as well as their sponsors had hoped. While the institutional barriers to voting have been reduced but not eliminated, minority turnout has increased. The emphasis on grassroots organizing, especially the use of new communication technologies, has helped generate that increase have more competitive elections and more money raised and spent in them. But the increase in private funding has also undercut public financing of presidential elections, giving an advantage to wealthy candidates and those who have the ability to raise large amounts of money. It has also contributed to the public perception that money influences election outcomes.

The problem of nonvoting has resisted easy solutions. It is as much an attitude problem as anything else, and changing attitudes is difficult. Legislation alone cannot do so. It will require a major effort by those in and outside of government to reconstitute the civic culture and reestablish trust between the voters and their elected officials. There are no easy and quick fixes for the root causes of the nonvoting—public alienation and cynicism, mistrust of politicians and public officials, and the haphazard way in which elections are conducted in the states and local precincts.

Now It's Your Turn

Discussion Questions

1. Can the public's will be expressed in an election if all adults—or most—do not vote?

2. Should voting be an obligation of citizenship? If so, should that obligation be enforced by penalties for those who do not comply?

3. Should people with little interest in the election and information about it be encouraged (or even entitled) to vote?

4. Should registration be made automatic for citizens in the states in which they officially reside?

5. Should electoral systems, voting rules, and the administration of elections for national officials continue to be set by the states and counties or should the federal government determine these?

6. Should election day be a holiday or a non-workday, such as Sunday, or should voting be extended for a longer period of time? If so, which level of government—federal, state, or local—should pay for that extension?

Topics for Debate

Challenge or defend the following statements:

1. Universal suffrage is neither necessary nor desirable.

2. Nonvoting is really not a major problem for American democracy.

3. Literacy tests should be instituted in a nondiscriminatory manner to ensure that people have sufficient information about the candidates and issues to make an informed judgment.

4. States should permit voting via mail, the Internet, or telephone, if there is a secure way to do so.

5. The right to vote should not be abridged by conviction for a crime or during or after periods of incarceration.

6. Truly competitive electoral districts should be required in a democratic political system.

Exercises

1. Rock the Vote, a public interest organization dedicated to increasing voter turnout, particularly among younger citizens, has run a public relations campaign during recent presidential elections to increase electoral awareness, to provide potential voters with more information about the candidates and their campaigns, and, most important, to get more people registered to vote. It plans to run another educational campaign during the next election cycle. If that organization asked you for advice on how to organize and orchestrate such a campaign, what would you recommend?
   a. To whom should it direct its campaign?
   b. What should its principal appeals be, and how should they be articulated to achieve maximum impact?
   c. Should the content of those appeals change over the course of the campaign?
   d. What should be the principal means of communication?
   e. In addition to a public appeal, what else could the group do to enhance its educational efforts and achieve its principal objectives?

2. The National Commission on Federal Election Reform has proposed making election day a national holiday, establishing statewide systems of voter registration, replacing punch cards with ballots that can be optically scanned, and banning election-night predictions on the major networks until voting is completed within the continental United States. Assess these recommendations on the basis of

   a. their likelihood of increasing voter turnout;
   b. their costs to the governments that run the elections and to individuals who vote in them;
   c. their benefit to the major parties, third parties, and independent candidates;
   d. their constitutionality.

   On the basis of your assessment, indicate which (if any) of the recommendations of the commission you support and which (if any) you oppose.

INTERNET RESOURCES

- Center for Voting and Democracy: www.fairvote.org

  Organization devoted to making American elections more democratic by constitutional and legislative reforms.

- Common Cause: www.commoncause.org

  Public interest group concerned with electoral reform, media and democracy, and accountability in government.

- Election Assistance Commission: www.eac.gov

  Created by the Help America Vote Act, this national commission allows people to download a national voter registration form and provides information on where to send it. It also collects useful data on registration and turnout.

- League of Women Voters: www.lwv.org

  Established public interest group that publishes books and pamphlets on election activities, including information about the candidates and ballot initiatives. The league also lobbies Congress for campaign reform.

- Pew Center on the States: http://www.pewstates.org/issues/election-administration-328132

  Sponsored by the Pew Charitable Trusts, the Pew Center on the States does research on election administration and information on new election initiatives.

- Project Vote Smart: www.vote-smart.org

  Another public interest group dedicated to educating the electorate, particularly younger voters, on the issues, the candidates, and the records of public officials. The group distributes free toolkits for citizens and lots of information online.

- Public Citizen: www.citizen.org

  Public interest group started by citizen-activist Ralph Nader that is concerned with the rules and procedures that govern elections in the United States, openness of government, and accountability of those in office.

- Rock the Vote: www.rockthevote.org

  Getting people to register and vote is the primary goal of this public interest organization. Its Web site provides a short form that can be used to begin the registration process. Rock the Vote will even remind those who registered through its site to vote on election day.

SELECTED READINGS

American Political Science Association Task Force on Inequality and American Democracy. "American Democracy in an Age of Rising Inequality." *Perspectives on Politics* 2 (December 2004): 651–666.

Berinsky, Adam J. "The Perverse Consequences of Electoral Reform in the United States." *American Politics Research* 33 (July 2005): 471–491.

Burnham, Walter D. "The Turnout Problem." In *Elections American Style*, edited by A. James Reichley. Washington, DC: Brookings Institution, 1987.

Crigler, Ann N., Marion R. Just, and Edward J. McCaffery, eds. *Rethinking the Vote: The Politics and Prospects of American Electoral Reform*. New York, NY: Oxford University Press, 2004.

Gelman, Andrew, David Park, Boris Shor, Joseph Bafumi, and Jeronimo Cortina. *Red State, Blue State, Rich State, Poor State: Why Americans Vote the Way They Do*. Princeton, NJ: Princeton University Press, 2008.

Gerken, Heather K. *The Democracy Index: Why Our Election System Is Failing and How to Fix It*. Princeton, NJ: Princeton University Press, 2009.

Gilens, Martin. "Inequality and Democratic Responsiveness." *Public Opinion Quarterly* 69 (December 2005): 778–796.

Gomez, Brad T., Thomas G. Hansford, and George A. Krause. "The Republicans Should Pray for Rain: Weather, Turnout, and Voting in U.S. Presidential Elections." *Journal of Politics* 69 (August 2007): 649–663.

Iverson, Torben, and David Soskice. "Electoral Institutions, Parties, and the Politics of Class: Why Some Democracies Distribute More Than Others." *American Political Science Association* 100 (May 2006): 165–181.

Jacobs, Lawrence R., and Theda Skocpol, eds. *Inequality and American Democracy: What We Know and What We Need to Learn*. New York, NY: Russell Sage Foundation, 2005.

Kaufman, Karen M., John R. Petrocik, and Daron R. Shaw. *Unconventional Wisdom: Facts and Myths about American Voters*. New York, NY: Oxford University Press, 2008.

Leighley, Jan E. *Strength in Numbers? The Political Mobilization of Racial and Ethnic Minorities.* Princeton, NJ: Princeton University Press, 2001.

McDonald, Michael P. "The Return of the Voter: Turnout in the 2008 Presidential Election." *The Forum* 6, no. 4 (2008): article 4.

McDonald, Michael P., and Samuel Popkin. "The Myth of the Vanishing Voter." *American Political Science Review* 95 (December 2001): 963–974.

Overton, Spencer. *Stealing Democracy: The New Politics of Voter Suppression.* New York, NY: Norton, 2006.

Piven, Frances Fox, and Richard A. Cloward. *Why Americans Don't Vote.* New York, NY: Pantheon, 1988.

Powell, G. Bingham. *Elections as Instruments of Democracy: Majoritarian and Proportional Visions.* New Haven, CT: Yale University Press, 2000.

Rosenstone, Steven J., and John Mark Hansen. *Mobilization, Participation, and Democracy in America.* New York, NY: Macmillan, 1993.

Schlozman, Kay Lehman. "Citizen Participation in America: What Do We Know? Why Do We Care?" In *Political Science: The State of the Discipline,* edited by Ira Katznelson and Helen V. Milner. New York, NY: W.W. Norton, 2002.

Soss, Joe, and Lawrence R. Jacobs. "The Place of Inequality: Non-Participation in the American Polity." *Political Science Quarterly* 124 (Spring 2009): 99–125.

Teixeira, Ruy A. *The Disappearing American Voter.* Washington, DC: Brookings Institution, 1992.

Verba, Sidney, Kay Lehman Schlozman, and Henry E. Brady. *Voice and Equality: Civic Voluntarism in American Politics.* Cambridge, MA: Harvard University Press, 1995.

Wolfinger, Raymond E., and Jonathan Hoffman. "Registering and Voting with Motor Voter." *PS: Political Science and Politics* 34 (March 2001): 85–92.

NOTES

1. Noncitizens, such as legal and illegal immigrants who are residents of the United States, also have a stake in the system. They have common interests, needs, and obligations, including the payment of taxes on income earned in the United States. They are not afforded voting rights, however, until they become American citizens. For people who entered the country illegally, it is often difficult and takes considerable to meet the legal requirements for citizenship.

2. For an excellent study of turnout since the beginning of the Republic, see Walter Dean Burnham, "The Turnout Problem," in *Elections American Style,* ed. A. James Reichley (Washington, DC: Brookings Institution, 1987), 97–133.

3. In every southern state, a majority of African Americans were *not* eligible to vote until the mid- to late 1960s. Earl Black and Merle Black, *The Vital South: How Presidents Are Elected* (Cambridge, MA: Harvard University Press, 1992), 217.

4. Susan Welch et al., *American Government,* 3rd ed. (St. Paul, MN: West, 1990), 196.

5. Michael X. Delli Carpini and Ester R. Fuchs, "The Year of the Woman? Candidates, Voters, and the 1992 Elections," *Political Science Quarterly* 108 (Spring 1993): 30.

6. Two years later, the Supreme Court extended this prohibition to the election of state and local officials. It did so through its interpretation of the Fourteenth Amendment's equal protection clause, which holds that every person's vote should be equal: one person–one vote.

7. The Justice Department used this provision to challenge laws in Texas and South Carolina in 2012. The Supreme Court is expected to make a decision on these challenges in 2013.

8. Benjamin I. Page and Robert Y. Shapiro, *The Rational Public: Fifty Years of Trends in Americans' Policy Preferences* (Chicago, IL: University of Chicago Press, 1992), 166.

9. Lydia Saad, "Americans Would Swap Electoral College for Popular Vote," Gallup Poll, October 24, 2011. www.gallup.com/poll/150245/Americans-Swap-Electoral College-Popular-Vote

10. Christopher Uggen, Sarah Shannon, and Jeff Manza, "State-Level Estimates of Felon Disenfranchisement in the United States, 2010," The Sentencing Project, 2012. http://sentencing project.org/doc/publications/fd_State_Level_Estimates_of_Felon_Disen_2010.pdf

11. Michael P. McDonald, "Every Eligible Voter Counts: Correctly Measuring American Turnout Rates," n.d., www.brookings.edu/views/Papers/20040909mcdonald.pdf.

12. Janelle Carter, "Election Panel Submits Report to Bush," Associated Press, July 31, 2001. For an analysis of the recommendations of this report, see Brennan Center for Justice at NYU School of Law, Wendy R. Weiser Justin Levitt, Catherine Weiss, and Spencer Overton, "Response to the 2005 Commission on Federal Election Reform," Brennan Center for Justice. www.brennancenter.org

13. Uggen, Shannon, and Manza, "State-Level Estimates."

14. U.S. Commission on Civil Rights, as reported in Robert E. Pierre and Peter Slevin, "Florida Vote Rife with Disparities, Study Says," *Washington Post,* June 5, 2001, sec. A.

15. David Stout, "Study Finds Ballot Problems Are More Likely for Poor," *New York Times,* July 9, 2001. http://www.nytimes.com/2001/07/09/us/study-finds-ballot-problems-are-more-likely-for-poor.html

16. Robert F. Kennedy Jr. alleged in "Was the 2004 Election Stolen?" *Rolling Stone,* June 1, 2006, www.rollingstone.com/news/story/10432334/%20was_the_2004_election_stolen, that President George W. Bush's victory in 2004 was fraudulent. Kennedy cited numerous irregularities, ranging from absentee ballots not received to Democratic registration materials being destroyed to more than one million ballots voided. He also claimed that 350,000 Democratic voters in Ohio were prevented from casting their ballots or having them counted. This number would have been sufficient to reverse the official results in that state.

   Other irregularities also were reported. In the governor's race in the state of Washington, a race that was decided by 129 votes, it was alleged that ineligible ex-felons voted, as well as people who voted in the name of deceased persons. In Wisconsin, one hundred people were alleged to have voted twice. See "Building Confidence in U.S. Elections," *Report of the Commission on Federal Election Reform,* September 2005, 4.

17. Eight states have a strict photo-ID rule. In these states (Georgia, Indiana, Kansas, Mississippi, South Carolina, Tennessee, Texas, and Wisconsin), voters who do not bring a photo-ID to the polls may only cast a provisional ballot, which is counted in the official results only if they bring a photo-ID to election officials within a few days of the election. Other states that have a photo-ID law allow other forms of verification in the absence of the photo-ID.

18. Michael P. McDonald, "General Election Turnout Rates," http://elections.gmu.edu/Turnout_2012G.htm

19. Michael P. McDonald, "2006 General Election Turnout Rates," http://elections.gmu.edu/Turnout_2006G.html; Michael P. McDonald, "2010 General Election Turnout Rates," http://elections.gmu.edu/Turnout_2010G.html.

20. Rhodes Cook, "Democratic Primary Turnout: Comparing 2004 with Previous Highs," www.rhodescook.com/primary.analysis.html; Chris Cillizza and Zachery A. Goldfarb, "Primary Turnout Low," *Washington Post,* October 8, 2006, sec. A.

21. Stephen J. Wayne, "When Democracy Works: The 2008 Presidential Nominations," in *Winning the Presidency,* ed. William J. Crotty (Boulder, CO: Paradigm Publishers, 2009), 50.

22. Michael P. McDonald, "2012 Presidential Nomination Contest Turnout," http://elections.gmu.edu/Turnout_2012P.html

23. Frances Fox Piven and Richard A. Cloward argue that ethnic and religious identities reinforced partisan loyalties to mobilize the vote, particularly among the working class. Similarly, sectional issues and party competitiveness also contributed to the high turnout in the nineteenth century; see their book *Why Americans Don't Vote* (New York, NY: Pantheon, 1988), 26–29.

24. Keith Melder, *Hail to the Candidate* (Washington, DC: Smithsonian Institution Press, 1992), 69–100; Gil Troy, *See How They Ran* (New York, NY: Free Press, 1991), 20–30.

25. The influx of immigrants, first predominantly from northern Europe during the period from 1840 to 1860, and later from southern Europe from 1880 to 1910, provided fertile ground for parties to recruit new partisans by providing them with social services and other benefits in exchange for their votes.

26. For a discussion of the impact of registration reforms on voter turnout, see Michael J. Hammer, *Discount Voting: Voter Registration Reforms and Their Effects.* (New York, NY: Cambridge University Press, 2009).

27. Surveys report a higher rate of voter turnout than do official government records. The reason given for this discrepancy has been that people lie because they think that they should have voted—in other words, they believe the right answer to the question, Did you vote, is "yes." However, political scientists Matthew Berent, Jon A. Krosnick, and Arthur Lupia have uncovered evidence that people who participate in surveys are more likely to vote than those who do not participate. Hence, there may be less lying than was originally thought. See Matthew K. Berent, Jon A. Krosnick, and Arthur Lupia, *The Quality of Government Records and "Overestimation" of Registration and Turnout in Surveys: Lessons from the 2008 ANES Panel Study's Registration and Turnout Validation Exercises.* Working Paper no. nes012554. August 2011Version. Ann Arbor, MI, and Palo Alto, CA: American National Election Studies. http://www.electionstudies.org/resources/papers/nes012554.pdf

28. Pew Research Center for the People and the Press, "American Values Survey," June 4, 2012. http://www.people-press.org/values-questions//q41w/i-feel-its-my-duty-as-a-citizen-to-always-vote/#total

29. Pew Research Center for the People and the Press, "Trends in American Values: 1987–2012," June 4, 2012. http://www.people-press.org/2012/06/04/partisan-polarization-surges-in-bush-obama-years

30. Ibid.

31. Some express doubts about the accuracy of the vote tabulation. Confidence in that accuracy has declined although it varies among states and partisans. Lower confidence is expressed by those whose party and candidates lose.

32. Princeton Survey Research Associates, national survey conducted from October 21 to November 2, 1996.

33. Martin P. Wattenberg and Craig Leonard Brians, "Negative Campaign Advertising: Demobilizer or Mobilizer?" *American Political Science Review* 93 (December 1999): 891–899.

34. Steven Finkel and John Greer, "A Spot Check: Casting Doubt on the Demobilizing Effect of Attack Advertising," *American Journal of Political Science* 42 (April 1998): 573–595; Kim Fridkin Kahn and Patrick J. Kenny, "Do Negative Campaigns Mobilize or Suppress Turnout?" *American Political Science Review* 93 (December 1999): 877–889.

35. Massachusetts Institute of Technology and California Institute of Technology, "Voting: What Is and What Could Be," July 17, 2001; MIT, "Caltech-MIT Team Finds 4–6 Million Votes Lost in the 2000 Election; Nationwide Reforms Outlined in Report," News release, July 16, 2001, http://web.mit.edu/newsoffice/2001/voting2.html.

36. "Inaccurate, Costly, and Inefficient: Evidence that America's Voter Registration System Needs an Upgrade," Pew Center on the States, February 14, 2012. http://www.pewstates.org/research/reports/inaccurate-costly-and-inefficient-85899378437

37. For a detailed discussion of the problems, politics, and consequences of the presidential vote in Florida in 2000, see Charles L. Zelden, *Bush v. Gore: Exposing the Hidden Crisis in American Democracy* (Lawrence: University Press of Kansas, 2008).

38. Martin P. Wattenberg, "Getting Out the Vote," *Public Perspective* (January/February 2001): 16–17.

39. Paul R. Abramson, John H. Aldrich, and David W. Rohde, *Change and Continuity in the 2008 and 2010 Elections* (Washington, DC: CQ Press, 2012), 106–107.

40. Pew Research Center for the People and the Press has conducted polls over the past 15 years that show declining trust and confidence in government. These results were collected in *Deconstructing Distrust*, which Pew published in 1998 and updated in "Public Votes for Continuity and Change in 2000," February 25, 1999. Another survey, "Expecting More Say: The American Public on Its Role in Government Decisionmaking," this by the Center on Policy Attitudes and issued on May 10, 1999, found strong support (74.5 percent) for the proposition that "the government is pretty much run by a few big interests looking out for themselves."

41. Paul R. Abramson, John H. Aldrich, and David W. Rhode, *Change and Continuity in the 2008 and 2010 Elections* (Washington, DC: CQ Press, 2012), 105–106.

42. Raymond E. Wolfinger and Steven J. Rosenstone, *Who Votes?* (New Haven, CT: Yale University Press, 1980), 13–26.

43. Levels of education in the United States have increased since the end of the World War II, but turnout has fluctuated. It decreased from the middle to the end of the twentieth century, but has increased in the twenty-first century, particularly in presidential elections. Reliance on mass media advertising and weakening party organizations contributed to the decrease, while more effective targeting of voters and grassroots organizations by the parties and candidates, beginning in 2004, have resulted in a larger turnout. See Richard A. Brody, "The Puzzle of Participation in America," in *The New American Political System*, ed. Anthony King (Washington, DC: American Enterprise Institute for Public Policy, 1978); Robert D. Putnam, *Bowling Alone: The Collapse and Revival of the American Community* (New York, NY: Simon and Schuster, 2000; Cindy D. Kam and Carl L. Palmer, "Reconsidering the Effects of Education on Political Participation," *Journal of Politics* 70, no. 3 (2008): 612–631.

44. Delli Carpini, Michael X. and Scott Keeter, *What Americans Know about Politics and Why It Matters* (New Haven, CT: Yale University Press, 1996).

45. Abramson, Aldrich, and Rohde, *Change and Continuity*, 95.

46. Professors Joe Soss and Lawrence R. Jacobs describe this gap:

> In a perfectly egalitarian society, each fifth of the population would receive 20 percent of a country's income. Today, the most affluent fifth of Americans receive about 48 percent of the total family income, a sum that is approximately double the proportion received by each of the two quintiles immediately below them (approximately 22.9 percent and 15.3 percent, respectively) and more than fourfold greater than the bottom two quintiles, which each received less than 10 percent of total family income.

Joe Soss and Lawrence R. Jacobs, "The Place of Inequality: Non-Participation in the American Polity," *Political Science Quarterly* 124 (Spring 2000): 101.

47. Ibid., 122.

48. Ibid., 121–122.

49. Ruy A. Teixeira, *The Disappearing American Voter* (Washington, DC: Brookings Institution, 1992), 95. See also Jack Citrin, Eric Schickler, and John Sides, "What If Everyone Voted? Simulating the Impact of Increased Turnout in Senate Elections," *American Journal of Political Science* 47 (January 2003): 75–90; Benjamin Highton and Raymond E. Wolfinger, "The Political Implications of Higher Turnout," *British Journal of Political Science* 31 (January 2001): 179–223; Michael D. Martinez and Jeff Gill, "The Effects of Turnout on Partisan Outcomes in U.S. Presidential Elections, 1960-2000," *Journal of Politics* 67 (November 2005): 1248–1274.

50. Teixeira, *The Disappearing American Voter,* 100.

51. "The ANES Guide to Public Opinion and Electoral Behavior: Voter Turnout, 1948–2008." American National Election Studies, http://www.electionstudies.org/nesguide/2ndtable/t6a_2_2.htm

52. Jane E. Leighley and Jonathan Nagler, "Socioeconomic Class Bias in Turnout, 1964–1988: The Voters Remain the Same," *American Political Science Review* 86 (September 1992): 725–736; Andrew Gelman, David Park, Boris Shor, Joseph Bafumi, and Jeronimo Cortina, *Red State, Blue State, Rich State, Poor State: Why Americans Vote the Way They Do* (Princeton, NJ: Princeton University Press, 2008); James DeNardo, "Turnout and the Vote: The Joke's on the Democrats," *American Political Science Review* 74 (June 1980): 406-420; James DeNardo, "Does Heavy Turnout Help the Democrats in Presidential Elections," *American Political Science Review* 80 (December 1986):1291–1304; Thomas G. Hansford and Brad T. Gomez, "Estimating the Electoral Effects of Voter Turnout," *American Political Science Review* 104 (May 2010): 268-288.

53. DeNardo, "Turnout and the Vote"; DeNardo, "Does Heavy Turnout Help the Democrats?" Jack H. Nagel and John E. McNulty, "Partisan Effects of Turnout in Presidential Elections," *American Political Science Review,* 90 (December 1996): 780-793; Jack H. Nagel and John E. McNulty, "Partisan Effects of Voter Turnout in Presidential Elections, *American Politics Quarterly* 28 (July 2000): 408-429; Hansford and Gomez, "Estimating the Electoral Effects of Voter Turnout," *American Political Science Review.*

54. Bernard Grofman, Guillermo Owen, and Christian Collet, "Rethinking the Partisan Effects of Higher Turnout: So What's the Question?" *Public Choice* 99 (June 1999): 357–376.

55. Sidney Verba, Kay Lehman Schlozman, and Henry E. Brady, *Voice and Equality: Civic Voluntarism in American Politics* (Cambridge, MA: Harvard University Press, 1995).

56. John D. Griffin and Brian Newman, "Are Voters Better Represented?" *Journal of Politics* 67 (November 2005): 1206–1227.

57. Task Force on Inequality and American Democracy of the American Political Science Association, "American Democracy in an Age of Rising Inequality," 2004, 1, www.apsanet.org/imgtest/taskforcereport.pdf.

58. "The ANES Guide to Public Opinion and Electoral Behavior: Voter Turnout, 1948–2008." American National Election Studies, http://www.electionstudies.org/nesguide/2ndtable/t6a_2_2.htm

59. "Census Bureau Reports Hispanic Voter Turnout Reaches Record High for Congressional Election," Census Bureau, September 28, 2011. www.census.gov/newsroom/releases/archives/voting/cb11-164.html

60. This argument was advanced by Bernard Berelson, Paul F. Lazerfeld, and William McPhee in their book *Voting* (Chicago, IL: University of Chicago Press, 1954); see also Lester Milbrath, *Political Participation* (Chicago, IL: Rand McNally, 1965).

61. Blame tends to be greater than credit. Political scientists have found that people seem more motivated to turn out to vote during bad times than during good ones. See Howard Bloom and H. Douglas Price, "Voter Response to Short Run Economic Conditions: The Asymmetric Effects of Prosperity and Recession," *American Political Science Review* 69 (December 1975): 1240–1254; and Morris P. Fiorina, "Economic Retrospective Voting in National Elections: A Microanalysis," *American Journal of Political Science* 22 (May 1978): 426–433.

62. See "Why Don't Americans Trust the Government," *Washington Post*, Kaiser Family Foundation, and Harvard University, 1996; and *Deconstructing Distrust* (Washington, DC: Pew Research Center for the People and the Press, 1998).

63. The Supreme Court heard a Texas redistricting case in 2012 in which the U.S. Department of Justice challenged a redistricting plan drawn by the state legislature on the grounds that it did not create enough districts in which minorities would be in the majority, a requirement of the Voting Rights Act of 1986.

64. The term "gerrymander" owes its origin to the creative districting in the state of Massachusetts following the enactment of the Constitution. Governor Elbridge Gerry and his supporters created a legislative district in the western part of the state that looked like a salamander. A Massachusetts newspaper, critical of the political motives that shaped the district lines, called it a gerrymander, and the term stuck.

65. Iowa and Colorado have done so.

66. The three qualifications are age, residence, and U.S. citizenship. The Supreme Court decided that state-imposed term limits adds a fourth qualification that can be accomplished only by a constitutional amendment.

67. Teixeira, *The Disappearing American Voter,* 106–147; and Wolfinger and Rosenstone, *Who Votes?,* 73.

68. Heather K. Gerken, *The Democracy Index: Why Our Election System Is Failing and How to Fix It* (Princeton, NJ: Princeton University Press, 2009), 1.

69. Ibid., 28–29.

70. "New Pew State Identifies Seven States with Best Election Administration Performance in 2008 and 2010," Pew Center on the States, February 5, 2013. www.pewstates.org/news-room/new-pew-study-identifies-seven-states-with-best-election-administration

71. Moreover, churches are often polling and voting stations in the United States.

72. Democrats allege that there is a partisan motive as well, claiming that the changes, tightening rules for registering new voters, reducing the period for voting, and in some cases, requiring photo identification cards, are designed to reduce the size of the electorate to the advantage of the Republicans.

73. Another change that might facilitate voting would be to redesign the form and shape of the ballot. Some states still use a party-column ballot, in which all of a party's candidates are listed together below the party's label. Partisans have no difficulty discerning their candidates.

The office-column ballot, on which candidates are listed by the position for which they are running, may confuse people not familiar with the names of all the candidates. In addition, ballots also may contain complex policy initiatives on which voters are asked to decide quickly so as not to delay those waiting in line to vote.

74. A recent study by the Pew Research Center for the People and Politics found electoral confidence in the accuracy of national vote count declining. In 2012, 31 percent said they were very confident in the accuracy of the count compared to 43 percent in 2008 and 48 percent in 2004. "Low Marks for the 2012 Election," Pew Research Center for the People and the Press, November 15, 2012. www.people-press.org/files/legacy-questionnaires/11-15-12%20Topline%20for%20release.pdf

chapter 3

How Representative Are American Elections?

Did you know that . . .

- the constitutional system was designed to protect the rights of minorities, and the electoral system has evolved to reflect the influence of majorities (or at least pluralities)?
- drawing the shape of a legislative district to advance the party in power is an old American tradition that goes back more than two hundred years? *Gerrymandering ↓ hasn't been addressed?*
- for most of U.S. history, the Supreme Court regarded the drafting of legislative districts as a political, not a judicial, issue and thus stayed away from this type of representational question?
- the redrafting of congressional districts to gain more representation for African American and Hispanic voters in the 1990s contributed to increasing the number of conservative Republican members of Congress? *reverse effect?*
- most democracies automatically register their citizens who reach voting age and the United States does not? *WHY DON'T WE*
- the Electoral College was originally designed to ensure that the most qualified, not necessarily the most popular, candidates were selected as president and vice president? *does it serve that purpose today*
- fifteen states currently have laws that place limits on the number of terms their state legislative representatives can serve?
- women make up 51 percent of the electorate but only 20 percent of the Senate and 18 percent of the House of Representatives? *gender bias?*
- most members of the House of Representative usually face little or no opposition for renomination?
- in the twenty-first century, more than three out of four members of the House of Representatives have won reelection by 60 percent or more of the vote?
- most groups that are less well represented in government support a stronger role for government than do those that are better represented? *more passive people?*

Is this any way to run a democratic election? *What is it*

In a representative democracy, all citizens are entitled to have their interests represented. Is the U.S. electoral system, in which candidates are chosen by plurality vote in single-member districts, fair and equitable for all groups in the society? Many people say no. They claim that the system overrepresents the majority and underrepresents the minority.

This chapter addresses the issue of representation. It examines how the electoral system affects the representative character of government. Beginning with a discussion of the concept of representation, the chapter then turns to the relationship between the structure of elections and the type of representation that this structure produces. Those who have benefited from this representational struggle and those who have not are identified and their attitudes toward government and public policy outcomes discussed. The chapter also explores the necessity and desirability of imposing legal qualifications for office and their effect on a democratic electoral process.

THE CONCEPT OF REPRESENTATION

The concept of representation is central to the democratic belief that government should reflect the values and policy preferences of its citizens. This belief became the principal justification for the American Revolution. "Taxation without representation is tyranny!" was the rallying cry of those who wanted their representational rights as English citizens restored.

Although the issue for the colonists was their lack of representation in the British Parliament, for the framers it was devising a system that would permit diverse representation but not reflect every mood of the people, much less convert those moods into public policy. The majority of delegates at the Constitutional Convention feared that the largely uneducated citizenry would vote on the basis of emotions and self-interest, that such a reaction would encourage candidates to promise whatever they believed was necessary to get elected and elected officials to satisfy short-term interests at the expense of longer term national concerns. They also were concerned that minority interests and rights could not be adequately protected if the dominant public mood always carried the day. By overlapping constituencies between the federal government and the states and within the federal government itself, the delegates hoped to achieve both state and popular representation without domination by a single interest, region, or group. To do so, they designed a system in which parts of the polity were better and more effectively represented than was the polity as a whole. Their artful constitutional framework has shaped the representational character of the American electoral system ever since, as have the structure and administration of elections and the creation and evolution of the two major political parties.

The Constitution gave the states the authority to determine how their representatives would be chosen. Most states used their discretion to create institutions that paralleled those of the national government, in which representatives were chosen from clearly defined geographic areas. Within these areas, voters selected candidates directly by popular vote or indirectly by voting for state legislators who in turn selected the state's senators and presidential electors.

How the election was to be conducted, voter eligibility determined, and candidates chosen were left to the states to decide. The Constitution specified only a few qualifications for federal office: a minimum age, a geographic residence requirement at the time of election, citizenship for a specified number of years, and, in the case of the president, being both native born and a fourteen-year resident of the United States before the election. The Constitution also prohibited religious tests as a condition for holding public office.

separation of church & state

Types of Representation

In choosing their representatives, the states selected candidates from their pool of eligible voters: initially white, male Christians who owned property. Most elected officials were better educated than the average male citizen and usually prominent within their communities. As the country became more diverse and as suffrage expanded, so too did the acceptable qualifications for being elected to office. However, what qualifications were deemed acceptable changed much more slowly than did the composition of the electorate. Even today, most of the initial dominant characteristics still prevail: white, male, with above-average education and income.

Herein is part of the representational dilemma for the United States. If one purpose of representation is to reflect the needs and interests of the society as a whole, then how can a government dominated by white males provide fair and equal representation?

Many say that it cannot. They argue that only a person who shares the characteristics of a particular constituency can effectively represent that constituency. Knowing how it feels to live in a community; having interests and needs similar to those of the people who reside there; and sharing the values, political beliefs, and perceptions of these residents are thought to be keys to effective representation. Taken to its conclusion, this argument contends that the best representative for most people most of the time is a person who resembles themselves demographically, attitudinally, and politically.

It follows that the composition of government also should reflect the composition of society if the government is to be representative of that society. In other words, if a particular group, such as African Americans, constitutes a certain proportion of the voting-age population, about 13 percent, then that group should constitute a similar proportion of the government. When Bill Clinton promised in his 1992 campaign to appoint an administration as diverse as America, he was subscribing to this tenet of equal and fair representation for all.[1]

but this is not the reality

Getting their fair share has become a goal of underrepresented groups and a hot-button political issue for them. Not only do the underrepresented want their needs addressed, their interests satisfied, and their values incorporated into policy decisions, but many also want to be represented by people like themselves. They see representation as a symbol of acceptance and equality.

In addition to **descriptive representation,** or how well the government reflects the demographic composition of society, there is also the issue of **substantive representation,** which is how well public policy decisions reflect the values, interests, and desires of the various groups that comprise the American polity. If there is a consensus, does public policy incorporate it? If there is not one, does the policy reflect the varied preferences of the society?[2]

Whereas descriptive representation is reflected in the "who" of government (the people in office), substantive representation is reflected in the "what" of government (public policy and its impact on society). The distinction between these two types of representation arises in part because people who have the same demographic characteristics may hold different beliefs, beliefs in some cases that do not reflect the dominant sentiment of that group.

Although substantive representation is more difficult to evaluate than descriptive representation, it is every bit as important. Not only do people want to see their own reflection in government, they also want that government to be responsive to their needs and interests.

Roles of Representatives

How to achieve equitable representation is an important issue; what role representatives should play in office is another. People want their representatives to serve their constituency and the nation. But serving both may be difficult if the interests of the constituency and nation diverge. For years, members of Congress earmarked special projects for their districts while complaining about the amount of government spending. They provided short-term fixes for their constituents that exacerbated longer-term budgetary problems for the country.

The electoral system reinforces the representational function. To be reelected, representatives must demonstrate that their behavior in office reflects the partisan and ideological orientation of their constituents.[3] For the chief executive, president, governor or mayor, external conditions are correspondingly more important although partisan and ideological congruity is still a factor.[4]

There are other representational issues: disagreements among constituents as well as differences in the intensity of their feelings and disagreements between constituents and their elected representatives. How should an elected representative act if these differences persist?

There are basically two schools of thought about what the representative's proper role should be.[5] The democratic school perceives the representative as a **delegate** of the people and, as such, duty bound to discern and reflect the dominant opinion. If such an opinion is discernible, the representative should follow it; if it is not, then a representative may be able to exercise more personal discretion in deciding what to do, particularly if that representative has the information and expertise to make an informed judgment.

The other representational role is that of a **trustee,** a person charged with using the information and expertise at his or her disposal to make the best possible decision. Edmund Burke, a British politician and scholar, defended this approach in a speech to the people of Bristol who elected him to Parliament:

> Parliament is not a congress of ambassadors from different and hostile interests; which interests each must maintain, as an agent and advocate, against other agents and advocates; but Parliament is a deliberative assembly of one nation, with one interest, that of the whole; where, not local purposes, not local prejudices ought to guide, but the general good, resulting from the general reason of the whole. You choose a member indeed; but when you have chosen him he is not a member of Bristol, but he is a member of Parliament.[6]

Those who argue for a trustee role contend that the public does not have the desire, ability, or knowledge to focus on policy matters, much less make good policy decisions. This is why people elect representatives to make those decisions for them. Representatives have greater interest and desire (as indicated by their candidacy) in public policy making and, it is hoped, more knowledge and ability to do the job effectively. Moreover, this school of thought sees legislative institutions as deliberative bodies in which internal debate should inform a representative's policy judgments.

But the roles of delegate and trustee, while conceptually distinct, are not nearly as separated in practice. Neither is inert. Both are capable of acquiring new information that affects their interests, needs, and political judgments. Here's how the process of representation works.

The Process of Representation

Representation is a dynamic process with considerable interaction between the representative and the represented. Both are influenced by communications that flow between them, sometimes directly and sometimes indirectly through political parties, nonparty groups, and the news media.

Learning occurs. Although the process is a continuous one, an election may be considered a point at which authoritative judgments are made. In the campaign, candidates make promises and demonstrate their qualifications and the electorate makes a decision, based in part on these promises and qualifications. What follows is an expectation that the winning candidate will and should behave in a manner consistent with what that candidate said and did during the campaign. In short, campaign promises should guide initial public policy decisions so long as the conditions on which those promises were based remain as they were during the election period.

But we know conditions change; hopefully elected officials learn in office, not only because they have access to more and better information than they did as candidates, but also because policymaking is deliberative. They learn from their colleagues and also usually need to compromise to find enough common ground to forge a policy consensus. So elected officials, as representatives of the people, have to educate their constituents and simultaneously be responsive to their needs, interests, and opinions. Representation is a two-way street.

Public officials engage in what political scientists Lawrence Jacobs and Robert Shapiro refer to as "crafted talk," communication intended to explain and persuade.[7] The danger is that this communication can be manipulative, intentionally or unintentionally. That danger is minimized by maintaining a free and open society in which diverse groups can express their views and generate public debate. That debate helps to prevent those in power from imposing their views on a less knowledgeable public; although it may not prevent them from making poor policy decisions, it does increase the odds that there may be electoral consequences for those decisions.

The next election provides an opportunity for constituents to review the rhetoric and behavior of their representative, expressing approval or disapproval by their vote if that representative seeks reelection. Thus, particularly when an incumbent is running, the electorate looks backward and makes primarily a retrospective judgment unless voters have reason to believe that future performance will not mirror past behavior.

Whereas the electorate looks back, the representative looks forward, anticipating future constituency issues. This anticipation is motivated by the desire that most representatives have for reelection and public approval.[8] Of course, most representatives do not wait until the next election to monitor their constituents' opinions. They consult public opinion polls, establish focus groups, and review and respond to the communications they receive. In short, representatives exercise a prospective judgment on how they think their constituents will react to their performance in office. The next election will let them know whether the judgment is correct.

There have been several trends that have affected the process of representation in the United States during the last half century. One is that the American people have been somewhat ambiguous about the role they want representatives to play. They prefer leaders to followers, but they also want their leaders to stay in touch with popular sentiment. They expect their elected officials to look out for their interests, but they also think that their representatives are too sensitive to special interests, and they believe that most members of Congress are too parochial for the good of the country. Nonetheless, they continue to reelect most of them anyway.

There has also been increasing skepticism about the truthfulness of those in positions of power, whether their description of events and conditions has been accurate and whether their policy prescriptions would achieve the results they promise. This skepticism has been fueled by revelations of false statements that have been made by presidents and members of Congress, as well as policy decisions seemingly motivated more by personal interests than public needs and interests.

People think their representatives would make better decisions if they did what most of the people want, but they do not believe that officials do so most of the time.[9] Moreover, they are also skeptical of public opinion polls as accurate measures of public opinion. Most people do not understand how a poll of about one thousand people can accurately measure the sentiment of an entire country.[10] Their skepticism about polling extends to the motivation that prompts officials to rely on them. More people believe that officials in government use polls to stay popular and get reelected than because they want to give the public a say in what the government does.[11] This belief is a component of the increasing cynicism toward government, especially elected officials, which Americans have been expressing since the late 1960s.

THE STRUCTURE OF ELECTIONS AND THE UNDERREPRESENTATION OF MINORITIES

How elections are structured shapes the representative character of the American political system—particularly its descriptive representation. The boundaries of legislative districts, the number of officials selected within them, and the procedure by which the winner is determined all affect the character of representation.

As noted in Chapter 2, the structure, rules, and procedures of elections aren't neutral. Plurality voting in single-member districts disproportionately benefits those in the majority. It also benefits the two major parties at the expense of third parties and independent candidates. Similarly, the way the Electoral College operates today favors the large and more competitive states and groups within them.

Plurality Voting in Single-Member Districts

The Constitution does not prescribe single-member legislative districts. What it does require is a reapportionment, every ten years, of the members of the House of Representatives on the basis of the national census. States gain or lose seats depending on how their proportion of the population compares with that of the country as a whole. There is one proviso, however, that every state must have at least one representative in the House.

As mentioned in the previous chapter, the single-member-district system has generally prevailed since the Constitution was ratified. In such a system, the state drafts the boundaries of its legislative districts; each district is represented by one legislator, elected on the basis of the popular vote within the district. In 1967, Congress enacted a law to require such a system for election to the House of Representatives. One reason for the passage of this legislation was to prevent southern states from reducing the vote of African Americans by conducting state-wide, at-large elections for members of Congress. A second reason was to prevent the courts from ordering at-large elections in states in which districting plans were in dispute.[12]

A voting system in which the candidate with the most votes wins favors those in the majority, both candidates and parties. It does so within each district as well as cumulatively among the districts within the state. It is difficult for a minority group to gain representation unless it constitutes a majority or near majority within a district or state.

The best evidence to support the proposition that a system which results in plurality winners from single-member districts adversely affects minority groups is the composition of most legislative bodies today.

Take Congress, for example. Table 3.1 shows the percentages of African Americans, Latinos, and Asian Americans elected to Congress since 1985. Although African Americans constitute 12.7 percent of the voting-age population, Latinos 15.6 percent, and Asian Americans 4.6 percent, these groups have traditionally been underrepresented in Congress, although more so in the past than at present.[13]

Not only has the underrepresentation of minority groups become a political issue, but it also has become a legal one because the Fourteenth Amendment requires that states not deny their citizens equal protection of the laws. Equal protection, in turn, implies equal influence on and representation within the body that makes the laws.

Not until the 1960s, however, did the judiciary begin to address constitutional issues associated with minority representation. In 1962 the Supreme Court decided in the case of *Baker v. Carr* (369 U.S. 186) that malapportioned state legislatures may violate the equal protection clause of the Fourteenth Amendment. The Court's judgment that legislative districting can be a judicial matter, not simply a political one, opened the floodgates to lawsuits by those who believe that the size and shape of their districts discriminate against them and thus deny them fair representation.

In cases arising from these lawsuits, the Supreme Court ruled that all districts that elect representatives, except for those for the U.S. Senate and the Electoral College, had to be apportioned on the basis of population according to the one person–one vote principle.[14] Additionally, the Court said that the size of congressional districts within a state cannot vary very much, no more than one-half of 1 percent.[15]

The configuration of districts, however, wasn't subject to judicial scrutiny until 1986, when the Supreme Court ruled in the case of *Davis v. Bandemer* (478 U.S. 109) that gerrymandering, the drafting of legislative district boundaries to benefit the party in power, could also become a constitutional issue if groups of people were denied equal representation—that is, if the drafting was done in a discriminatory fashion.

By the 1980s, the battle over representation had spread to all institutions of the national government. Congress got involved when it amended

TABLE 3.1	**Minority Members of Congress, 1985–2013 (percentages)**

Congress/Year	African Americans	Hispanics	Asian Americans
House of Representatives			
99th/1985	4.4	2.5	1.1
100th/1987	5.1	2.5	1.4
101st/1989	5.3	2.5	1.4
102nd/1991	5.7	2.3	1.1
103rd/1993	8.7	3.9	1.6
104th/1995	9.0	4.1	1.6
105th/1997	8.5	4.1	1.4
106th/1999	9.0	4.4	1.6
107th/2001	8.3	4.4	1.6
108th/2003	8.5	5.3	1.1
109th/2005	9.1	5.3	1.1
110th/2007	9.1	5.7	1.4
111th/2009	9.0	5.7	1.6
112th/2011	9.7	7.0	2.0
113th/2013	10.1	6.2	2.3
Senate			
99th/1985	0	0	2
100th/1987	0	0	2
101st/1989	0	0	3
102nd/1991	0	0	2
103rd/1993	1	0	2
104th/1995	1	0	2
105th/1997	1	0	2
106th/1999	0	0	2
107th/2001	0	0	2
108th/2003	1	0	2
109th/2005	1	2	2
110th/2007	1	3	2
111th/2009	1	2	3
112th/2011	0	2	2
113th/2013	1	3	2

Source: U.S. Census Bureau, Statistical Abstract of the United States: 2009, Table 390; Members of Congress: Selected Characteristics, 1985–2007, www.census.gov/prod/2008pubs/09statab/election.pdf; and updated by author.

the Voting Rights Act in 1982 to encourage states to create districts in which racial and ethnic minorities were in the majority. Subsequently, the Justice Department has pressured the states to follow the dictates of the legislation when they redraft their legislative districts following a census.[16]

The redrafting of state congressional districts has resulted in an increase in minority representation in Congress (see Table 3.1), but it has also contributed to a more Republican and conservative Congress. Many of the newly crafted districts were in the South and Southwest. Because African Americans and Hispanics are predominantly Democratic, concentrating these groups in so-called majority–minority districts resulted in "whiter" districts in other parts of the state, which benefited the Republicans at the expense of the Democrats.

The gain in GOP seats helped the Republicans win control of Congress in 1994 and allowed them to institute a more conservative policy agenda, which has been opposed by the minority groups that the voting rights legislation was designed to help. Thus, in effect, the establishment of more districts in which a minority within the state became a majority within the district improved the descriptive representation for these minority groups but adversely affected their substantive representation.[17]

Legal challenges to these new minority districts were quickly initiated by Democrats and others who believed that they amounted to racial gerrymandering. A divided Supreme Court agreed. By a majority of one, the Court held that race could not be a primary factor in drafting the boundaries of legislative districts.[18] The Court's decision was seen as a major setback for those desiring greater minority representation of elected officials.

Not only does minority underrepresentation contribute to a racial and ethnic bias, it also reinforces economic inequality within the political system given the lower levels of income and higher levels of unemployment among people in the two largest minority groups, African Americans and Hispanics.

In short, districts represented by a single person, referred to as single-member districts and chosen by winner-take-all voting, work to favor the demographic and partisan majorities in those districts. Aspiring politicians have to run on the Democratic or Republican labels if they are to have a reasonable chance of being elected in competitive districts. In noncompetitive ones, where the primary is effectively equivalent to the general election, they have to vie for the nomination of the dominant party.

Sometimes, to improve their chances, Democratic and Republican candidates in the general election seek a third-party endorsement to get an extra line on the ballot and garner support from those who do not identify with either of the major parties. But rarely does a candidate who is endorsed only by a third party, or who runs as an independent, win. In the twenty-first century, there have been only a very few members of Congress who have been elected as independents, and most had a major party affiliation before declaring themselves independent.

In this sense, plurality voting in single-member districts contributes to a stable two-party system.[19] It also has the advantage of simplicity, since the candidate who receives the most votes wins accords with the principle of majority (plurality) rule, a basic tenet of a democratic electoral process in which all votes are equal.

The problem is the un- or underrepresentation of minorities. The more heterogeneous the society, the more minority groups that may be adversely affected by the winner-take-all system. Moreover, as we have noted, such a system encourages the party in control to draft or redraft electoral districts to its political advantage. More partisan districts tend to be less competitive, which reduces motivation for voting, particularly for those in the minority.[20]

These electoral issues have prompted consideration of multi-member districts represented by more than one person in which the winners are determined by the proportion of votes they or their party receives.

Improving Minority Representation

What can be done to improve demographic and partisan minority representation? There are several answers, but none of them affords much immediate hope of rectifying the representational problem for certain groups. The principal structural change that would contribute to minority representation would be to create multi-member districts and use a proportional system of voting in which candidates are chosen roughly in proportion to the vote they or their parties receive.

Many countries, especially those with a parliamentary form of government, have such voting systems. Most of the newer democracies in Eastern Europe have adopted proportional representation. Others, such as Italy, Japan, and Mexico, mix proportional and plurality voting systems for their legislative representatives. (Table 3.2 lists the electoral systems of a variety of other democratic countries.) Some of the states in the United States use proportional voting methods in multi-member districts to choose state legislators, city council members, and school board members. Both Democratic and Republican parties require proportional voting in all or part of their presidential nominating processes.

The principal advantage of proportional voting is that demographic and partisan minorities can gain representation roughly in proportion to their strength within the electorate. And as we noted in Chapter 2, it also encourages turnout. Voters have more and wider choices. Gerrymandering is eliminated.

If political parties receive legislative seats in proportion to the vote they get, they determine which of the candidates they put forth will be chosen. Presumably, the parties will present and choose a balanced slate in order to broaden their appeal and maximize their vote. In this way, some of the malrepresentation which a straight majority vote produces can be reduced or ended entirely.

There are other benefits of multi-member districts and proportional voting. Public debate is extended, and voters have more options. Moreover, the

TABLE 3.2 **Electoral Systems of Selected Democratic Countries**

Country	System of Representation
Australia	Single-member districts (SMD) with preferential voting, but uses proportional representation (PR) for senate elections
Austria	Proportional representation
Belgium	Proportional representation
Canada	Single-member districts
Czech Republic	Proportional representation
France	Single-member districts with a runoff if no one gets at least 50% in the first round
Germany	Combination of SMD and PR
Greece	Proportional representation
Ireland	Proportional representation
Israel	Proportional representation
Italy	Combination of SMD and PR
Japan	Combination of SMD and PR
Korea (Rep. of)	Combination of SMD and PR
Mexico	Combination of SMD and PR
Netherlands	Proportional representation
Romania	Proportional representation
South Africa	Proportional representation
Spain	Proportional representation
Sweden	Proportional representation
United Kingdom	Single-member districts
United States	Single-member districts

Source: Data from "Voting in Major Democracies." The Center for Voting and Democracy, http://fairvote.org/pr/nations.htm

governing coalitions formed after the election will represent a wider variety and usually a larger number of the electorate. Such representation tends to broaden public support for legislative policy outcomes.

On the negative side, a proportional election might require more complicated voting instructions and more complex ballots. It could also make it easier for candidates and parties with extreme political views to gain a platform and even a voice in government. Another disadvantage is that the winning party—the one receiving the most legislative seats—may not constitute a legislative majority, forcing the leader of that party to try to form a governing coalition with other parties. A multiparty coalition is more fragile than a government composed of a single party. A vote against the coalition government on a major issue frequently topples it and either forces new elections or requires a new party leader to try to form a viable government. Pragmatism is the order of the day, and political compromise a necessity. It is also harder to pinpoint accountability in a multiparty government.

In a multiparty system, small parties that do not represent major groups, can benefit disproportionately. Take Israel, for example, a country in which its small religious parties, some of which have strong fundamentalist beliefs, exercise considerable influence because their support has been necessary to form a governing majority.

One way to reduce the fractionalization a multiparty system produces is to require a minimum proportion of the vote which parties or candidates must receive in order to benefit from the election results. In the United States, the Democratic Party has adopted a threshold of 15 percent for candidates for its presidential nomination to receive delegates at its national nominating convention. The other way to achieve fairer and more equal representation for minorities is to eliminate the allegiances and attitudes (some consider them biases and prejudices) that favor the majority. But major attitudinal change takes time, usually several generations, and judging by the demographic composition of elected public officials the United States has some way to go.

AMERICAN POLITICS AND
THE UNDERREPRESENTATION OF WOMEN

Women outnumber men in the U.S. population today, composing almost 52 percent of the voting-age population. They are also a majority of the electorate, although that is of more recent origin. Women won the right to vote in 1919, but it took another sixty years for them to vote in equal proportion to men. Today, the proportion of women voting is slightly higher than that of men. Yet women represent a substantially lower proportion of members of Congress and of state legislative and top executive officials than do men. Why?

For most of the nation's existence, men dominated politics, and that domination, to some extent, still exists. Incumbency advantage in elections reinforces this domination. It will take time for women to gain the electoral positions or professional status from which they can more successfully seek office. Moreover, women still take time off from their careers, far more often than do men, to raise a family, and are disadvantaged politically for doing so. Women have also been hurt by the persistence of gender stereotypes that they are weaker, more emotional, and less rational than men—stereotypes that lack empirical verification but that conflict with public images of successful political leadership.

A proportional voting system would probably help women gain greater representation in government. Gender balance tends to improve when multiple candidates are chosen in electoral districts. In the presidential nomination process, Democratic Party rules require proportional voting and gender balance; Republican rules permit both, with the result that women constitute about half the delegates at Democratic nominating conventions and between 40 and 45 percent at recent Republican conventions.

Table 3.3 lists the gains women have made since 1991 in Congress, top state executive positions, and state legislatures; it also indicates that they have a way to go to achieve gender parity. The fact that women constitute a majority of the electorate, turn out to vote at a slightly higher rate than men, and are more likely to support women candidates suggests that the gap will continue to decline, but how fast it will do so remains to be seen.

TABLE 3.3 **Women in Elective Office, 1991–2013 (percentages rounded)**

Level of office	Year											
	1991	1993	1995	1997	1999	2001	2003	2005	2007	2009	2011	2013
Congress	6	10	10	11	12	14	14	16	15	17	17	18
Statewide executive	18	22	26	25	28	28	26	26	24	24	24	23
State legislature	18	21	21	22	22	22	22	23	24	24	24	24

Source: Center for Women and Politics, Eagleton Institute of Politics, Rutgers University, www .cawp.rutgers .edu/fast_facts/index.php.

THE ELECTORAL COLLEGE SYSTEM AND THE OVERREPRESENTATION OF LARGE COMPETITIVE STATES

The Electoral College system also creates a representational bias. Initially designed as a dual compromise between the large and small states and between proponents of a federal structure and of a more centralized national government, it provided an alternative to the other methods considered for choosing the president: legislative selection or a direct popular vote. The framers did not want Congress to select the president because they feared that legislative selection would jeopardize the executive's independence. Nor did they want the people to do so because they lacked faith in the average person's judgment and in the states' ability to conduct fair and honest elections. Moreover, the delegates at the Constitutional Convention wanted a leader, not a demagogue, a person selected on the basis of personal qualifications, not popular appeal. Finally, they hoped that their electoral system, which had electors voting at the same time in their respective states, would limit the potential for cabal, intrigue, and group dominance over the election outcome. Given the state of communications and transportation in 1787, distance provided safety, or so the framers thought.

According to the original plan, states would be allocated electors in proportion to their congressional representation in the House and Senate, thereby giving some advantage to the smallest states because of their equal representation in the Senate, an advantage that remains in place today. Wyoming, the least populous state, has a population that is less than 1.5 percent of California's, but Wyoming has 5.6 percent of California's electoral votes. Other inequities result from the apportionment of House seats. Montana's population is almost twice the size of Wyoming's, yet both states have the same representation in the Electoral College.

The original plan also allowed the states to choose their electors in any manner they saw fit. In the first election, in which ten states participated, half of them had their legislatures select the electors and the others chose them in some form of popular vote. The Constitution stated that after the electors were selected they would meet in their respective states and vote for two people, at least one of whom could not be an inhabitant of their state.

The person with the most votes would be president, provided the plurality winner had a majority;[21] the person with the second-highest number of votes would be vice president. In this way the framers hoped to ensure that the two most qualified people would be chosen for the top two offices.

The system worked according to the original design for the first two elections in 1788 and 1792. Washington was the unanimous choice of the electors, but there was no consensus on the other candidate. John Adams, the eventual second choice, benefited from some informal caucusing prior to the vote.

Partisanship and Winner-Take-All Voting

The development of the party system in the mid-1790s transformed voting in the Electoral College. Instead of making an independent judgment, each elector began to exercise a partisan one. Electors became partisan agents. Selected on the basis of their loyalty to a party, they were expected to vote for its candidates. And with a very few exceptions, they did. Since 1787, there have been only 156 "faithless electors" (out of more than 22,000 votes cast) who did not vote for their party's nominee as was expected. None of these errant votes affected the elections' results.[22]

In the early part of the nineteenth century, there was a movement in many of the states to directly elect the electors. In 1800, ten of the fifteen states had their legislatures choose the electors. By 1832, all but South Carolina elected them by popular vote. That state began to do so in 1864.

The popular selection of electors made the Electoral College more democratic than it had been and was intended to be. However, the movement of states to a winner-take-all system, in which partisan slates of electors competed against one another, created a plurality-rule scenario. It also created advantages for some states and disadvantages for others.

The large states, whose electoral votes are magnified by winner-take-all voting, benefit the most. Within these states, groups that are geographically concentrated and unified in their voting behavior also are helped because they can exercise an influence disproportionate to their numbers. Moreover, these groups tend to get candidates to focus on their issues and the positions they favor: Iranians living in California want to maintain pressure on the Iranian government to conduct free and fair elections and allow political protests; Jews in New York want to continue economic and military aid for Israel; and Hispanics in the Southwest are concerned about immigrant rights and immigration reform. The list goes on.

If the large states were equally competitive, the electoral system would encourage candidates to concentrate their campaigns in these states. The seven largest states combined have almost 39 percent of the entire electoral vote. But some of these states are not as competitive as some of the middle-size and smaller states. In this age of polling and targeting, candidates concentrate their campaigns, advertising, and voter mobilization efforts in states that are the most competitive.[23] At the beginning of an election cycle, this can be as many as one-third of the states; by the end of the cycle, that number is usually reduced to single digits. In the last three presidential elections, the major battleground states that received the most attention and campaign activities were Florida, Michigan, Ohio, and Pennsylvania. In 2012, the Center for Voting and Democracy reported that all the events in which the major party candidates participated occurred in only 11 states.[24]

Concentrated campaigning makes strategic sense, but it also undercuts the democratic and national character of presidential elections. It undermines the democratic process by discouraging turnout in the states not considered battleground states and by neglecting or downplaying the issues and interests of people who live in those states. It makes a mockery of the only national election in the United States for the only nationally elected public officials, the president and vice president. If that election were truly national, then the campaigns should be national as well, and the parties should devote their efforts to getting all eligible voters out to vote, not just focus on those in the key, competitive states. Moreover, to create or sustain a national agenda, a national mandate, and a national coalition for governing, it is necessary to think about issues in national terms; make national appeals; and mount a national campaign with candidate appearances, advertising, and grassroots activities held across the country rather than concentrated in only a few states.

In addition to the unequal representation in the Electoral College, made worse by the general ticket system that produces a winner-take-all outcome in forty-eight of the fifty states and the District of Columbia, the Electoral College system also can produce an undemocratic result. Three times in American history, in 1876, 1888, and 2000, the winning candidate did not receive a plurality of the popular vote.[25] Many more times, the shift of a relatively small number of votes in a few states would have changed the outcome of the election.

The most likely situation in which the candidate with the most popular votes would lose in the Electoral College is that of very close competition between the major parties, along with a strong third-party candidate who captures sufficient electoral votes to deny the leading candidate a majority. The elections of 1968, 1992, and 2004 could have produced such a scenario but did not. The election of 2000 did: there were six states (Florida, New Hampshire, Iowa, New Mexico, Oregon, and Wisconsin) in which the winning candidate's margin of victory was less than the votes that third-party candidates Ralph Nader and Pat Buchanan received.[26] If the Electoral College provides unequal representation to the states, if this system encourages the candidates to mount highly concentrated campaigns in only a few of the states, and if the election can result in an undemocratic outcome, then why keep it?

would we be more democratic without?

Supporters contend that it has worked reasonably well. It has been decisive and reflective of the popular vote most of the time, even enlarging the winning candidate's margin of victory in the Electoral College. They claim that the system reflects the country's federal structure, requires the winner to have support across the country, protects concentrated minorities, and compartmentalizes and thereby reduces the impact of fraudulent voting practices and vote-counting errors.

Opponents note that the system has not worked as the framers intended since the two-party system developed, producing three nonplurality winners and several close calls in other elections. They contend that it was never based on the principle of federalism, nor would its demise affect the federal character of the United States, and that its benefits to any one group are offset by costs to other groups, thereby undermining the principle of equal protection of the laws.

Nor do its opponents perceive the electoral system as more likely to contain the evils of cabal, intrigue, and voter fraud. On the contrary, they argue, the more complex the electoral system, the more likely it is to be subject to deals among the electors and those who support them; the smaller the electoral unit, the more likely a dispute over relatively few votes could make a difference. They point to Florida in 2000 as an example. In the national popular vote, Gore won by about 540,000 votes; in Florida, the final tally gave Bush a 537-vote victory. Which of these two situations, the national vote or the Florida vote, is more likely to result in controversy?

can these states have more leverage?

Reforming the Electoral College System

What are the options? Most Americans favor a direct popular vote. Gallup polls preceding recent presidential elections report that a majority of the population supports a constitutional amendment to elect the president by direct popular vote.[27] There has been a partisan cleavage in the support for this reform, with more Democrats in favor of it than Republicans.[28]

In 1969, the House of Representatives voted for a constitutional amendment to directly elect the president, but the Senate did not follow suit. In 1979, fifty-one Senators supported a joint resolution for a direct popular vote, not the two-thirds necessary for a constitutional amendment. Since then, members of Congress have repeatedly introduced direct election amendments, but to no avail.

The tradition of the Electoral College, the reluctance of states that are advantaged by the current system to change it, and the Republican Party's hesitancy, based in part on philosophy and in part on the difficulties that Republican candidates have encountered in appealing to the growing number of minority voters, have thus far prevented a direct election amendment from being passed by Congress and put to the states for a vote. Even in the aftermath of the controversial 2000 election, Florida vote, and Supreme Court decision, Congress, at that time controlled by the Republicans, did not even hold public hearings on the matter.

Congress's reluctance to address the issue, combined with the increasing public dissatisfaction with the Electoral College and the way campaigns are conducted within it, have prompted a variety of citizen proposals for changing the current system. One of the most innovative is a state-based plan for electing the president by a national popular vote. States would enter into an interstate compact in which they would agree to join together to pass identical laws that awarded all of their electoral votes to the presidential candidate who received the most popular votes in the country as a whole. The compact would not take effect, however, until it was agreed to by enough states to cast a majority of the electoral votes, thereby ensuring that the candidates with the most popular votes would win in the Electoral College.[29] The practical merits of this proposal are that it does not necessitate a constitutional amendment, which is unlikely at this time, and would continue to allow the states to retain the authority for determining their electors and how they voted. By the election of 2012, however, only eight states plus the District of Columbia with a total of 132 electoral votes had agreed to join the compact.[30]

A direct election of the president and vice president would certainly be consistent with a democratic election process; it would encourage turnout across the country, not just in the battleground states; it would prevent a discrepancy between the popular vote and the electoral vote; and it would force the candidates to campaign in population centers, appeal to urban-suburban interests, and provide a national agenda and more justification for claiming a national mandate.

Critics, however, see a direct, popular vote, particularly a close one, as more likely to nationalize and thereby aggravate such problems as voter (in) eligibility, possible vote fraud, and ballot tabulation errors such as the ones in Florida in 2000. A national election would probably cost more than the focused presidential campaigns of the late twentieth and early twenty-first centuries. Less-populated rural areas, particularly in the mountain states and the Midwest, might be neglected. An election decided primarily by voters concentrated on the Atlantic and Pacific coasts would not provide the geographic balance and reflect the federal character as much as does the current system.

Finally, a plurality winner might not receive a majority of the total vote as the Electoral College requires today. In seven out of the twenty-five elections in the twentieth century and one out of four in the twenty-first century, the winner did not receive 50 percent of the popular vote. One way to deal with this problem is to have a runoff election between the top two candidates if neither receives a majority;[31] another is to have Congress select the winner from the top two vote-getters; a third alternative would be to elect the plurality winner if that candidate received at least 40 percent of the total vote. Only Abraham Lincoln in 1860 fell below this percentage. In a four-candidate contest, he received 39.8 percent of the vote.

Other proposals, such as allocating a state's electoral votes in proportion to the popular vote that the candidates received in that state, have been advanced. Known as the **proportional plan,** such a voting system would more closely reflect the diversity of views across the country and encourage turnout among the population, but it also might result in a proliferation of votes among different candidates and parties, thereby making it more difficult for any one of them to get a majority. Third-party and independent candidates would exercise more influence under a proportional voting system. Moreover, unless all the states move to such a system, those that allocate their electoral votes in proportion to their popular votes would be disadvantaged. Candidates would not concentrate their efforts on proportional voting states because the payoff in electoral votes would be much smaller than in winner-take-all states—a principal reason that Colorado voters rejected a proportional voting initiative in 2004.

Another option, known as the **district plan,** currently is used in the states of Maine and Nebraska. This option gives two at-large electoral votes to the candidate who wins the popular vote in the state and one electoral vote to the candidate who wins the vote in each legislative district in the state. In the 2008 election, one district in Nebraska voted for Obama while the other two and the state overall voted for McCain. The district plan would produce closer presidential elections than the current system, but it also might align the presidential election more closely to that of Congress, particularly the House of Representatives. Moreover, the uncompetitive nature of many congressional districts does not provide an incentive for candidates to campaign in these less-competitive districts unless the overall state vote were competitive. Despite the results in 2000, the present Electoral College system, with its winner-take-all voting in forty-eight of the fifty states, has tended to enlarge the winning candidate's margin of victory, thereby giving the victor a larger mandate in the Electoral College than that candidate would have received from a direct popular vote. However, acting on the basis of such a mandate can be hazardous.

OTHER REPRESENTATIONAL ISSUES

Term Limits

The Twenty-second Amendment, ratified in 1951, limits a president to a maximum of two elected terms in office, or to only one if the president serves more than half his predecessor's term. Lyndon Johnson, who became president after John F. Kennedy's assassination in November 1963, would have been eligible for two elected terms; Gerald Ford, who succeeded Richard Nixon in August 1974, was eligible for only one.

The movement for term limits, which peaked in the 1990s, was spurred by dissatisfaction with the performance of government and the behavior of public officials. The public's perception continues to be that elected officials are unduly influenced by special interests, that they become increasingly self-interested and self-promoting, and that they use the perquisites of their office to gain an unfair advantage—thus, the argument goes, the only effective way to ensure turnover in office is to limit the terms of office to a specified number of years or elections.[32]

Those who support this argument contend that legislatures were initially designed to be popular assemblies in which concerned citizens represented their brethren when formulating and overseeing public policy. The idea of an assembly composed of political professionals with job security gained through significant incumbency advantages is anathema to this original design and its intent. Rotation in office keeps elected officials more in touch with the needs and interests of the electorate. It also creates more non-incumbency elections in which competition is stimulated and more voters turn out. It is argued as well that term limits prevent special-interest groups from becoming too cozy with those in power and thus less likely to use their resources to "buy, rent, or influence" elected officials.

The anti-term-limits crowd contends that limits are unnecessary, undesirable, and undemocratic.[33] They are unnecessary because there is sufficient turnover in most legislatures, undesirable because they result in the election of less knowledgeable and less experienced public officials who initially lack the skills to be effective in office and thus become more dependent on staff, and undemocratic because they prevent the electorate from reelecting a particular representative who may have served well in office. Moreover, limits remove the incentive for an incumbent to be responsive in his or her last term and may contribute to the phenomenon of declining influence in that term.[34]

The Twenty-second Amendment is a good example of the negative impact term limits can have and the power vacuum it can create. The amendment that prohibits presidents from running for a third term weakens them as their second term progresses. The term "lame duck" is frequently used to describe their predicament. As power flows away from them, they usually seek refuge in ceremony, travel, and speeches; concentrate on foreign policy; and make much more use of their unilateral instruments of executive authority.

Supporters of term limits believe that the loss-of-power argument is overblown and that presidents are reelected to continue their policies already in place, not to create a lot of new domestic programs. The greater danger, they contend, is that the cult of personality can upset the balance of power and effectively undercut the democratic electoral process, as Republicans claim occurred when Franklin Delano Roosevelt was reelected in 1940 and 1944 after having served two full terms in office.

Some states have also sought to impose restrictions on how long their members of Congress could serve. Not only did they believe that turnover would bring new ideas to government, but they also wanted to provide more electoral opportunities for their term-limited state legislators. The Supreme Court, however, ruled that state-imposed limits on members of Congress were unconstitutional because they added an additional qualification for eligibility to serve in Congress, thereby conflicting with Article I of the Constitution, which specifies only age, citizenry, and residence requirements for members of Congress. The Court's decision effectively derailed the term-limits movement.

Age, Residency, and Citizenship Requirements

In addition to term limits, there are several other constitutional qualifications that limit public choice. At the national level, these include minimum-age and residency requirements for Congress and the presidency and a native-born requirement for the president. Are such qualifications still necessary and desirable? Does it make sense to have a minimum-age requirement but not a maximum-age one? Ronald Reagan, the oldest president, suffered memory loss in his second term. Senator Strom Thurmond, the oldest member of Congress, was reelected at the age of ninety-two and stood fourth in line for the presidency as President Pro Tempore of the Senate. About one-third of the electorate thought that Senator Robert Dole's age of seventy-four was a factor that could affect their voting decision when considering him in 1996; Senator John McCain's age of 72 was also cited by 39 percent as a factor in voting in the 2008 general election.[35]

these qualifications still necessary?

The president has to be a native-born American. Being born in the United States might have been important in 1787, when the nation was young and people's patriotic ties to it were weaker, but is it still relevant? The issue was raised and kept alive during and after the 2008 presidential election by people who questioned whether Barack Obama had actually been born in United States. These "birthers," as they had come to be known, questioned the legitimacy of the shortened form of Obama's Hawaiian birth certificate. To quell the matter which building magnate, Donald Trump, raised in his brief quest for the 2012 Republican nomination, the president released an extended copy of the actual hospital certificate, confirming his birth in Honolulu on August 4, 1961.

Several prominent citizens have been precluded from the presidency by this requirement. They held high positions in government, some were in the official line of succession and would have been considered qualified in every other respect, but they were born in other countries. Included in this group have been secretaries of state Henry Kissinger (born in Germany) and Madeleine Albright (born in Czechoslovakia) and California governor Arnold Schwarzenegger (born in Austria).

Similarly, what is the purpose of a residency requirement, particularly in an age of international commerce in which business executives employed by multinational corporations often have to spend considerable time living abroad? Although the Constitution mandates residence in a state before a person can represent that state, it is still possible to achieve residency by moving there and declaring residence some time before the election. Former attorney general Robert Kennedy and then first lady Hillary Rodham Clinton both moved to New York to be candidates for the U.S. Senate. Both were elected, although Kennedy hadn't lived in the state long enough to vote.

REPRESENTATION AND POLICY OUTCOMES

Representational inequalities have contributed to public policy outcomes that favor those who are already economically and educationally advantaged. Inequalities also fuel attitudes toward government. These attitudes have become more negative. Distrust of government and public officials have increased over the last half century.

Contemporary public opinion surveys by the Pew Research Center indicate that a majority of Americans believe that government is inefficient and wasteful, that government is not run for the benefit of all, and that a smaller government with fewer services is preferable to a larger government with more services.[36] Yet when asked whether the federal government does enough for older people, children, poor people, and the middle class, a majority said "no."[37] And people still believe that it is the responsibility of government to guarantee every citizen enough to eat and a place to sleep and to take care of people who cannot take care of themselves (although the proportion that adheres to these beliefs has declined).[38]

Within American society, women, young people, African Americans, and Hispanics are more supportive than others of government's involvement in social and economic matters. Larger proportions of these groups believe that "government needs to do more to make health care affordable and accessible,"[39] and government should lead the fight against childhood obesity.[40]

The different attitudes of different groups present an interesting dialectic. Those who have been less well represented in government favor a larger role for government while those who have been more effectively represented favor a more limited role. Since the 1930s, people with the greatest needs have tended to be more sympathetic to the Democratic Party and its pro-government agenda.

Inequality in terms of election results and demographic representation makes an impact on public policy outcomes, particularly in a governmental system that impedes rather than facilitates change, a system in which it is easier to prevent policy change than achieve it. Remember that the status quo is no friend to the disadvantaged. Existing policy tends to reinforce conditions in which those with economic, social, and political power continue to reap more benefits than do others.[41]

The relatively smaller percentages of women and minorities in government compared with their proportion in the general population make it less likely that the unrepresented or underrepresented will be heard, that their issues become salient, their opinions considered, and their policy goals achieved. Joe Soss and Lawrence R. Jacobs cite evidence indicating " . . . that on issues where the policy preferences of rich and poor diverge, governmental policy is substantially more responsive to the preferences of more affluent individuals and groups,"[42] groups that are better represented and have greater access to those in power.

Representational inequality lessens support for policy change. Sometimes it also raises questions about the legitimacy of government actions; it may even encourage the circumvention of those actions. Unequal representation can also lead to cynical views about government, the officials who run it, and the politicians who compete for public office.

Although the evidence presented here suggests that a major attitudinal shift toward a larger role for government has not occurred in the United States, the terrorist attacks of September 11, 2001, natural disasters such as hurricanes, droughts, earthquakes, and other environmental disasters, health emergencies, such as plagues, pandemics, and food and drug-related medical problems, the availability and costs of energy, and law and order issues have all led people to turn to government for help when they have nowhere else to turn.

In short, representation is a critical link in the problem-resolution process. Representation holds the relationship between people and their elected representatives together. When representation is inequitable or its process manipulated by elites, the policy outcomes, if any, are likely to be skewed toward those who enjoy the most political influence.

SUMMARY: REPRESENTATIONAL DILEMMAS IN A NUTSHELL

American democracy rests on the concept of representative government. In such a government, all citizens have the right to be equally and fairly represented. But theory and practice diverge. Structural biases affect the representative character of the U.S. political system.

Plurality voting in single-member districts overrepresents majorities at the expense of minorities, but it also contributes to stability and accountability in government by maximizing the number of seats that the majority party holds and its ability to exercise power. A proportional voting system in multi-member districts increases minority representation, but frequently at the price of a coalition government.

Women are underrepresented but not as a consequence of structural bias. Their failure to achieve representation equal to their proportion of the population is largely a residue of the restrictions placed on women's suffrage before 1920, voting prejudices, differing gender career patterns, partisan recruitment practices that favored men, and the advantages that incumbents, who are still overwhelmingly male, have in getting reelected.

Winner-take-all voting in the Electoral College inflates the clout of the large states and the cohesive groups within them. More important, it encourages candidates to concentrate their campaigns in populous areas deemed by historical voting patterns and current public opinion polling to be most competitive and neglect much of the rest of the country. As a consequence, presidential elections are national, but presidential campaigns are not.

If states with more than half the electoral votes required their electors to vote for the national popular vote winner, an undemocratic result could not occur in the Electoral College. Under the current arrangement, however, it can and has. It also could occur if states were to apportion their electors on the basis of statewide and legislative district voting or on the proportion of the vote that candidates received in the state, although the results of the Electoral College vote would probably be closer than it has been in the current winner-take-all system.

Electoral and representational outcomes are affected by restrictions placed on eligibility. Age and residency requirements shrink the pool of eligible candidates. Limits on tenure contribute to turnover of elected officials, which can adversely affect the operation of government.

The underrepresentation of certain groups has been a source of discontent and feeds into the perspective of many people in these groups that public policy outcomes benefit those in power and the groups that support them. People who are economically disadvantaged and thus underrepresented in the electorate and in government tend to want a larger and more active government because they have nowhere else to turn. Public perceptions and evaluations of government, its role and performance, are also driven by partisanship and the state of the economy.

To address representational bias and the policy problems that flow from it, elected officials have to be more cognizant of the need for more equitable representation and willing to adjust the electoral system or voting behavior to achieve it—a tall order, to be sure, and one that is not readily embraced by those who benefit from the current system.

elected officials must change, but would they?

Now It's Your Turn

Discussion Questions

1. Is it possible to have a democratic electoral system in which the majority decides and minorities are fairly represented and their rights protected?

2. If women constitute a majority of the voting-age population, why do fewer women than men get elected to positions in government?

3. What difference might it make if there were a more equitable gender balance among elected officials?

4. Is it important for a representative democracy to have demographic, issue, and ideological groups represented in proportion to their percentages in the population? If so, how can this representation be achieved?

5. What consequences do you think a direct election of the president would have on the electorate, the electoral process, the operation of government, and national public policy?

6. Are age, residency, and place-of-birth requirements consistent with a democratic electoral process in which the people are supposed to be able to choose their elected leaders? Should there be a maximum age requirement for voting or service in government?

7. Why do people who are worse off and less well represented in government want it to do more, whereas those who are better off, well represented, and more likely to benefit from public policy outcomes want government to do less?

Topics for Debate

Challenge or defend the following statements:

1. Descriptive representation is irrelevant and may be harmful to substantive representation and effective government.

2. The system of plurality voting in single-member districts is inconsistent with the Supreme Court's interpretation of the Fourteenth Amendment's equal protection clause.

3. The underrepresentation of women in elected positions does not adversely affect public policy.

4. The direct election of the president is neither necessary nor desirable.

5. Term limits are a good idea and should be imposed for all elected officials, regardless of position.

6. Age qualifications for office are unnecessary, undesirable, and undemocratic and should be eliminated.

7. Periodic tests of mental competency should be required for voting and government service.

8. Persons incarcerated for crimes should at least be permitted to vote for law enforcement officials and judges.

Exercise

A congressional committee is holding a hearing on how to improve representation in the national government. As an expert on representational issues, you've been invited to testify. Your assignment is to prepare and present your testimony. In your testimony, note the following:

1. how well the society is currently represented in the federal government;

2. the principal groups that suffer representational bias;

3. the source of their representational problems and what it would take to fix them;

4. the pros and cons of changing the system to remove these representational problems (including any unintended consequences which you think might occur); and

5. your recommendation to the committee on what (if anything) it should propose to Congress as a legislative solution to the problem.

INTERNET RESOURCES

- Center for the Study of Women in Politics: www.camp.rutgers.edu

  Part of the Eagleton Institute of Rutgers University that provides information on women and elective office.

- Center for Voting and Democracy: FairVote: www.fairvote.org

  Contains a wealth of information on various voting systems, especially proportional representation.

- Joint Center for Political and Economic Studies; www.jointcenter.org

  A think tank that provides information and analysis on African Americans and other people of color and their political involvement.

- National Popular Vote: www.nationalpopularvote.com

  Puts forward a proposal and arguments for the direct election of the president accomplished by an interstate compact and not by a constitutional amendment.

- Pew Hispanic Information Center: pewtrusts.org/our_work_category .aspx?id=212

  A source of information on Hispanic public opinion.

- The Pew Research Center for the People and the Press: www.people-press .org

  Conducts surveys on public knowledge, attitudes, and opinions toward candidates, government, and the media.

- U.S. Term Limits: www.termlimits.org

  Promotes term limits; provides information on states that have legislated or had initiatives on term limits.

SELECTED READINGS

American Political Science Association. "Task Force on Inequality." (2004). http://www.apsanet.org/content_62119.cfm?navID=812
Bartels, Larry. *Unequal Democracy: The Political Economy of the New Gilded Age*. Princeton, NJ: Princeton University Press, 2008.
Brunell, Thomas L. *Redistricting and Representation: Why Competitive Elections Are Bad for America*. New York, NY: Routledge, 2008.

Disch, Lisa. "Democratic Representation and the Constituency Paradox." *Perspectives on Politics,* 10 (September 2012): 599–616.

—. "Toward a Mobilization Conception of Democratic Representation," *American Political Science Review* 105 (Feb. 2011): 100–114.

Edwards, George C., III. *Why the Electoral College Is Bad for America.* New Haven, CT: Yale University Press, 2004.

Gallagher, Michael, and Paul Mitchell, eds. *The Politics of Electoral Systems.* Oxford, England: Oxford University Press, 2005.

Gilens, Martin. "Inequality and Democratic Responsiveness." *Public Opinion Quarterly* 69 (December 2005): 778–796.

Guinier, Lani. *The Tyranny of the Majority.* New York, NY: Free Press, 1994.

Lublin, David. *The Paradox of Representation.* Princeton, NJ: Princeton University Press, 1997.

Malbin, Michael J., and Gerald Benjamin, eds. *Limiting Legislative Terms.* Washington, DC: CQ Press, 1992.

Mansbridge, Jane J. "Rethinking Representatioin," *American Political Science Review* 97 (Nov. 2003): 515–528.

Nye, Joseph S., Jr., Philip D. Zelikow, and David King. *Why People Don't Trust Government.* Cambridge, MA: Harvard University Press, 1997.

Pitkin, Hanna F. *The Concept of Representation.* Berkeley: University of California Press, 1967.

Rehfeld, Andrew. "On Quotas and Qualifications for Office." In *Political Representation and Democratic Self Rule,* edited by Ian Shapiro, Susan Stokes, and Elisabeth Wood. New York, NY: Cambridge University Press, 2009.

—. "Representation Rethought: On Trustees, Delegates, and Gyroscopes in the Study of Political Representation and Democracy." *American Political Science Review* 33 (May 2009): 214–230.

Urbinati, Nadia. *Representative Democracy: Principles and Genealogy.* Chicago, IL: University of Chicago Press, 2008.

Urbinati, Nadia, and Mark E. Warren. "The Concept of Representation in Contemporary Democratic Theory." *Annual Review of Political Science* 11 (2008): 387–412.

Vermeule, Adrian. *Mechanisms of Democracy: Institutional Design Writ Small.* New York, NY: Oxford University Press, 2007.

Washington Post, Kaiser Family Foundation, and Harvard University. "Role of Government Survey." (October 2010). www.kff.org/kaiserpolls/8112.cfm

NOTES

1. Although Clinton did appoint a more diverse administration than his predecessors, he did not achieve his objective of appointing an administration as diverse as America.
2. Alfio Cerami, "From Electoral to Policy Representation: A Comparison of 34 Democracies," paper presented at the seminar ECOPOL, Centre d'études Européennes, Sciences Po, Paris, France (February 17, 2007). www.policy-evaluation.org/cerami/docs/cerami_electoral.pdf

3. Brandice Canes-Wrone and Kenneth W. Shotts, "When Do Elections Encourage Ideological Rigidity? *American Political Science Review* 101, no. 2 (May 2007): 273–288; Justin Fox, "Government Transparency and Policy Making," *Public Choice* 131, no. 1 (2007): 23–44 .

4. Justin Fox and Kenneth W. Shotts, "Delegates or Trustees? A Theory of Political Accountability," *Journal of Politics* 71 (October 2009): 1225–1237.

5. For a deeper discussion of the representational issue, see Andrew Rehfeld, "Representation Rethought: On Trustees, Delegates, and Gyroscopes in the Study of Political Representation and Democracy," *American Political Science Review* 33 (May 2009): 214–230.

6. Edmund Burke, "Speech to the Electors," *Burke's Politics,* quoted in Hanna F. Pitkin, *The Concept of Representation* (Berkeley: University of California Press, 1967), 171.

7. Lawrence Jacobs and Robert Shapiro, *Politicians Don't Pander: Political Manipulation and the Loss of Democratic Responsiveness* (Chicago, IL: University of Chicago Press, 2000), 27.

8. The reelection motive is evident in the increasing amount of time, energy, staff, and more resources that legislative and elected executives have been devoting to servicing constituency needs. Members of Congress have received greater allowances for home travel, and even the legislative calendar has been adjusted to permit representatives to spend more time in their home districts.

9. In a national survey conducted for the Center on Policy Attitudes, people were asked whether "elected officials would make better decisions if they thought more deeply about what they think is right." Almost 80 percent of the respondents said yes. They were also asked, "When your Representative in Congress votes on an issue, which should be more important: the way voters in your district feel about that issue, or the Representative's own principles and judgment about what is best for the country?" A majority of 68.5 percent answered, "The way voters feel." Steven Kull, "Expecting More Say: The American Public on Its Role in Government," Center on Policy Attitudes, May 10, 1999, 35; Frank Newport, "Americans Want Leaders to Follow Public's Views More Closely," Gallup Poll, September 23, 2011. www.gallup .con/p011.149636/Americans-Leaders-Follow-Public-Views-Closely.aspx

10. "Polling and Democracy," *Public Perspective* (July/August 2001): 24. They also believe that public officials place too much attention on polls. Gallup Poll, "Public Opinion Polls," April 15, 1999.

11. "Polling and Democracy," 23.

12. "The History of Single Member Districts for Congress," The Center for Voting and Democracy. http://archive.fairvote.org/?page=526

13. U.S. Census Bureau, *Statistical Abstract of the United States: 2012* (Washington, DC: Government Printing Office, 2012), Table 6: Resident Population by Sex, Race, and Hispanic-Origin: 2000–2009. http://www.census.gov/compendia/statab/cats/population/estimates_ and_projections_by_age_sex_raceethnicity.html

14. *Reynolds v. Sims,* 377 U.S. 533 (1964).

15. *Wesberry v. Sanders,* 376 U.S. 1 (1964).

16. A Supreme Court decision on this issue is expected in 2013.

17. For an excellent discussion of this quandary, see David Lublin, *The Paradox of Representation* (Princeton, NJ: Princeton University Press, 1997).

18. *Shaw v. Reno,* 509 U.S. 630 (1993); *Miller v. Johnson,* 115 S.Ct. 2475 (1995); *Bush v. Vera,* 116 S.Ct. 1941 (1996); and *Meadows v. Moon,* 117 S.Ct. 2501 (1997).

19. Maurice Duverger, *Political Parties* (New York, NY: Wiley, 1954).

20. Other systems, such as preferential or cumulative voting, can be used in single-member districts. In preferential voting, candidates are ranked by voters in order of preference. The candidate who receives the least number of first-place votes is eliminated, with his or her votes redistributed on the basis of that candidate's second-place rankings. The process is repeated

until only one candidate is left. Australia and Brazil use variations of the preferential voting if no candidate receives at least 50 percent of the votes in the first round.

Another system designed to help minorities is cumulative voting. In this system, voters are given as many votes as there are candidates and allowed to distribute them any way they choose. They could, for example, give all the votes to one of the candidates, perhaps a person who shares their demographic characteristics or attitudinal views, or they could divide them among several of the candidates. Lani Guinier, a professor of law, contends that such a system would accord with the one person–one vote principle but would not involve the state in racial districting. Without such a system, she argues, the prejudices of the majority will dominate. Lani Guinier, *The Tyranny of the Majority* (New York, NY: Free Press, 1994).

21. If no candidate received a majority, the House of Representatives would choose from among the top five candidates. The Twelfth Amendment later reduced this number to three when it provided for separate ballots for the president and vice president. In the event of a House election, voting would be by state, with each state delegation possessing one vote.

22. "Faithless Electors," The Center for Voting and Democracy." www.archive.fairvote.org/e_college/faithless.htm

23. Even incumbent presidents keep their eye on the most competitive states when deciding where to travel and hold public events. Fifty-six percent of George W. Bush's non–White House events in his first year in office were held in states he won or lost by 10 percent of the vote or less in 2000; similarly, Barack Obama also concentrated his domestic travel months in the states that were most competitive in 2008 and promised to be in 2012. Brendan J. Doherty, "The Politics of the Permanent Campaign: Presidential Travel and the Electoral College," *Presidential Studies Quarterly* 37, no. 4 (2007): 749–773. "Presidential Events Held," Center for Voting and Democracy. http://www.fairvote.org.

24. Center for Voting and Democracy, "Presidential Tracker," www.fairvote.org/presidential-tracker

25. In 1876 a dispute over twenty electoral votes and the resolution of it by a congressionally established commission resulted in the election of Republican Rutherford B. Hayes, who had fewer popular votes than his opponent, Samuel J. Tilden. In 1888 Republican Benjamin Harrison received a majority of the electoral votes; his opponent, President Grover Cleveland, received a majority of the popular votes. In 2000 Republican George W. Bush won a majority of the electoral vote; Democrat Al Gore had a plurality of the popular vote.

26. According to the Voter News Survey exit poll, 47 percent of Nader voters said they would have voted for Gore, 21 percent for Bush, and 30 percent indicated that they would not have voted at all. Had Nader not run, Gore would have won Florida and the presidency.

27. In 2011, Gallup reported that 71 percent of Democrats, 61 percent of Independents, and 53 percent of Republicans supported abolishing the Electoral College for a direct popular vote. Lydia, Saad, "Americans Would Swap Electoral College for Popular Vote: Majority of Republicans Now Agree with Most Democrats that Constitution Should Be Amended," Gallup Poll (October 24, 2011). http://www.gallup.com/poll/150245/Americans-Swap-Electoral-College-Popular-Vote.aspx

28. Ibid.

29. *Every Vote Equal,* 243–274.

30. "The National Popular Vote Bill Is Now at Half-way Point," National Popular Vote. www.nationalpopularvote.com

31. Two elections would be costly, might result in the candidate who came in second in the first round winning in the second, and would be time-consuming, thereby shortening the transition.

32. For arguments in favor of term limits, see Mark Petracca, "Rotation in Office: The History of an Idea," in *Limiting Legislative Terms,* ed. Michael J. Malbin and Gerald Benjamin (Washington, DC: CQ Press, 1992), 19–52; and George Will, *Restoration: Congress, Term Limits, and the Recovery of Deliberative Democracy* (New York, NY: Free Press, 1992).

33. Malbin and Benjamin, eds., *Limiting Legislative Terms,* 198–221.

34. John R. Hibbing, *Congressional Careers: Contours of Life in the U.S. House of Representatives* (Chapel Hill: University of North Carolina Press, 1991), 180; and John M. Carey, *Term Limits and Legislative Representation* (Cambridge, England: Cambridge University Press, 1996), 193–194.

35. Edison Research, "National Exit Poll," is available on most major news networks' Web sites.

36. Pew Research Center for the People and the Press, "The Generation Gap and the 2012 Election" (November 3, 2011). http://www.people-press.org/2011/11/03/the-generation-gap-and-the-2012-election-3

37. Pew Research Center for the People and the Press, "Generations Survey; Final Topline" (September 22–October 4, 2011), Question 21. http://www.people-press.org/files/legacy-questionnaires/toplines%20for%20release.pdf

38. In a 2012 survey, a majority of Americans said that they opposed going into further debt to help the needy. Pew Research Center for the People and the Press, "Trends in American Values: 1987–2012" (June 4, 2012). http://www.people-press.org/2012/06/04/partisan-polarization-surges-in-bush-obama-years; Pew Research Center for the People and the Press, "The People and Their Government: Distrust, Discontent, Anger and Partisan Rancor" (April 18, 2010). www.people-press.org/files/legacy-pdf/606.pdf.

39. Pew Research Center for the People and the Press, "Independents Take Center Stage in Obama Era: Trends in Political and Core Attitudes—Section 2: Views of Government and the Social Safety Net" (May 21, 2009). http://www.people-press.org/2009/05/21/independents-take-center-stage-in-obama-era/

40. Pew Research Center for the People and the Press, "Most See Role for Government in Reducing Childhood Obesity" (March 8, 2011). http://www.people-press.org/2011/03/08/most-see-role-for-government-in-reducing-childhood-obesity/2/

41. Americans are also becoming more conscious of political divides along economic lines among the rich and the poor. See Rich Morin, "Rising Share of Americans See Conflict between Rich and Poor," Pew Social and Demographic Trends (January 11, 2012). http://www.pewsocialtrends.org/2012/01/11/rising-share-of-americans-see-conflict-between-rich-and-poor/

42. Joe Soss and Lawrence R. Jacobs, "The Place of Inequality: Non-participation in the American Polity," *Political Science Quarterly* 124 (Spring 2009): 99; see also Martin Gilens, "Inequality and Democratic Responsiveness," *Public Opinion Quarterly* 69 (December 2005): 778–796; Larry Bartels, *Unequal Democracy: The Political Economy of the New Gilded Age* (Princeton, NJ: Princeton University Press, 2008).

chapter 4

Has Money Corrupted Our Electoral Process?

Did you know that . . .

- Richard Nixon spent six times as much in his last race for the presidency in 1972 (and more than twice as much as his Democratic opponent, George McGovern) as he spent for his first in 1960? *[increasing influence of $]*
- Barack Obama's 2008 campaign spent almost twice as much as did McCain and the Republican National Committee combined; in 2012, both the Obama and Romney campaigns and their supporting groups spent about the same amount, over $1 billion each?
- the more money congressional incumbents spend in the general election the more likely they are in trouble? *interesting idea*
- approximately 1 percent of the population contributed almost 25 percent of the money spent in the 2010 congressional elections? *[rights of privileged few]*
- there may be no direct, causal relationship between campaign spending and electoral success? *but their representation is greater*
- the party that controls Congress tends to receive a larger proportion of its funds from nonparty groups than does the party in the minority?
- fewer than 7 percent of taxpayers checked off the box that allows $3 of their taxes to go to a Federal Election Campaign Fund prior to the 2012 presidential election cycle? *[does anyone care?]*
- Super PACs, permitted by the Supreme Court's *Citizens United* decision in 2010 raised and spent an estimated $645 million during the 2012 election? *[but are they the problem]* *partisanship influence not on elections?*
- Industry associations, labor unions, and corporations spend much more money lobbying elected officials at the national level than they do trying to influence their election victories or defeats?
- people believe that members of Congress are more beholden to special interest groups than to their own electoral constituents? *officials are accessed by the wealthy vs. the mass of the electorate*
- the Federal Election Commission seems permanently immobilized by its partisan composition of three Democrats and three Republicans? *but isn't that a better objective?*

Is this any way to run a democratic election?

MONEY AND DEMOCRATIC ELECTIONS

What does money have to do with democracy? The answer is "a lot" if it:

- gives wealthy people and groups an unfair advantage in influencing the election;
- affects who votes and how they vote;
- conditions who runs for office and who does not;
- affects information the electorate receives about the candidates and their issue positions;
- affects public perceptions of how the electoral system is working, whether it is fair or unfair, and whether it contributes to or detracts from responsive government;
- affects how elections are administered: the period of time in which citizens may vote, the places at which they can do so, the length of time it takes them to complete the voting process, the form and clarity of the ballots, the timeliness and accuracy of the vote tabulation, and the number of election officials available to help citizens deal with problems, oversee the process, and plan for the next election.

Money can and does affect the democratic character of elections in the United States. If a basic tenet of an electoral democracy is the right of every adult citizen to have an equal opportunity to influence an election outcome, then the unequal distribution of resources within society threatens that right. Does the average citizen have the same opportunity to affect an election campaign as do multibillionaires Bill Gates, George Soros, and Sheldon Adelson, or to run for office as multimillionaires George W. Bush and John Kerry did in 2004 and Mitt Romney in 2012? Do two equally qualified candidates have the same chance to win if one is wealthy and willing to use a personal fortune to advance personal political ambitions while the other begins with much more modest means? Is everyone equally protected by the laws if some people are able to gain more access to policymakers by virtue of their campaign contributions and expenditures than those who cannot or do not contribute?

The difficulties in providing equal opportunities for all citizens stem in large part from the value Americans place on personal freedom and private property. The Constitution protects the right of people to use their own resources as they see fit, provided they do so legally. Moreover, the Supreme Court has equated campaign spending with freedom of speech. In 1976, in the case of *Buckley v. Valeo* (424 U.S. 1), the Court held that the independent expenditures by individuals and groups are protected by the First Amendment, as is the advocacy of issues by party and nonparty groups.

Not only does the Constitution protect the rights of people and groups to express their beliefs and "petition the government for grievances," but the electoral and governing systems are designed to allow them to do so, to enable those who feel most strongly about a candidate or issue to try to convince others of the merits of their opinions and the arguments supporting them.

Freedom to spend and the freedom to speak are not the only two freedoms that produce inequality in the electoral process. Freedom of the press is another. Should giant corporations that control the communication industry be able to shape the scope, content, and spin of the information the electorate receives? Should they be subject to any government control? Should the mass media profit from their performance of a public service—covering election campaigns?

This chapter explores the impact of money on elections. It begins with a description of the rising costs of political campaigns, the problems associated with these costs, and the ways Congress and other governments have attempted to deal with these problems. It then assesses the intended and unintended consequences of recent election laws and Supreme Court decisions on the conduct of campaigns and the democratic character of the electoral system. Subsequent sections of the chapter deal with the relationship between money and electoral success, public perceptions of the money issue, and proposals for campaign finance reform.

CAMPAIGN FINANCE LEGISLATION AND ITS CONSEQUENCES

The costs of elections have skyrocketed in the last forty-eight years. In 1960 Richard Nixon spent about $10 million in his race for the presidency. Eight years later, he spent $25 million. Running for reelection against a weak opponent in 1972, he spent more than $61 million. Since then, campaign expenditures have risen dramatically. The Center for Responsive Politics, a public interest group that tracks campaign spending, estimated that $3.1 billion during 1999–2000, $4.1 billion during 2003–2004, $5.3 billion during 2007–2008, and about $6 billion during 2011–2012.[1] An increasing proportion of those expenditures have been spent on the race for president.[2] In 2012, they were over 40 percent of all spending on federal elections.[3]

A variety of factors have contributed to this rapid increase in spending. The nomination process has become more competitive and has lasted longer. Today, successful candidates have to run in two elections that occur over a two-year period. The techniques of modern campaigning—television advertising, survey research, direct-mail and e-mail fund-raising, database compilations, grassroots organizing, and networking on the Internet—have added to the costs.

The Federal Election Campaign Act

Fearing that the election process had become too expensive, that candidates had to spend too much time raising money, they had become too dependent on large donors, and money was being given secretly and, perhaps, illegally to candidates and parties, Congress went into action. Legislation was enacted in the 1970s to reduce the costs of elections, decrease dependence on wealthy donors, reduce the amount of time candidates spend fund-raising, increase the number of viable candidates, make the races more competitive, and make contributions and expenditures subject to full public view. The Democratic Congress had an additional objective in passing this legislation—to reduce the Republican Party's financial advantage in federal elections.

The new laws were primarily directed at the presidential election, but some restrictions were also placed on congressional elections. The amount of money that individuals and groups could give to candidates for federal office as well as to the political parties was strictly limited. In addition, a restriction was placed on how much money candidates could contribute to their own campaigns. The law also allowed corporations and labor unions, previously banned from contributing money, to encourage their employees, members, and stockholders to form political action committees (PACs) and contribute up to $5,000 per candidate per election.[4] Federal subsidies and grants for major-party presidential candidates and funds for the major parties were provided, and spending limits for candidates in the presidential campaign that accepted these funds were established. The Federal Election Commission (FEC), composed of six members, initially to be appointed by both the president and Congress, was set up to monitor and police election activities.

The Federal Election Campaign Act (FECA) was the first comprehensive law to regulate campaign finance activity and the first to provide partial public funding for the presidential nomination and general election.[5] Previous legislation had prohibited direct business and labor contributions but had done little to regulate the source and amount of campaign contributions and expenditures.

Prior to the 1970s the only public funding was at the state level, and it paid for the administration of the election. In providing public subsidies, the United States followed the practices of several European countries that also subsidized candidates or their parties' elections. (Table 4.1 summarizes the grants and subsidies of other democratic governments.)

The FECA, scheduled to go into effect after the 1972 elections, was immediately challenged as unconstitutional. Critics charged that the limits placed on contributions and spending violated the constitutionally guaranteed right to freedom of speech, that the funding provisions unfairly discriminated against third-party and independent candidates, and that appointment of some of the commissioners by Congress violated the separation of powers.

In 1976, the Supreme Court declared two parts of the law unconstitutional. Although the Court upheld the right of Congress to regulate campaign contributions for candidates who seek federal office, it held that independent spending by individuals and groups was protected by the First Amendment to the Constitution and thus could not be regulated. It also voided Congress's selection of four of the six election commissioners as an intrusion on the president's executive authority.

TABLE 4.1	Public Subsidies and Spending Limits for Elections in Countries				
Country	Direct subsidy	Free media access	Tax relief for parties	Tax relief for donors	Ceiling on party expenditures
Argentina	Yes	Yes	Yes	Yes	Yes
Australia	Yes	No	No	Yes	No
Austria	Yes	No	No	No	No
Belgium	Yes	Yes	No	No	No
Brazil	Yes	Yes	Yes	No	Yes
Canada	Yes	Yes	No	Yes	Yes
Chile	No	Yes	Yes	Yes	No
Czech Republic	Yes	Yes	Yes	Yes	No
France	Yes	Yes	No	Yes	Yes
Germany	Yes	Yes	Yes	Yes	No
India	No	Yes	No	No	No
Israel	Yes	Yes	Yes	Yes	Yes
Italy	Yes	Yes	Yes	Yes	Yes
Japan	Yes	Yes	Yes	Yes	No
Mexico	Yes	Yes	Yes	Yes	Yes
New Zealand	No	Yes	No	No	Yes
Peru	No	Yes	No	No	No
Russia	Yes	Yes	No	No	Yes
South Africa	Yes	Yes	No	No	No
Spain	Yes	Yes	Yes	No	Yes
United Kingdom	Yes	Yes	No	No	Yes
United States	No	No	No	No	No

Source: Institute for Democracy and Electoral Assistance, Political Finance Database, www.idea .int/parties/finance/db.

The Court's decision forced Congress back to the drawing board in the midst of another presidential election cycle. A new law was enacted at the start of the 1976 presidential nomination campaign. It retained the contribution and spending limits and public funding of the presidential campaign, but the funding was to be voluntary. Candidates did not have to accept government funds; if they did, however, they were limited in how much they could contribute or lend to their own campaign and how much their campaigns could spend. The FEC was reconstituted with all six members, specified as three Republicans and three Democrats, to be nominated by the president and appointed with the advice and consent of the Senate.

With limited money available, the candidates decided to spend the bulk of their resources in 1976 on television advertising to reach the widest possible audience. As a consequence, much of the political paraphernalia that normally accompanies presidential campaigns—buttons, bumper stickers, yard signs, campaign literature, and the like—was missing or in short supply. Voter turnout continued to decline. Congress was concerned that the funding limitations, the emphasis on television advertising and on media-oriented events, and the drop in turnout were all related.

The 1979 Amendment and the Soft-Money Loophole

An amendment to the law was enacted in 1979 that enabled the parties to raise and spend unlimited amounts of money for their voluntary efforts to promote voting through educational campaigns, get-out-the-vote drives, and other party-building efforts. The only prohibition on the expenditure of this money was that it could not be spent advocating for a specific candidate's election.

Known as the "soft-money amendment," it created a gigantic loophole in the law, permitting, even encouraging, the solicitation of large contributions. Unlike the "hard money" that was strictly regulated and reported, soft money was not regulated and, initially, not even unreported.[6]

In the first two presidential elections after the soft-money amendment was passed, the Republicans enjoyed a financial advantage. Helped by negative reaction to the Jimmy Carter presidency, Ronald Reagan's appeal among wealthy conservative donors and business interests, and, subsequently, his own general popularity, the GOP raised three times as much soft money as the Democrats in 1980 and 1984.

The race for soft money increased exponentially in the 1990s. It did so as a consequence of a clever plan conceived by President Bill Clinton's political advisers. Clinton needed to improve his public standing and image in the aftermath of the Republicans' victory in the 1994 midterm elections, the failure of his health care initiative, and scandals that beset his administration. To do so, the president's political strategists recommended an advertising campaign in which the president's moderate policy positions were contrasted with the more conservative Republican stands.

Launched in the summer of 1995, the campaign was expensive. In the first two months, almost $2 million was spent on it. Fearful that the continued expenditure of large sums of money could deplete Clinton's reelection treasury and leave him with insufficient funds to respond to an attack by the Republicans and their nominee, the president's advisers decided to raise and spend soft money for the advertising campaign rather than depend on the money that had been or would be contributed to his official reelection committee.

The Clinton fund-raising effort, in which the president, vice president, senior White House officials, and the First Lady participated, raised the ante on soft-money contributions. It also embroiled the president and his staff in questionable fund-raising tactics, especially their use of public facilities for the purposes of private solicitation. It undercut the spending limits which the original legislation had imposed on federal candidates who accepted government funds.

public vs private

The Republicans protested the actions of Clinton and his staff but to no avail. Unable to stop them from using their position in government to raise money, the Republicans then conducted their own soft-money campaign. After the election, the Republican-controlled Senate investigated Democratic fund-raising activities. No new campaign finance legislation was enacted, however.

Sen. John McCain kept the soft-money issue alive during his 2000 quest for the Republican presidential nomination. Other principal candidates in that election, notably Democrats Al Gore and Bill Bradley, also said that they favored campaign finance reform to close the soft-money loophole. After the election and several high-profile accounting frauds, business failures, and illegalities by corporate executives, Congress, swept up by public indignation over these fraudulent actions, enacted the Bipartisan Campaign Reform Act (BCRA) in 2002. *But did it solve the problem?*

The 2002 Bipartisan Campaign Reform Act

A principal purpose of the new law was to ban the national political parties from raising soft money. Another was to prevent them and nonparty groups from using advocacy advertising as a not-so-subtle vehicle for promoting particular candidates. A third objective was to increase the amount that individuals were permitted to give to candidates and their parties.

candidates, not party

stop such partisanship

The BCRA prohibited the national parties from soliciting unregulated contributions. To compensate for their potential loss of revenue, the law raised the individual contribution limits from $1,000 to $2,000 and indexed the higher amount to inflation. Party and nonparty groups were not allowed to mention candidates by name in their advocacy ads thirty days or less before a primary and sixty days or less before the general election. Finally, the BCRA allowed candidates for Congress facing self-financed opponents to raise additional funds to level the playing field—the so-called millionaires' amendment.

but did it level the playing field

As with FECA, the BCRA was immediately challenged by those who opposed the law and believed that it violated their First Amendment right of freedom of speech. In December 2003, in the case of *McConnell v. FEC* (540 U.S. 93), the Supreme Court upheld the major provisions of the law, allowing the legislation to shape the financial aspects of the 2004 and subsequent election campaigns.

Opponents of the law had feared that the political parties would be unable to make up the loss of soft money. The Democrats, most of whom had supported the legislation, were particularly nervous since their party had relied on these non-regulated contributions to offset the Republicans' traditional fund-raising advantage. Moreover, being in the minority, the Democrats could not use the White House or Congress as they had in previous elections to bolster their fund-raising efforts.

To deal with this potential shortfall, Terry McAuliffe, then chair of the Democratic National Committee, created a task force of party operatives and supporters and charged them with designing a strategy to deal with the expected shortage of funds. The task force recommended that nonparty, non-profit groups, which Internal Revenue Code provisions, 527 and 501(c), permitted to be involved in political activities, be used as vehicles for raising and spending soft money. The spending, however, could not be coordinated with the party or candidates; it had to be done independently.

Beginning in 2003, these nonparty groups started to raise money for Democratic candidates. They were aided in their efforts by millions of dollars in seed money donated by wealthy Democrats. Outraged by the ruse, the Republicans appealed to the FEC, but unsuccessfully. The commissioners, by a 4–2 vote, decided not to intervene during the 2004 election campaign. As a consequence, the Republicans belatedly set up their own 527 and 501(c) organizations to raise and spend soft money. In the end, more than $400 million was collected and spent by these groups.[7]

The parties also took advantage of changes in the law to raise more money than they had in previous election cycles. The increase in the amount that individuals could contribute to candidates for national office, the computerization of their fund-raising databases, and the deepening partisan divisions in the country fueled this effort.

Thus, the BCRA had a mixed impact on the parties. It encouraged them to improve and broaden their fund-raising base, largely as a product of Internet solicitation. It also increased the number of small donations, those in the amount of $200 or less. In 2000, 25 percent of the total contributions came from gifts of $200 or less; in 2004 that percentage had increased to 34; by 2008, it had increased 40.4 percent.[8] The provision that limited advocacy advertising in the final thirty days before primaries and sixty days before the general election motivated the parties and groups to take up the slack and spend more money on grassroots efforts. The spending had the desired result; it helped increase voter turnout.

However, soft money—lots of it—continued to find its way into the federal election campaign, especially by virtue of the fund-raising activities and expenditures of party-oriented nonparty groups.[9] Table 4.2 lists the revenues and expenditures of nonparty groups since 2000.

Nonparty groups, created to supplement their party's efforts, actually reduced the control the candidates and their parties had over their own campaigns.

		Independent	Electioneering	Communication
Cycle	Total	Expenditures	Communications	Costs
2012	$1,062.7	$1,030.9	$26.3	$5.5
2010	304.7	210.9	80.0	13.8
2008	301.7	156.8	119.3	25.6
2006	68.9	37.4	15.2	16.3
2004	200.1	100.2	31.2	68.7
2002	27.3	16.6	0	10.7
2000	50.8	33	0	17.8

TABLE 4.2   **Campaign Spending by Nonparty Groups, 2000–2012 (in millions)**

Source: Center for Responsive Politics, "Outside Spending." http://www.opensecrets.org/outsidespending/index.php

The prohibition against coordinating party and nonparty activities resulted in the conduct of separate, presumably uncoordinated campaigns. But the BCRA also allowed the parties to engage in independent spending, which they could coordinate with candidate campaigns, so both coordinated and noncoordinated election activities increased.

The BCRA had another effect, partly anticipated and partly not. By doubling the amount that candidates could receive from individual donors and adjusting that amount to the rate of inflation, the law stimulated candidate fund-raising and quickly increased the amount of money available to them. They had more, so they could spend more. The BCRA did not, however, raise the spending limits for presidential candidates who accepted federal funds, except for an annual inflationary adjustment. Thus, a large spending gap began to develop between federally funded and privately funded candidates for their parties' presidential nominations.

Those who accepted federal matching grants were handicapped in three ways: They were restricted in what they could spend in individual states, limits that were most harmful in the important early contests which attract so much media attention and tend to weed the fields of candidates quickly. Second, federally funded candidates had overall spending limits that could be debilitating during an extended nomination process. In 2000, Senator McCain, fighting George W. Bush for the Republican Party nomination, had come to within $1 million dollars of his nomination cap by the first Tuesday in March, whereas Bush, who did not accept federal funds, had no cap. The third problem was the lack of sufficient money during the three- to five-month period after the nominee was effectively settled but before the nominating convention was held.[10] How do candidates who have reached the limit continue to stay in the news, extend their base, and respond to criticism from the opposing party's presidential candidate? These handicaps prompted Howard Dean and John Kerry not to accept matching grants in 2004 so they would not be at a disadvantage against an unchallenged incumbent, George W. Bush. Both Bush and Kerry accepted the federal grant in the general election and, with the help of their parties and nonparty groups, had about the same amount of funds to spend in the general election.[11]

With no incumbent president or vice president running in 2008, the nomination contest started earlier than in previous years. The early start complicated the problem for federally funded candidates in two ways. It extended the period during which their expenditures counted against the state and overall limits, but it also extended the period for raising funds. Under the circumstances, there was even less incentive to rely on federal matching grants for the nomination or federal grants for the general election.

Barack Obama's successful fund-raising during the 2008 nomination period (he raised $326 million through the end of June 2008, when the primary season concluded) prompted him to reject federal funds for the general election.[12] John McCain was forced to take the $84.1 million in public support, however, because he did not think he could raise nearly the amount that Obama could privately. Besides, McCain believed in public financing and had drafted much of the 2002 BRCA legislation—also called the McCain-Feingold Act. In the general election Obama's privately funded campaign enjoyed an almost five-to-one spending advantage over McCain's, about a two-to-one advantage if Republican Party expenditures were combined with McCain's federal funds. The irony for McCain was also obvious. An opponent of soft money and architect of the legal structure which banned it, McCain's BCRA undermined his own presidential campaign and, with it, the public funding provision of presidential elections that he so strongly advocated.

As far as federal funds are concerned, the lesson is clear for future nominations and elections. Unless the spending limits imposed on government-funded candidates are modified or lifted entirely, public financing of presidential elections is practically dead. It will be used only by lesser-known or fringe candidates who have no other option.

The financing floodgates have been opened even wider by the Supreme Court's decision in *Citizens United v. Federal Election Commission,* 558 U.S. 08–205 (2010). The Court ruled that corporations and, by implication, labor unions, could raise and spend unlimited amounts of money on election activities so long as it was not done in coordination with the candidates' campaigns. A subsequent, unanimous Court of Appeals judgment held that other nonparty groups as well, including those created for the purpose of supporting or opposing particular candidates, could raise unlimited amounts of money as well, so long as they do not coordinate with the candidate's campaign.

TABLE 4.3   **Major Party Revenues and Expenditures, 2000–2012 (in millions)**

	2000		2004		2008		2012	
	Revenue	Expenditures	Revenue	Expenditures	Revenue	Expenditures	Revenue	Expenditures
Democrats	$520.4	510.7	824.4	816.8	961.2	956.0	1,051.6	1,036.0
Republicans	$715.7	679.8	894.3	877.2	920.5	792.2	1,003.8	985.2

Source: Center for Responsive Politics, "Political Parties Overview." http://www.opensecrets.org/parties/index.php?cmte=&cycle=2012

This ruling has encouraged candidates, or more precisely, their aides, friends, and financial backers, to establish their own Super PACs to supplement their own campaign activity.

During the 2011–2012 election cycle, Super PAC money greatly increased the amount of campaign spending. Most of it was devoted to negative television advertising.

CONTINUING CAMPAIGN FINANCE ISSUES

Of the approximately $6 billion spent on the 2012 federal elections, $2.3 billion was spent on the presidential contest alone, and the rest on the races for Congress.[13] Is it necessary to spend such large sums to educate the public about the candidates and issues? Given the length of campaign, the relatively low level of public knowledge, the costs of mass media advertising, the expense of creating and maintaining a large campaign organization with a nucleus of paid staff and the instruments of modern technology, the answer apparently is "yes." Clearly, candidates, managers, the parties, and nonparty groups believe it is.

From a candidate's perspective, having a large war chest can often dissuade a credible challenger. In their quests for reelection, Presidents Clinton, George W. Bush, and Obama raised millions of dollars to discourage a quality challenger in their own party from running against them for the nomination. These presidents also wanted the money so they could respond quickly to attacks made against them by their partisan opponents.

From the party's view, raising and spending more money helps fund their political organizations and extends their influence over the election. Political parties have become stronger today in large part because of their fund-raising and turnout activities

Campaigns are more costly today because of the revolution in communications technology and the need to hire professional communicators, mass marketers, and election law accountants and attorneys. Polling, media advertising, grassroots organizing, computer programming, data acquisition, social networking, Web site design, and the equipment on which these technologies depend require considerable upfront costs. In the past, political parties provided their nominees with campaign services and the personnel to run them. Today, most of these operations are undertaken by the candidates' campaigns.

Having money up front allows candidates to jump-start their campaigns. It also gives them greater opportunities to develop and expand their donor base. They can set up more field offices. In 2008, Obama had 770 state offices, the majority of which were concentrated in the most competitive battleground states, compared to only 370 for McCain; in 2012, Obama had 790 field offices, of which 690 were in key targeted states compared to 284 overall for Romney, with 262 of them in the battleground states.[14]

Upfront money also gives candidates greater flexibility in deciding when and where to campaign. It helps them get press coverage because the news media view money as an early sign of electability. Coverage follows the dollar, and that coverage, in turn, can generate more dollars. The front-loading of the nomination process has contributed to the need for early money.

Money buys recognition, hires political professionals, and satisfies other needs, such as fund-raising, staff support, and grassroots organizing, but it may not buy much more than that. It certainly does not guarantee electoral success, as self-financed campaigns by Ross Perot and Steve Forbes attest. It is interesting to note that the candidates who had the largest revenues in the year before the 2004 and 2008 nominations did not win their party's nomination. After Barack Obama surpassed Hillary Clinton in fund-raising in 2008 and exceeded her expenditures by margins of two or three to one, he, too, was unable to parlay his financial lead into popular vote victories in the big primaries of Texas, Indiana, and Pennsylvania. Had he spent less, however, he might have done worse.

In the general election, there seems to be a stronger relationship between the expenditure of money and electoral success. Between 1860 and 1972, the winning presidential candidates outspent the losers twenty-one out of twenty-nine times. Republican candidates spent more than their Democratic opponents in twenty-five out of twenty-nine elections during this period. The four times they did not, the Democrats won. According to political scientist Larry Bartels, "campaign spending has had a significant electoral impact in presidential elections over the past half century [1952–2004]."[15] It has generally benefited the party that has spent the most, the Republicans. Bartels concludes that campaign spending increases the probability of voter support, particularly among the most affluent voters.[16]

The relationship between money and electoral success holds even when independent expenditures, partisan communications, and soft money are considered. In the 1980s, considerably more was raised and spent on behalf of Republican nominees than on their Democratic opponents. In the 1990s, the Democrats narrowed the gap but still did not eliminate the GOP's fund-raising advantage. George W. Bush was the financial as well as electoral victor in 2000, but in 2004 the spending by and for the major-party candidates was about equal. In 2008, the money advantage shifted strongly to the Democrats.

Although it returned to near equality in 2012, the Obama campaign raised and thus controlled the spending of more money in the presidential election, an advantage that contributed to Obama's victories, in the key battleground states.

In congressional elections, the relationship between money and electoral outcomes presents a similar picture. The candidate with the most money usually wins. Incumbents can usually raise more money than challengers, but they need less money to win reelection. When incumbents spend a lot of money, however, it is usually a sign that they are in trouble, not that they are assured of victory; open seats in competitive districts tend to attract the most donors and dollars. In short, fund raising and perceived electability go hand in hand. Money flows toward the perceived winner, which discourages quality challengers and, for incumbents, extends their electoral advantages.

money ↑ electoral advantage ↑

Who Contributes to Campaigns and What Do Donors Get for Their Money? *⟹ representation*

In addition to the inequality that unequal resources create for the candidates, there is another problem many consider equally troubling and harmful to a democratic electoral process: that is the problem of a political payoff. Do the contributors, directly or indirectly, receive a personal or policy benefit for their contributions?

Contributors are unequally distributed in the society. Only a small percentage of the population regularly gives to the candidates and the parties and a much smaller proportion of these donors give a substantial proportion of all the money donated. The Sunlight Foundation, a nonprofit, public interest group, reported that in the 2010 congressional elections:

> 26,783 individuals (or slightly less than one in ten thousand Americans) each contributed more than $10,000 to federal political campaigns. Combined, these donors spent $774 million. That's 24.3% of the total from individuals to politicians, parties, PACs, and independent expenditure groups.[17]

Most of these people were corporate executives, lawyers, and lobbyists. Although Barack Obama received a record number of small contributions ($200 or less) in both elections, (34 percent in 2008 and 57 percent in 2012), many of his donors gave multiple times. In contrast, only 26 percent of Romney's contributions were less than $200.[18]

The concentration of contributors among wealthy individuals and campaign expenditures among corporations, trade associations, labor unions, and Super PACs raises important issues for an electoral democracy. To what extent can and do the people and groups influence who runs and wins, and to whom are the winning candidates likely to be most responsive and beholden once in office? From the public's perspective the answers are clear: the big contributors

rich get their wishes heard

to Super PACs and individuals—called "bundlers"—who raise large amounts of regulated money for the candidates. The advocacy groups that spend substantial resources during the election campaign are also likely benefactors.

Rightly or wrongly, the perception is that money buys access and influence. Similarly, people believe that members of Congress are more likely to respond to campaign donors outside of their districts than to nondonors within their districts, that they support policies primarily because these policies are desired by their donors and not because elected officials believe them to be in the best interests of the country, and that the government is pretty much run by a few big interests rather than for the benefit of all the people.[19] (The public has also been periodically troubled by the accusations of foreign money being spent in U.S. elections to influence the outcome and the implications that those expenditures may have for national security.[20])

The issue is one of equity. If the groups that contribute and spend the most money were representative of the population as a whole, the situation would be better than if they represented a particular economic stratum within society. But, alas, they do not. Business interests spend the most; the expenditures of consumer groups pale in comparison. Organized labor spends less, directs most of it to the Democrats, and represents the interests of blue-collar union workers. Who represents the interests of nonunionized blue-collar workers, white-collar employees, or the unemployed? As the people see it, politicians are also winners in the money game. Although the public thinks of both parties and their candidates as involved in excessive and even questionable fundraising activities, Republican and Democratic partisans differ over the most egregious campaign finance problems. Republicans direct their outrage at the incipient influence of labor unions and the liberal establishment, whereas the Democrats see special-interest money, flowing in large part from business and conservative advocacy groups to Republicans, as the problem that most needs rectifying. The creation, growth, and activity of Super PACs has fueled and extended this debate.

According to national surveys, the public wants the financial system to be reformed and the abuses ended, but people doubt that politicians in Washington will do so. Nor does the public want to use taxpayer funds to pay the costs of political campaigns.[21]

Why Has Congress Been So Slow to Deal with These Problems?

The unintended consequences of campaign finance legislation have made members of Congress reluctant to act quickly. Some members are reluctant to legislate at all because they are philosophically opposed to government regulation in general and campaign finance regulation in particular. They see spending as free speech protected by the First Amendment. Some also object to using taxpayer money to fund national elections, partially or wholly. Some may also believe that public funding undercuts their advantage that they as incumbents have when they seek reelection, although that proposition has been subject to debate among political scientists and politicians.[22]

Besides which, members of Congress are probably the most inappropriate group to fix a problem from which they have professionally and personally benefited. They are hardly disinterested policymakers. As incumbents, they can raise more money. This built-in advantage naturally makes them hesitant to change the system and level the playing field. Whichever party has been able to raise the most money tends to oppose legislation that would reduce its competitive edge.

In addition to the partisan and ideological opposition, there also has not been much recent public pressure on Congress to act. Although people say that they desire campaign finance reform, most do not regard it as a major policy priority. It was not even mentioned on the Gallup poll's most important problems facing the United States during 2004–2012.[23]

As a consequence, although propositions have been introduced in recent Congresses, primarily by Democrats, to rectify some of these issues—preventing foreign money from U.S. elections, prohibiting government contractors from electoral activity, requiring sponsors of ads to identify the groups that pay for them, and forcing mass media companies to charge the lowest advertising rates for political commercials—they have not advanced to serious consideration, much less been enacted into law.

What Else Could Congress Do?

Is there anything else Congress can and should do to promote campaign finance equity? Should it reduce or eliminate PAC contributions to candidates, prohibit corporations and companies with substantial foreign ownership from donating money, and/or ban election activity by companies bidding for federal contracts?

In addition to litigation that such actions might initiate, there are supplementary policy concerns as well. PAC contributions are relatively insignificant for presidential candidates. Although they are more important for congressional candidates, the maximum amount allowed, $5,000 from any one PAC, is a relatively small portion of most campaign war chests. Campaign spending by nonparty groups cannot be restricted, so their interests would be represented regardless in the electoral process. The coordination of Super PACs' electoral activities with candidate campaigns is still prohibited but candidates' political backers have found ways to circumvent this restriction. Nor has foreign influence been much of a problem. Under the existing law, contributions are restricted to U.S. citizens and noncitizens who are permanent residents. American subsidiaries of foreign-owned companies also may create PACs or make contributions, provided they do so with money earned in the United States. A foreign company cannot give its American subsidiary money to spend in U.S. elections. Congress could prohibit any contribution from a person who is not a U.S. citizen. It also could prevent foreign-owned companies from making contributions. It probably could not, however, prevent American employees of these companies from forming PACs and making contributions, nor would Congress want to do so because this could potentially discriminate against American workers.[24]

The federal contracting issue also raises freedom of speech concerns and could have an adverse effect on the competitive bidding as well as the outsourcing of government services. In 2007 Congress enacted the Honest Leadership and Open Government Act, which limited gifts members of Congress could receive and travel that was paid for by others; it required lobbyists to disclose election contributions they or the group they represented made, as well as any bundling activities in which they engaged on behalf of candidates.

In short, increased regulatory activity generates considerable partisan pushback, may conflict with recent Supreme Court decisions, and does not have a record of success in eliminating the equity issues that have plagued U.S. elections. Is there another way to deal with this problem?

Increase Election Funding. The grant for the federal election could be increased and would need to be, given the higher costs of election campaigns, the increased expenditures by candidates and their parties, and the greater opportunities and incentives for raising private funds instead of taking government money. Candidate expenditures have risen at a rate greater than inflation since the initial campaign finance legislation went into effect in the 1970s. Yet the amount of money that the major-party candidates can receive if they accept federal funds is still tied to the $10 million figure established in 1974, adjusted by the rate of inflation.

Providing candidates with more money or allowing them to supplement federal funds with private contributions in the general election would make federally funded candidates more competitive with privately financed opponents and also less dependent on their parties and nonparty groups, which now regularly supplement presidential campaigns. It would also enlarge the field of potential candidates during the nomination process and level it more equitably, thereby giving lesser known and less–well funded candidates opportunities that they had lacked in the past, an initial goal of the public funding legislation. Candidates might spend less time raising money and more time campaigning, another objective of the Federal Election Campaign Act.

The Campaign Finance Institute (CFI), a nonprofit public interest organization devoted to financial disclosure and reform during elections, has proposed increasing the one-for-one grant that candidates competing for their party's presidential nomination receive to up to six times that amount, as well as providing the grant earlier, the year before the election, but basing it on individual contributions of $100 or less. The CFI argues that doing so would broaden the field and might extend the nomination campaign; however, increasing federal funding would also require more money be placed in the Treasury's election fund. The CFI proposes that the income tax checkoff be raised from $3 to $5 a person. Given all the other policy issues that must be addressed, rising concern about the magnitude of annual budget deficits and the national debt, the relatively tepid support for government-financed elections in the United States, and the increasing willingness of the public to permit funding with private contributions, it is extremely unlikely that Congress and the general public would support such an increase. Fewer than 7 percent of taxpayers currently check the box to put money into the fund.

Enlarge Spending Limits for Federally Funded Candidates. Another way in which public funding system could be revitalized is to raise the limits on spending for candidates who accept federal funds. Those limits are too low because of the BCRA's increase in amount that individuals can contribute, the development of Internet technology which facilitates continuous, broad-based fund-raising, and supplementary spending by candidate-oriented Super PACs. In addition to increasing the spending limits, private funding in the general election might also be permitted, thereby reducing but not eliminating financial inequities.

Increasing the expenditure limits substantially would make federal funds a more viable option for candidates faced with the dilemma of not being able to raise or spend as much as their primary and general election opponents. It could help extend the contested phase of the nomination and make that phase more equal. Easing or eliminating the contribution and spending limits after the nominee was effectively determined also would equalize the preconvention campaign in the period after the primaries and before the national nominating conventions.

Raising the spending limits, however, would force the candidates back into the fund-raising game for extended periods of time. More fund-raising by the candidates would create greater competition for funds within the party and among allied groups and even congressional candidates. Cohesion between the party and nonparty groups and the nominee might suffer as a result.

One proposal that has received considerable attention would set voluntary ceilings for House and Senate elections, such as $600,000 for House races (about $1 per person in the district) and $950,000 to $5.5 million for the Senate, depending on the population of the state. Candidates who abide by these limits would receive free or reduced-cost time on television and cheaper mailing rates, a proposal that is likely to be strongly opposed by traditional for-profit communication companies, notably those in television, radio, and print. Countries such as Germany, Mexico, and the United Kingdom require their television broadcasters to provide free time to political parties but not to individual candidates; the United States could do the same as a condition for renewal of television licenses. But what about minority parties and independent candidates? What about stations that do not use the airwaves but operate via cable or satellite? Lowering mail rates is another option, but one that would also require an additional subsidy for a government corporation, the U.S. Postal Service, which is already in financial difficulty.

Voluntary limits with inducements for compliance would equalize spending and keep costs from getting out of hand. Incumbents who can raise more money might seem disadvantaged by this arrangement, but most would not be. Challengers usually need more money to balance the incumbent's advantages of recognition, constituency service, and accomplishments in office. But voluntary spending limits also could give greater advantage to wealthy candidates who do not have to abide by them. *So what can we actually do?*

SUMMARY: CAMPAIGN FINANCE DILEMMAS IN A NUTSHELL

$

American elections are getting more and more expensive. For some candidates it seems as if the sky is the limit when it comes to raising and spending campaign funds. Each election has become more costly than the previous one.

NEED UNEQUAL REP.?

The need for money has become an obsession for candidates and has encouraged them to devote increasing amounts of time, energy, and money raising it. Their drive to fill their own campaign coffers, often well in advance of the election, has created (at least in the public's mind) a political system in which the wealthy exercise the most influence, thereby undermining the equity principle in a democracy.

For the past forty years, Congress and the president have had to contend with a range of campaign finance issues stemming from the need to fund more and more campaign expenditures, many of which resulted from the professionalization of campaign operations, weakening of party control, and the introduction of new communication technologies. Initially, the solution was thought to lie in requirements that limited individual and group contributions to candidates for federal office, established spending limits for presidential candidates who accepted government funds, and mandated detailed public reports on revenues and expenditures to the FEC.

LEGISLATION HAS HAD NOT DESIRED EFFECT

The legislation enacted in the 1970s achieved some of these objectives. It broadened the base of campaign contributions, initially decreased the perceived influence of the wealthy, lessened the amount of time and energy that presidential candidates had to spend on fund-raising, and leveled the playing field and thereby gave more candidates an opportunity to demonstrate their qualifications for office and electability. Very importantly, it also brought campaign finance into the open, to full public view.

CONSTITUTIONAL RIGHTS STRIKE DOWN

But some of these achievements have been short-lived. The Supreme Court's judgment that campaign spending is free speech and protected by the First Amendment has undercut the goal of cutting campaign expenses. Although limits can be legally placed on contributions to federal candidates, expenditure limits on individuals and certain groups cannot be. Nor can spending limits be placed on candidates who do not accept federal funding. For those who do, however, the limits have become too restrictive to make federal funds a viable option. As a consequence, unless the law is changed, candidates will not accept government money if they have any other options.

Resource inequities undercut the democratic character of elections. The wealthy gain advantage by virtue of the money they have and are willing to spend. Similarly, candidates with the greatest personal resources or access to those of others are also disproportionately benefited. Successful candidates are beholden to their benefactors and the interests they represent. They curry their favor and reward them with access and influence, which in turn, affects their public policy decisions—at least that is how the public perceives it. It is a vicious circle that undermines democratic governance.

[handwritten margin note: WEALTHY HAVE ADVANTAGE]

[handwritten note: NOT QUITE DEMOCRATIC INTERESTS OF FEW HEARD]

Now It's Your Turn

Discussion Questions

1. Is money as corrupting an influence on politics and government as people believe?

2. Do the wealthy exercise disproportionate influence on election outcomes and, as a result, on government?

3. Are American elections too expensive? What would be a reasonable criterion by which to evaluate whether the costs of elections are excessive?

4. Can money in elections ever be regulated as long as the Supreme Court considers the expenditure of resources to be protected by the First Amendment's free speech provision?

5. Does money buy electoral success? Has it in recent presidential and congressional nominations and elections?

Topics for Debate

Challenge or defend the following statements:

1. All laws regulating campaign finance, except for the reporting requirements, should be abolished.

2. All federal elections should be publicly funded.

3. Congress should increase the matching grants on small contributions and decrease the spending limits on candidates who accept federal funds during the presidential nominating process.

4. The required political composition of the Federal Election Commission should be abolished and replaced by independent, nonpartisan commissioners who are nominated by the president and confirmed by the Senate.

5. The Constitution should be amended to exclude campaign spending from the free speech protection of the First Amendment.

Exercise

This exercise has two parts. The first is to design a nonpartisan public relations campaign on the need for campaign finance reform in the United States. In formulating your campaign, indicate why the system must be reformed and what those reforms should be. Make sure that you try to anticipate the objections that different groups may raise to your proposals.

For the second part of the exercise, assume that your campaign has been successful and generated enough of a public outcry to move Congress into action. At this point, assume the role of a Democratic or Republican member of a committee (your choice) charged with investigating the issue and proposing a legislative solution.

1. Outline the major points of a bill that addresses the problems you have cited in your public relations campaign. (Remember, you are now a partisan, so your bill should not adversely affect the interests of your party. If it is to be enacted into law, however, it must still pass the House and receive 60 votes in the Senate.) In your statement, anticipate the criticisms that members of the other party on the committee are likely to make and respond to them.

2. With your class as the full committee, have a vote at the end to see whether your proposals should be sent forward to the floor of Congress. Would the current administration support such a bill? Would the Supreme Court?

INTERNET RESOURCES

- Campaign Finance Institute: www.campaignfinanceinstitute.org

  This nonprofit, nonpartisan institute collects and analyzes detailed finance information from recent federal elections and makes recommendations on how to improve the electoral system.

- Center for Responsive Politics: www.opensecrets.org

  Focuses on money and elections; publishes alerts, news releases, and major studies on campaign finance issues.

- Common Cause: www.commoncause.org

  Considers itself a citizens' lobbying group; for years, it has been at the forefront of campaign finance reform.

- Public Citizen: www.publiccitizen.org

  This organization provides information about problematic relationships among money, elections to office, and governance.

- Federal Election Commission: www.fec.gov

  Official source for data on campaign revenues and expenditures for federal elections; puts candidate finance reports on its Web site, as well as analyzes data from these reports and makes them available to the public.

- Sunlight Foundation: http://sunlightfoundation.com

  The Sunlight Foundation is a nonprofit, nonpartisan organization that uses the Internet to promote ideas for openness and transparency in government.

SELECTED READINGS

Corrado, Anthony, and David B. Magleby, eds. *Financing the 2008 Election.* Washington, DC: Brookings Institution Press, 2011.

Corrado, Anthony J., Michael J. Malbin, Thomas E. Mann, and Norman J. Ornstein. *Reform in an Age of Networked Campaigns: How to Foster Citizen Participation through Small Donors and Volunteers.* Washington, DC: The Campaign Finance Institute, American Enterprise Institute and the Brookings Institution, 2011. http://www.cfinst.org/about/events/2010_01_14.aspx

Magleby, David B., Anthony Corrado, and Kelly D. Patterson, eds. *Financing the 2004 Election.* Washington, DC: Brookings Institution Press, 2006.

Malbin, Michael, ed. *The Election after Reform: Money, Politics, and the Bipartisan Campaign Reform Act.* Lanham, MD: Rowman & Littlefield, 2006.

Malbin, Michael, Peter W. Brusoe, and Brendan Galvin. "Public Financing of Elections after Citizens United and Arizona Free Enterprise." Campaign Finance Institute (July 6, 2011). http://cfinst.org/Press/PReleases/11–07–07/Public_Financing_of_Elections_after_Citizens_United_and_Arizona_Free_Enterprise.aspx

—. "Small Donors, Large Donors, and the Internet: The Case for Public Funding after Obama." Campaign Finance Institute, April 22, 2009. www.campaignfinanceinstitute.org/pr/prRelease.aspx?ReleaseID=228.

Mann, Thomas E. "The U.S. Campaign Finance System under Strain: Problems and Prospects." In *Setting National Priorities: 1999*, edited by Robert D. Reischauer and Henry J. Aaron. Washington, DC: Brookings Institution Press, 1999.

Panagopoulos, Costas, ed. *Public Financing in American Elections.* Philadelphia, PA: Temple University Press, 2011.

NOTES

1. "The Money Behind Elections," Center for Responsive Politics. http://www.opensecrets.org/bigpicture/index.php

2. David B. Magleby, "Adaptation and Innovation in the Financing of the 2008 Elections," in David B. Magleby and Anthony J. Corrado, eds. *Financing the 2008 Elections* (Washington, DC: Brookings Institution, 2011), 19.

3. Center for Responsive Politics, "The Money behind the Elections." http://www.opensecrets.org/bigpicture/index.php; Center for Responsive Politics, "2012 Presidential Race," http://www.opensecrets.org/pres12/index.php

4. In an effort to control spiraling media expenses, the law limited the amount that could be spent on advertising. That provision was later eliminated.

5. Theodore Roosevelt was the first president to propose publically funded presidential elections. He did so in 1907 in a message to Congress. Roosevelt proposed eliminating private contributions for candidates who accepted public funds.

6. Congress subsequently imposed a reporting requirement similar to the one that existed for all other contributions.

7. "527s Advocacy Group Spending," Center for Responsive Politics. http://www.opensecrets.org/527s/index.php

8. Michael J. Malbin, "A Public Funding System in Jeopardy: Lessons from the Presidential Nomination Contest of 2004," in *The Election after Reform: Money, Politics and the Bipartisan Campaign Reform Act,* ed. Michael J. Malbin (Lanham, MD: Rowman & Littlefield, 2006), 226–232. Percentage for 2008 calculated by author from data available from the Federal Election Commission, "Presidential Campaign Finance: Contributions to All Candidates," www.fec.gov/DisclosureSearch/mapApp.do.

9. Campaign Finance Institute, "501(c) Groups Emerge as Big Players Alongside 527s: Outside Soft Money Groups Approaching $400 Million in Targeted Spending in 2008 Election," October 31, 2008, http://campaignfinanceinstitute.org/pr/prRelease.aspx?ReleaseID=214.

10. During the almost five-month period after he effectively won the nomination and before the Republican Convention, McCain raised $112.5 million.

11. Kerry later said that accepting federal funds was one of the biggest mistakes he made in the 2004 race. John Kerry, "Interview," *Meet the Press,* NBC News, April 9, 2006. www.msnbe.msn.com/id/12169680/page4

12. Before he made the decision to reject federal funds, Obama asked the Federal Election Commission (FEC) at the beginning of the 2011 nomination process whether he could accept private contributions for the general election without waiving his eligibility for federal funds. The FEC ruled "yes." Similarly, John McCain used the matching funds he was entitled to receive in 2012 as collateral for a $4 million loan in 2011. He later chose not to accept the matching funds; the FEC ruled that in so doing he did not violate the law.

13. Center for Responsive Politics, "2012 Presidential Race." http://opensecrets.org/overview/index.php

14. Mark Silva, "Obama's Ground Game; 770 Field Offices," *The Swamp, Chicago Tribune, blog,* October 24, 2008. www.swamppolitics.com/news/politics/blog/2008/'10/obamas_ground_game_770_field_o.html; Andrea Levien, "Tracking Presidential Campaign Field Operations," The Center for Voting and Democracy, November 14, 2012. www.fairvote.org/tracking-presidential-campaign-field-operations

15. Larry M. Bartels, *Unequal Democracy: The Political Economy of the New Gilded Age* (Princeton, NJ: Princeton University Press, 2008), 120.

16. Ibid., 120–122.

17. Lee Drutman, "The Political One Percent of the One Percent," Sunlight Foundation, December 13, 2011. http://sunlightfoundation.com/blog/2011/12/132/the-political-one-percent-of-the-one-percent

18. "All CFI Funding Statistics Revised and Updated for the 2008 Presidential Primary and General Election Candidates," Campaign Finance Institute, January 8, 2010. www.cfinst.org/president/pdf/2010_1006_Table1.pdf

19. "A Generational Look at the Public: Politics and Policy," *The Washington Post,* Kaiser Family Foundation, and Harvard University, October 2002. http://kff.org/kaiserpolls/3273-index.cfm; "Role of Government Survey, *The Washington Post,* Kaiser Family Foundation, and Harvard University, October 2010. http://kff.org/kaiserpolls/upload/8112.pdf

20. "Financing Campaigns: Skepticism, and a Need for Change," *New York Times,* April 8, 1997, sec. A.

21. Public opinion on the issue of campaign finance depends largely on the wording of the survey item. When limits on large contributions are proposed, the public favors restrictions, but when the cost of elections is emphasized, majorities oppose public funding. Stephen R. Weissman and Ruth A. Hassan (with assistance from Jack Santucci), "Public Attitudes toward Public Financed Elections, 1972–2008," in *Public Financing in American Elections,* edited by Costas Panagopoulos (Philadelphia, PA: Temple University Press, 2011), 124–143.

22. See Kenneth Mayer, Timothy Werner, and Amanda Williams, "Do Public Financing Programs Enhance Electoral Competition?" in *The Marketplace of Democracy: Electoral Competition and American Politics,* edited by Michael P. McDonald and John Samples (Washington, DC: Brookings Institution, 2006), 245–267; Patrick Basham and Dennis Polhill, "Uncompetitive Elections and the American Political System," *Policy Analysis* (2005): 1–20; Peter Wallison and Joel Gora, *Better Parties, Better Government: A Realistic Program for Campaign Finance Reform* (Washington, DC: American Enterprise Institute, 2009).

23. Gallup Poll, "Trends A-Z: Most Important Problem," http://www.gallup.com/poll/1675/Most-Important-Problem.aspx.

24. Congress would probably not want to prevent what has become a widespread practice in the United States: having foreign corporations and governments hire American firms to represent their interests in the United States.

chapter 5

News Media
Watchdog or Pit Bull?

Did you know that . . .

- there are more free and accessible sources of campaign information than ever before, yet the level of public knowledge has not significantly increased?
- although Americans say they believe in freedom of the press, they are divided over the question, do news organizations help or hurt democracy?
- the more education people have, the less they trust the news media?
- a majority of the population wants to prevent the broadcast and cable networks from projecting a winner in presidential elections while people are still voting?
- the voting-age group least informed about campaigns is the youngest: people between the ages of eighteen and twenty-nine?
- television is the primary source of election news in almost every advanced democratic nation?
- Approximately one quarter of the 18- to 19-year-olds get their news from social networking sites?
- television news often covers campaigns and elections as if they were sporting events?
- when the public has been asked to evaluate news media's coverage of recent national campaigns, the average grade given is a C?
- the spin put on campaign coverage today is more negative than positive?
- television anchors and correspondents received six times more airtime than the candidates on the news shows of the major networks during recent presidential campaigns?
- people rate the honesty and ethical standards of funeral directors and accountants higher than those of journalists, while members of Congress and lobbyists are evaluated even lower?
- almost two out of three people believe the press is biased in reporting the news?

Is this any way to run a democratic election?

A free and fair press is essential to a democratic electoral process because they provide information to help citizens understand the issues, evaluate the candidates, and assess the longer-term implications of their policy positions. News coverage of elections can also generate political participation, affect public perceptions and voting decisions, and build confidence in the system and legitimize its outcomes.

Not only does the news media provide more information than would be directly available from the campaigns themselves, but they do so more objectively than self-interested candidates and parties. Reporters make it easier for the electorate to compare people running for office, place the campaign in some historical and contemporary perspective, and gain knowledge required to make an enlightened electoral judgment. For all these reasons, press coverage of election campaigns is important, more so as the electorate has expanded and the number of news sources has proliferated.

In the course of covering elections, however, the news media have also become part of the story. They affect the campaign by the news they present and the manner in which they present it. They help focus the electoral agenda for the campaign, emphasize certain qualifications of the candidates, and report on the statements those candidates make and the public policy positions they take. The news media analyze how the candidates are doing, how the public is reacting to the campaign, and how the election may turn out. After the election is over, they explain who voted for whom and why. In addition, the press speculate on the impact the election is likely to have on government and public policy in the years ahead. The news media then become watchdogs, holding elected officials accountable for the promises they have made and for their decisions in office. Both during the election and after it, these reporting and evaluative functions give the press enormous power.

But who is accountable for the media?

To the extent that the information the news media present is accurate, comprehensive, relevant, and impartial, the electorate is well served. To the extent that the information is incomplete, inaccurate, incomprehensible, truncated, skewed, biased, or in any other way unfair, the electorate is shortchanged, and the democratic electoral process suffers as a result. In short, the scope, content, and spin of the news can enhance or warp the public's vision, energize or turn off voters, facilitate or impede electoral decisions, and provide realistic or unrealistic policy expectations. All of this newsworthy information can and does affect public opinion and, over time, political attitudes, and support for democratic electoral processes.

Has the United States been well served by the way the news media cover campaigns, assess candidates, monitor public opinion, and explain election outcomes? To answer this complex question, the chapter begins by examining the evolution of the press in American elections, with an emphasis on the technological changes of the last several decades. The second part of the chapter explores the consequences of those changes on news organizations, news distribution, and news coverage. Part III turns to the format of electoral journalism, the ways in which campaigns are presented and assessed. The final section presents proposals for improving the scope and content of campaign communications, with the goal of better informing and involving the electorate.

THE EVOLUTION OF ELECTION NEWS

Newspapers were published in America long before the country gained its independence. They were not, however, neutral; in fact, the first paper, *Publick Occurrences, Both Foreign and Domestick,* was banned after only one issue by the British for its "offensive content." Since that time, newspapers have taken part in the debates on the country's most critical political, economic, and social issues.

The early newspapers, sold by subscription and delivered by mail,[1] were more like today's op-ed pages than papers that report on people and events. Intended for the educated and business classes interested in public affairs, most newspapers had a discernible political perspective that shaped the news they presented. These perspectives, written in the form of essays, debated controversial issues such as independence and the ratification of the Constitution. It was in such papers that James Madison, Alexander Hamilton, and John Jay published their famous essays, known as *The Federalist Papers.*

The audience for and content of newspapers began to change during the 1830s, as the political parties expanded their popular base. Technological improvements, a growth in literacy, and greater public involvement in political affairs contributed to the rise of the "penny press"—newspapers that sold for a penny and were profitable by virtue of their advertising and mass circulation. To sell more papers, stories had to be entertaining. Electoral campaigns fit this mold better than most other news about politics, government, and public policy. As a consequence, campaigns received extensive coverage, which may also have contributed to increased voter turnout during the nineteenth century.

Technology has played its part. The invention of the telegraph made it possible for an emerging Washington press corps to communicate information about national political issues to the entire country. Radio, which began operating in 1920, stayed as the principal electronic news medium from the 1920s to the 1950s. It allowed people to hear news from all over the world, sometimes as it was happening. The 1924 presidential election was the first to be reported on radio; the conventions, major speeches, and election returns were broadcast to a national listening audience. During the 1928 election, both major presidential candidates, Republican Herbert Hoover and Democrat Alfred E. Smith, spent campaign funds on radio advertising.

Television

Television started to become a major source for news reporting in the 1950s. As the number of television sets and the hours that people watched grew quickly, television supplemented radio as a primary source of fast-breaking news. The effect of television directly on campaigns was felt as early as 1952, when Republican vice presidential candidate Richard Nixon denied allegations that he had obtained and used campaign gifts for himself and his family. The speech, in which Nixon also vowed not to give up a dog named Checkers that had been a gift to the Nixon family from his political supporters, generated favorable public reaction and testified to the power of television if used effectively by candidates.

The year 1952 was also the first in which political advertising was aired on television by presidential candidates. Over the years that advertising has enabled campaigns to craft and project leadership images, prime and frame issues, and shape public debate. Televised debates between presidential candidates, which have now become a staple of nomination quests and general election campaigns, began in 1960 with the Kennedy-Nixon debates. This television debate and the ones that followed illustrated the importance of physical appearance, verbal articulateness, and knowledge of the issues as criteria for judging the qualities of the candidates.

The half-hour evening news shows on the three major broadcast networks became the primary source of news for millions of Americans in the 1960s. Events that occurred earlier in the day or the previous day were highlighted in relatively short news stories. The currency of the coverage combined with the size of the audience (over 50 million people watched these shows on a regular basis)[2] forced print news organizations to find other ways to distinguish their election news. Investigative journalism, political commentary, and in-depth reporting enhanced information about political campaigns.

Cable news began to challenge the dominance of the broadcast networks in the 1980s. Its 24–7 news cycle, begun by the Cable News Network (CNN) and later supplemented by MSNBC and Fox News, expanded the time frame in which news was reported. The ability of cable to cover stories as they were happening rather than waiting until a scheduled news program changed the viewing habits of news consumers. The expansion of programming options on cable as well as competition among cable providers that lowered the monthly rates for service increased cable's share of the news audience from about 20 percent of American households in 1980 to 56 percent in 1990, to approximately two-thirds by 2010.[3]

Cable had a similar effect on the broadcast news media as the broadcast media had had on print journalism. The broadcast networks had to modify their news programming. Their news got softer, "more sensational, more personality-centered, less time-bound, more practical, and more incident-based."[4] The evening news shows became the functional equivalent of news magazines rather than the initial sources of national news and analysis. Local stations also expanded their news coverage.

[handwritten margin notes: TV → more people reached, time people could access news greater, can see as well as hear candidates]

Audience size on the broadcast news networks declined, forcing them to reduce their staffs, downsize or eliminate foreign bureaus, and rely more on freelance journalists to report international events. Technology in the form of satellite dishes, cell phones, and the Internet, facilitated this form of news outsourcing. Newspaper readership also declined.

The Internet

As the 1990s progressed, people turned increasingly to the Internet for up-to-date news, first as a supplement and then as their primary source. By the year 2000, about 11 percent of the population indicated that the Internet was their major source of campaign news; four years later that percentage had risen to 21; by 2008, it had grown to one out of three and by 2012 almost one half. (See Table 5.1.)

Even cable news has begun to lose its viewers to the Internet. Although more people still say that they get their news from the three major cable news channels, CNN, FOX and MSNBC, than from the broadcast networks, cable news audiences have decreased by about 12 percent since 2000 while online news consumption has increased by 17 percent.[5] About one out of three Americans

TABLE 5.1	**Changing Sources of Campaign News, 1992–2012 (percentages)**					
Question: How did you get most of your election news?						
Year	1992	1996	2000	2004	2008	2012
Television	82	72	70	76	68	67
Newspapers	57	60	39	46	33	27
Radio	12	19	15	22	16	20
Magazines	9	11	4	6	3	3
Internet	n/a	3	11	21	36	47

Note: Numbers add to more than 100 percent because voters could list more than one primary source.

Sources: Pew Research Center for the People and the Press, "Low Marks for the 2012 Election," November 15, 2012. http://www.people-press.org/2012/11/15/low-marks-for-the-2012-election

Pew Research Center for the People and the Press, "Cable Leads the Pack as Campaign News Source," February 7, 2012. http;//www.people-press.org/2012/02/07/cable-leads-the-pack-as-campaign-news-source; Pew Research Center for the People and the Press, "Views of the News Media, 1985–2011: Press Widely Criticized, but Trusted More than Other Information Sources," September 22, 2011. http://www.people-press.org/2011/09/22/press-widely-criticized-but-trusted-more-than-other-institutions/

go online daily for news with an increasing number using mobile devices such as cell phones and tablets.[6] (See Table 5.2.) Newspapers and magazines have suffered the most, forcing the major news organizations to set up Web sites to make available their reports, analyses, and opinions, just to survive.[7]

TABLE 5.2	**Principal Sources of Television News, 2002–2012 (in percentages)**							
Year	Local	ABC	CBS	NBC	CNN	MSNBC	FOX News	Other/ DK	TV Not Main Source
2002	16	11	11	15	28	8	16	6	18
2004	15	11	9	14	20	6	19	6	26
2006	13	10	9	12	24	6	20	7	28
2008	15	12	9	10	23	8	17	6	30
2010	16	10	7	9	16	7	16	5	34
2012	21	13	11	12	19	11	22	6	21

Note: Numbers add to more than 100 percent because voters could list more than one primary source.

Source: Pew Research Center for the People and the Press, "Cable Leads the Pack as Campaign News Source," February 7, 2012. http://www.people-press.org/2012/02/07/cable-leads-the-pack-as-campaign-news-source; Pew Research Center for the People and the Press, "Political and Media Survey," Pew Research Center for the People and the Press, July 2011. http://www.people-press .org/2011/07/28/obama-loses-ground-in-2012-reelection-bid/

The changes have been rapid, with significant financial, informational, and civic consequences for the communications industry and the country as a whole.

THE COMMUNICATIONS REVOLUTION AND ITS CONSEQUENCES

The consequences of the communications revolution have been profound. Traditional news organizations are struggling to adjust to the new technologies and survive. Search engines, such as Google, Yahoo, and Bing, have gotten into the news business, potentially on a large scale with their own staffs, services, and transmission systems. Internet newspapers and Web sites such as *The Huffington Post, Real Clear Politics, The Beast,* and *Politico,* have been created to supplement and in some cases replace the services that the print newspapers provided. Along with social networking sites such as Facebook and Twitter, they have become the new intermediaries through which the traditional press have to gain and maintain their audience and distribute their news.[8]

[handwritten: but not always meant to be serious publications HuffPost all over Facebook]

More but Less Trustworthy Information

News has become easier and cheaper to obtain,[9] but it has also become less accurate and reliable. Rumors abound and are reported as facts. The rule of two, the independent source rule, which governed responsible journalism reporting for much of the twentieth century has been abandoned in the interests of speed, immediacy, and currency.[10] Much investigative journalism today is leak-driven, with bloggers and Internet surfers finding and revealing 'old' information about people and group activities, information that often is designed to raise questions about a person's integrity, consistency, or behavior. Much of this research is fueled by partisan and ideological agendas and beliefs.

Considerable classified information has also been placed in the public arena by individuals and groups, such as WikiLeaks, opposed to secrecy and policies that governments pursue. Privacy, security, and hacking into Web sites have now become matters of public concern.

Although more information has become accessible, the public has not become more knowledgeable. According to a survey conducted by the Pew Research Center in 2007, "citizens are about as able to name their leaders, and are about as aware of major news events, as was the public nearly 20 years ago."[11] Greater reliance on local news has actually reduced the exposure to national issues.[12] Despite extensive coverage of the nomination process in the late fall and early winter of 2011, the Pew Research Center reported that many people lacked information about the Republican candidates and the forthcoming primaries and caucuses.[13] In general, the public knows more political facts that are candidate-related than facts that are not.[14]

With more news outlets, why hasn't public knowledge about election campaigns increased? Part of the problem may have to do with the way news is presented, the attention devoted to a particular issue, the comprehensiveness of the story and depth of the analysis. Part may also have to do with the viewing habits of the audience, scanning the channels, getting news in bits and pieces rather than watching or listening to an entire news program.[15] There has also been a growing distrust of the news media, the accuracy of the information reported and the "spin," placed on the story.[16]

The Revitalization of the Partisan Press

The proliferation of news sources has rekindled partisan journalism. As previously noted, for much of its history, the American newspapers had a strong partisan orientation. They were organs of political parties, which used them to make and magnify their public appeals. As newspapers evolved from argumentative essays to the description and analysis of public events, the norm of objectivity grew in importance. The advent of broadcast radio and television, which required licenses to use the public airwaves, placed greater emphasis on nonpartisan reporting as did the use of surveys and statistics, designed also to reflect newer scientific methods of research. Public trust in the truthfulness and accuracy of the news increased. By the 1970s and early 1980s, the height of the broadcast network television news, almost 40 percent of the populace expressed great or quite a lot of confidence in the news media.[17] *what changed?*

Today that confidence has eroded. According to surveys conducted by the Gallup organization, a substantially smaller proportion of the population has a great deal or a fair amount of confidence in the media in 2012 (43 percent) than in 1972 (68 percent) and 2000 (51 percent).[18] Why the decline? The perception of partisanship may be part of the answer. ⇒ *polarized electorate*

People perceive more bias in news reporting, particularly from sources that do not reflect their political views.[19] They are more apt to distrust information from these sources and frequently extend their criticism to the news media as a whole.[20] In general, Republicans tend to be more critical of the press than Independents, who in turn are more critical than Democrats. After three years of the Obama administration, however, these partisan differences narrowed somewhat. (See Table 5.3.)

TABLE 5.3	**Perceptions of Political Bias of News Organizations (in percentages)**			
Year	1985	1999	2005	2011
Republican	49	69	73	76
Independent	44	53	59	63
Democratic	43	51	53	54

Source: "Views of the News Media. 1985–2011: Press Widely Criticized, but Trusted More than Other Information Sources," Pew Research Center on the People and the Press, September 22, 2011. http://pewresearch.org/pubs/2104/news-organizations-inaccurate-trust-cable-news-press-media-coverage

Put simply, people today find the press less believable, less accurate, and more biased than they did in the past. Figure 5.1 illustrates the growth of negative evaluations of the press' performance.

Niche journalism reflects and reinforces the political polarization in American society.[21] The expansion of news on the Internet, the breadth of sources, the ease of accessing them, and the public penchant for wanting news with or without a discernible point of view[22] could have reversed these polarizing trends but have not done so yet. In fact, the proliferation of partisan news sources has facilitated selective exposure and perception, the tendency of people to be attracted to information that reinforces rather than challenges their existing attitudes and beliefs. The Internet, especially, has attracted people with

⇒ *unspun*
people do this often

FIGURE 5.1   **Public Evaluation of Press Performance**

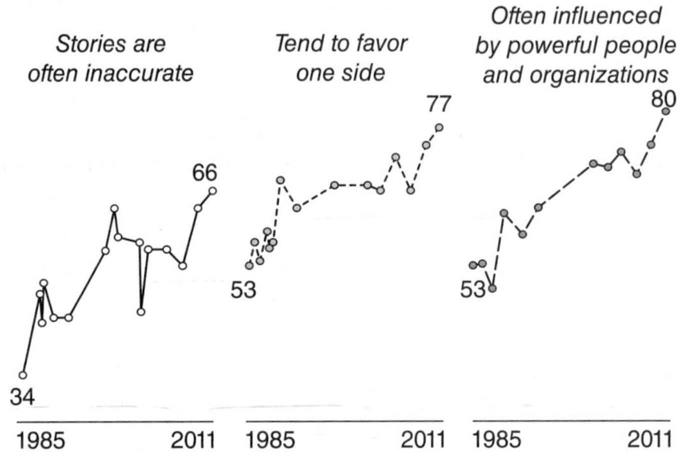

Stories are often inaccurate

Tend to favor one side

Often influenced by powerful people and organizations

77

80

66

53

53

34

1985   2011   1985   2011   1985   2011

Source: "Views of the News Media, 1985–2011: Press Widely Criticized, but Trusted More than Other Information Sources," Pew Research Center for the People and the Press, September 22, 2011. http://pewresearch.org/pubs/2104/news-organizations-inaccurate-trust-cable-news-press-media-coverage

---

more specialized interests and intense political feelings, as they are able to find sites that appeal to these interests and feelings.[23]

Partisan attitudes have not only affected perceptions of the press, they have affected views of the press' role in a democratic society. In theory, there is broad support for a free press. Although many people may not understand the protections that the First Amendment provides media in the United States today, they do believe that newspapers, radio, television, and news magazines are necessary for a democratic society. However, the numbers are not overwhelming. In a survey published in September 2011 by the Pew Research Center for the People and the Press, 44 percent agreed with the statement that the press protects democracy, but 36 percent did not.[24] A survey conducted by the Annenberg Public Policy Center found that most people also believe that a government may restrict the right of the press to report a story, a position to which most journalists obviously do not subscribe.[25]

To summarize, for many people the news has taken on a partisan coloration. People tend to rely on those sources with which they agree. It helps them sort out the issues, simplifying them by placing them within an ideological framework that clarifies their meaning, importance, and anticipated impact.

and probably be can't be justified monitored

Partisan media + people's bias + proliferation of media = uneducated electorate

It reinforces partisan differences and also narrows discussion, excludes information that does not accord with the political orientation of the news source and its audience, engages in hyperbole, and uses emotionally charged rhetoric, all of which affects the informed deliberative discussion in which learning occurs, common ground is recognized, and consensus is built.[26]

The public is affected by the information it receives. Although there is evidence that people can and do make rational judgments on the basis of this information they receive from partisan news sources,[27] there is also evidence that the more educated and informed people are, the more likely that they will use their cognitive skills to seek information that supports their views.[28]

[margin note: reinforces even more partisan views]

THE ADEQUACY OF CONTEMPORARY CAMPAIGN COVERAGE

Let's examine another type of bias, but not a primarily ideological one. It is a bias that stems from the format and content of election news reporting: the desire of news organizations to provide information that people want to desire, not necessarily they need to make informed voting decisions.

[margin note: → STORY vs. info]

Non-Ideological Journalistic Bias

[margin note: they need viewers + $ too]

In deciding what to report, the news media impose their journalistic perspective. It relates to the newsworthiness of information. All events, activities, and statements during elections are not considered of equal importance by the press. The criterion of audience interest is one of the main elements used to determine the type of coverage and the amount of it.

From the perspective of the press, if an item is new, surprising, exciting, different, dramatic, action oriented, or involving conflict, then it is more newsworthy than one that does not exhibit any of these characteristics. The first utterance is more newsworthy than the second one, the unexpected development more newsworthy than the anticipated outcome, the gaffe more newsworthy than the expected remark, the contest more newsworthy than the substance of the issues, and controversy is usually deemed more newsworthy than consensus (except when consensus is unexpected).

[margin note: exaggeration]

The journalist's orientation also extends to the format in which news is reported. It must be direct and, above all, clear. Positions are presented and contrasted as black or white; gray areas get less attention. The story usually has a single focus. There is a punch line or bottom line toward which the report is directed.

A Sound-Bite Mentality

[margin note: affects candidates' campaign]

The concepts of what is news and how news is reported create incentives for candidates to come up with new angles, new policies, and new events. It also encourages them to play it safe, not think out loud, and not take chances.

Words, expressions, and ideas are pretested in focus groups to gauge their likely impact before candidates express them in public. To combat a press eager to highlight the critical and the unexpected, candidates stage their events, recruit their audiences, and try to engineer an enthusiastic response from them. They speak in sound bites designed to capture public attention and and to be able to target these messages to specific groups. The size of the bite serves an additional need of the news media, particularly radio and television. It facilitates the compartmentalization of news, compressing it into proportions that the press believes the public can easily digest.

To the extent that the public gains its information about the campaign from these short, simple statements, the amount of knowledge and especially the depth of that knowledge suffer. Newspapers, particularly national ones such as the *New York Times* and *Wall Street Journal* and comprehensive regional dailies such as the *Chicago Tribune, Los Angeles Times,* and *Washington Post,* provide more extensive coverage. But only a small portion of the electorate regularly reads these papers, much less focuses on the election news in them, although people may access newspaper Web sites for individual stories. Nonetheless, the bulk of the electorate receives a snapshot, a partial and truncated piece of the campaign. Is it any wonder that people are poorly informed, that they retain so little of the news they see on television or read on the Internet?

Interpretive Reporting

There's another problem with contemporary campaign coverage in the mass media: it is highly mediated. People today see and hear more from the correspondents reporting the news than from the candidates making it. In fact, the candidates are seen and heard only briefly. The average length of a quotation from a candidate on the evening news since the 1988 presidential election has been less than ten seconds. Compare this with 42.3 seconds in 1968.[29] Today, to communicate their messages themselves, candidates seek alternative communication channels such as talk radio, entertainment television, their own Web sites, and social networking systems.[30]

Another problem with interpretive reporting is that many people believe that members of the news media allow their personal preferences to influence the way they cover the news. Interpretive reporting contributes to the perception of media bias. It has made voters more wary and less trusting of news correspondents, which in turn has contributed to the declining confidence people have in the accuracy and reliability of campaign news.

The press also operates as a pack despite the premium placed on new news. Increasingly lacking the personnel and resources to find new information on their own,[31] they follow the leader—these news organizations that have more resources, reliability, and reporters, such as the *New York Times, Wall Street Journal,* and the Associated Press. Such coverage tends to magnify and extend stories that are already in the news and to minimize others that do not make the mainstream media. It produces an echo effect. Here's how a report from the Pew Research Center's Project for Excellence in Journalism describes it:

> . . . the press first offers a stenographic account of candidate rhetoric and behavior, while also on the watch for misstatements and gaffes. Then, in a secondary reaction, it measures the political impact of what it has reported. This is magnified in particular during presidential races by the prevalence of polling and especially daily tracking. While this echo effect exists in all press coverage, it is far more intense in presidential elections, with the explosion of daily tracking polls, state polls, poll aggregation sites and the 24-hour cable debate over their implications.[32]

The ability of the pack to influence the campaign narrative forces candidates to anticipate and respond to news media coverage of campaign events. They do so by orchestrating and compartmentalizing their newsworthy activities and statements into morsels that they hope reporters will devour and then regurgitate. They also do so by researching and then leaking negative information about their opponent, faxing, texting, or phoning information to select reporters, staging media events, and crafting speeches with the sound bites they want included in the article. In 2012, only one quarter of the information presented by reporters about the candidates' characteristics and records came originally from journalists themselves. Most came from the campaigns and their political supporters [33] Candidates also use advertising as a ploy to get the media's attention as well as to reinforce or challenge perceptions that may have been created by news stories. Political advertising is not subject to the same standards for truthfulness and accuracy as is commercial advertising (see Chapter 8).

The Story Line

A major part of the media's interpretation of campaign news is the story into which most campaign events are fitted. That story is described as if it were a sporting event. The candidates are the players, and their moves (words, activities, and images) are usually described as strategic and tactical. Even their policy positions are evaluated within this game motif, presented as calculated attempts to appeal to certain political constituencies.

The metaphor used most frequently is that of the horse race. A race—especially if it is close and if the result isn't readily predictable—generates excitement. Excitement holds interest, which sells newspapers and magazines, increases the size of radio and television audiences, and generates more Internet "hits." Surprise, drama, and human-interest stories do the same. When these elements are present, elections get more coverage than when they are not.

In addition to conveying excitement and stimulating public interest, there is another reason why the media use the game format. It lends an aura of objectivity to reporting. It encourages the press to present quantitative data on the public's reaction to the campaign. Public opinion surveys, reported as news, are usually the dominant news item during the primaries and caucuses and share the spotlight with other campaign-related events during the general election.

Emphasizing the horse race is not a new phenomenon, but it often occurs at the expense of substantive policy debate. During the 2012 general election, there were almost twice as many horse race stories as policy stories,[34] a pattern evident in previous elections as well.[35]

What's the consequence of this type of coverage on the electorate? Simply put, it results in people's remembering less about the policy issues and the ways the candidates intend to deal with them. Although the candidates' positions get attention in the news media, the costs and consequences of their proposed policy solutions do not get nearly as much. A few national news organizations do provide this type of coverage, but in most news coverage, it is the horse race, the candidates themselves, and their strategies and tactics that are spotlighted.

All of this information from the press and candidates swirls about during the election campaign and creates a lot of noise that can confuse as well as inform voters. It's almost as if three interrelated campaigns are going on at once. In one, the candidates are appealing directly to the electorate for votes. In another, they're attempting to win over the media by controlling the agenda, spinning their news, leaking unfavorable stories about their opponents, and reacting quickly to controversies about themselves and their supporters. The third campaign is the one the media present to the electorate. It consists of entertaining news that commands the attention of their consumers rather than news intended primarily to educate the polity in the exercise of its civic responsibilities.

The Bad-News Campaign

Campaign news coverage also tends to be more negative than positive. There were twice as many negative than positive comments about congressional candidates of both parties on evening television news shows during the 2010 midterm elections. The spin on Tea Party candidates during that election was similarly negative.[36] It was more of the same during the Republican presidential primaries in 2011–2012 with none of the candidates, except Ron Paul, receiving more positive than negative commentary, until Romney built a large delegate lead and the press concluded that he would win. During this same period, the tone of Barack Obama's coverage was also primarily negative.[37]

In the 2012 general election both candidates received more negative than positive coverage. A comprehensive content analysis of news coverage between August 27 and November 5, 2012, by the Pew Research Center's Project for Excellence in Journalism found that 20 percent of the news stories about Obama were favorable compared with 29 percent unfavorable; Romney had only 15 percent favorable and 37 percent unfavorable.[38] The opinions expressed on Facebook, Twitter, and the blogs associated with news outlets were also more negative than positive, with Romney faring worse than Obama.[39]

Of course, negativity or criticism per se isn't harmful to a democratic electoral process; in fact, it is a necessary part of that process. Nonetheless, an overemphasis on the negative, particularly on personal and character dimensions, can disillusion voters,[40] decrease turnout, and make the election seem like a contest between the lesser of two evils.[41] *maybe about personal life*

Why all the negativism? Are the candidates less qualified now than they were in the past? Most scholarly observers do not think so. They offer three principal reasons for the press' underlying negativism: increasing skepticism about the motives and interests of politicians and elected officials, increasing emphasis on character issues combined with scrutiny of private behavior, and increasing competition with tabloid journalism in the news and entertainment marketplace. *– reinforce skepticism – scrutiny personal life – media attention*

The first of these reasons, skepticism about the rhetoric and actions of politicians, has always affected some press coverage. The Vietnam War and the Watergate scandal, however, ushered in an era of investigative journalism in which the media extended its distrust and disbelief in candidates and elected public officials and no longer gave them the benefit of doubt. The press assumed that politicians' statements and explanations were self-interested, and that it was the news media's job to reveal hidden motives, strategies, and goals.

Campaign coverage became more candidate-centered as investigative journalism began to focus more on the people seeking office than on their partisan connection. The line between public and private was obliterated, with the press trumpeting the importance of character as its rationale for reporting what used to be considered private (and therefore not reportable) behavior, such as family issues, sexual relationships, and addictive personal habits.

With the tabloids eager to highlight the personal foibles and relationships of prominent people, even if only rumored, the mainstream press found itself pressured to follow suit. They often used a report in the tabloid media, a news conference, or an unsubstantiated investigative story as the pretext for presenting this type of information as newsworthy. Thus, the allegations of Gennifer Flowers that she was Bill Clinton's lover for eleven years became front-page news during the 1992 Democratic nomination, as did facsimiles of memos questioning George W. Bush's service in the Alabama National Guard, claims disputing John Kerry's heroism in the Vietnam War, and allegations that Barack Obama was not born in the United States and thus did not meet the constitutional requirements for being president.

Opposition research by campaigns regularly stimulates and supplements this type of media coverage. Leaks have become a common and accepted way to alert the press to negative facts and rumors about one's opponents. Because the negative often is surprising and unexpected, this type of news feeds into the news media's addiction to information that grabs their audience. *negative surprising, juicy = media attention = media likes it, (more viewers?)*

From the candidates' perspective, the bad news is magnified by the fact that they don't get the opportunity to respond in kind, to explain their side of

NOT HEARING FROM CANDIDATES

the story in anywhere near the detail as the allegations that were made against them. Moreover, if the charges prove to be inaccurate, any corrections made by the press do not receive nearly the amount of coverage as the story that prompted them.

As a result, candidates are left with little alternative but to defend themselves against even the most reckless charges, thereby giving even more attention to those charges than they would otherwise merit. Not only must candidates respond quickly to allegations against them so as not to allow an unfavorable image to prevail, but they have an incentive to get dirt on their opponents as well. To make matters worse, candidates also have an inclination to reinforce negative personal news reported by the press by running negative personal advertising.

negative feedback loop

A number of unfortunate consequences for a democratic electoral process follow from this type of campaign behavior and media coverage. The electorate gets a jaundiced view of the campaign. Sometimes, it becomes more of a personal contest between two or more gladiators than an issue-oriented debate. The news is presented by television anchors, correspondents, and star newspaper reporters and not by the candidates themselves. It emphasizes the bad over the good.

How did coverage of the last two presidential elections fare? Was it more thorough, more objective, and more informative than previous elections? According to the Pew Research Center's Project for Excellence in Journalism, it was not. The coverage was similar to that of past campaigns.[42] The principal presidential candidates received about the same amount of attention during the general election, but the stories of the campaign were more favorable to Obama than to McCain and Romney.

Why did Obama receive more favorable coverage? The Pew Center's analysis concluded that it was due to the news media's horse race emphasis and the fact that Obama was in the lead for most of both general election campaigns:

> . . . winning in politics begat winning coverage, thanks in part to the relentless tendency of the press to frame its coverage of national elections as running narratives about the relative position of the candidates in the polls and internal tactical maneuvering to alter those positions. Obama's coverage was negative in tone when he was dropping in the polls, and became positive when he began to rise, and it was just so for McCain [and Romney] as well. Nor are these numbers different than what we have seen before. Obama's numbers are similar to what we saw for John Kerry . . . , and McCain's numbers are almost identical to what we saw eight years ago for Democrat Al Gore.[43]

In short, media coverage reports and thereby indirectly reinforces the polls. The candidate who is ahead gets a more favorable tone.[44]

cycle: polls ⇒ media tone ⇒ voters ⇒ polls

KNOWLEDGE AND VOTING

An Enlightened Decision?

Do people know enough to cast an intelligent vote? The electorate thinks so. After presidential elections, the Pew Research Center asks people whether they learned enough to make an informed choice. As Table 5.4 reveals, most people say "yes." What we don't know, however, is how much information people have, the kind of information it is, and how much of it is necessary to make an enlightened judgment.

who can decide who's educated enough?

Our limited knowledge of what the public knows stems from the fact that the vast majority of public affairs polls ask attitude and opinion questions rather than informational ones. In fact, information is frequently provided in the question or statement so that people can respond intelligently.

In short, campaign news coverage, political advertising, and coverage of such events as conventions and debates contribute to the learning process,[45] but how much people really learn is unclear. The critical question is whether they know enough to make an enlightened judgment on election day. Most people believe that they do, as indicated in Table 5.4. *but do they really...*

Information and Democracy: Three Views

How much public knowledge and activity are necessary to maintain the health and vitality of a democratic society? There are several schools of thought.

ELITIST:

Those who subscribe to the **elitist model** of democracy believe that as long as the leadership is informed, involved, and responsible to the people through the electoral process, the political system can function properly. This minimalist

if our leaders are educated

TABLE 5.4	**Voters' Perceptions of Information Adequacy, 1988–2012 (percentages)**						
Perception	1988	1992	1996	2000	2004	2008	2012
Learned enough to make an informed choice	59	77	75	83	86	85	88
Did not learn enough from the campaign	39	20	23	15	13	14	11
Don't know/refused	2	3	2	2	2	1	2

Sources: Pew Research Center for the People and the Press, "Low Marks for the 2012 Election," November 15, 2012. http://www.people-press.org/2012/11/15/low-marks-for-the-2012-election/; Pew Research Center for the People and the Press, "Voters Like Campaign 2004, but Too Much 'Mud-Slinging,'" November 11, 2004; Pew Research Center for the People and the Press, "High Marks for the Campaign, a High Bar for Obama: Republicans Want More Conservative Direction for GOP," November 13, 2008, http://people-press.org/report/471/high-bar-for-obama.

theory of public involvement maintains that democratic criteria are satisfied if the citizenry has the opportunity to participate in elections and enough basic information to do so. Citizens need to be able to differentiate among the candidates and their principal policy positions, factor in their own perceptions of reality, and make voting decisions. But not everyone has to be informed and participate in civic affairs for the system to work.

The **pluralist model** sees the system as democratic if it permits people to pursue their interests within the political arena. Elections are one of the political processes in which they can do so, but not the only one. Public demonstrations, letter-writing campaigns, e-mails, texting, and personal contacts are other means by which those outside of government can influence those in it. Again, the burden of being informed and involved rests primarily on the group leadership, on those in and out of power; the requirement for the populace is that its interests can be discerned, expressed, and pursued.

In both the elitist and the pluralistic models, the process by which people express their views is the main criterion for claiming that the system is democratic. The **popular, or plebiscitary, model** demands more. It requires a higher level of public involvement in politics and government. Within the electoral arena, this translates into more public debate, more interaction between the candidates and the electorate, and more people voting.

Those who adopt this perspective see the decline in public trust and confidence in politics and government as dangerous because it can lead to a concentration of power in the hands of a few. It also can reduce support for governmental decisions and for the people who make them and weaken the legitimacy of the rules and processes of the political system. One sign of alienation would be the growth of organized, armed vigilantes or militias, those who see it as their mission to take the law into their own hands. Another would be an increase in civil disobedience. A third might be the failure of significant portions of the population to participate in elections and to vote. A fourth would be the perception that special interests control election outcomes and government policymaking anyway, so votes do not matter and elections do not make a difference.

It is difficult to answer the question of how informed and involved a citizenry must be to maintain a democratic political system. But there is little doubt that the more information and involvement people have, and the more active support the general population gives to the candidates who run for office, the more attention they will pay to the party platforms on which those candidates run, to their qualifications for office, and their performance in it.

Of course, people do not get all their information about campaigns from the news media. Candidate advertisements are another source of information, as are personal contacts and experience, as well as social networking. News coverage, however, is still a very important component of the process of gathering sufficient information to make an informed voting decision—hence the issue addressed in the last part of this chapter: how to better educate the public about the campaign through the mass media.

WHAT CAN BE DONE TO IMPROVE ELECTION COVERAGE?

Criticizing contemporary press coverage of elections is much easier than making constructive suggestions for changing that coverage. The electorate may be getting what it wants but not necessarily what it needs. It is all well and good to berate the news media for not presenting a detailed discussion of the issues, but what good would it do to present such a discussion if the public were not interested in it, did not follow it, or was turned off by it? Besides, there is plenty of detailed and easily accessible information about the candidates and their campaigns, the parties and their platforms, and the voters and their interests and desires. And that information is readily available in national newspapers and magazines; on public radio and television; and on the Web sites of candidates, parties, nonparty groups, and news media organizations.

We can wring our hands and bemoan the fact that most people do not regularly consult these sources. We can say that they should, but we certainly aren't ready to reinstitute knowledge tests as a condition for voting. We can blame this state of affairs on the failure of civic education in the schools, a claim that probably has some merit, but shaking our heads sadly about underinformed, uninvolved, generally apathetic citizens will not change the situation, although it might enable some people to rationalize it more satisfactorily.

We can blame the problem on the news media, as does Thomas Patterson. Patterson believes that those who determine media markets have made a wrong-headed assumption that people interested in news want an endless diet of soft, tabloid-oriented pabulum to consume. Not so, he says. In a study of the news preferences of television audiences, he found hard news to be more appealing to more people than soft news. Moreover, he also discovered that consumers of hard news were less tolerant of soft news than consumers of soft news were of hard news.[46] Patterson concludes that in their effort to compete with the increasing variety and number of news-entertainment shows, the national news networks have done themselves and our democracy a disservice by increasing their emphasis on soft news, gossip, and celebrities.[47] The question then becomes what can be done to change contemporary media coverage of elections.

Redefine Election News

One suggestion is to convince those who control the scope and methods of election news coverage to change their definition of news, their standards for reporting it, and their game-oriented emphasis. A task force on campaign reform has urged such an approach in 1988. The task force suggested that the press "use the campaign controversies as spring boards for reporting on the real substance of politics and political careers, rather than treating them as self-contained episodes."[48] Similarly, instead of entertaining horse race stories that report polls of who is ahead and by how much, the task force recommended more analysis of why different groups seem to be supporting different candidates, more in-depth reporting—be it on character qualifications or substantive policy concerns—and more emphasis on the big issues that transcend day-to-day events. The report also made the observation that election news could be more repetitive, that news does not always have to be new, and that the test for including information should be the level of public knowledge on a subject, not the level of the press's knowledge about it.[49] Too often the catalyst for a story is the desire to scoop other journalists for something new and different rather than the salience of the issue to the voters and the country.

Thomas Patterson reaches much the same conclusion when he argues that the hard news component must be strengthened if people are to have the information they need to make an informed judgment when voting. "What is good for democracy is also good for the press," he writes.[50]

These are excellent suggestions, but they require the news media to change their journalistic orientation. Such changes tend to come slowly, if at all, and they are usually dictated by the economics of the marketplace, not by politics. Citizens could vote for these reforms with their television remotes, radio dials, and Web site hits by tuning in to news programs that provide more in-depth, policy-oriented coverage, such as public radio and television, two media outlets whose audiences have increased during the past two decades.[51] The bottom line is that without a massive, negative reaction to contemporary election coverage in the form in which it is accessible to the general public, that coverage is not likely to change.

Shorten the Campaign

A different type of suggestion, proposed by Thomas Patterson many years ago in his book *Out of Order,* was to shorten election campaigns, particularly the long and arduous nomination contests that now consume more time than the general election.[52] A more compact campaign, he believes, would of necessity focus the news media on the more important issues, cut down their interpretations and negativity, and force the political parties to play a greater role in communicating with the voters.[53] But it also would provide less time for an inattentive public to learn about the candidates and issues.

Although the major parties have prohibited delegate selection from occurring before the election year, that prohibition has not discouraged early campaigning. National legislation would probably be required. Not only would such legislation increase the regulatory role of the federal government in elections, possibly conflicting with the free speech protections of the First Amendment, but it would also limit the authority of the states to conduct elections for federal officials. Unless campaign finance laws were changed, candidates would still have to raise considerable sums of money and do so before the official campaign began. Besides, what guarantee would there be that the news media would become any less interpretive or negative?

Communicate More Directly with Voters

Another recommendation, made in some campaign finance proposals as well as by several bipartisan groups and commissions, is to conduct more of the campaign spontaneously and directly though the mass media. That could be done by extending the number of debates among the candidates and also by providing them with free broadcast time.

Most European democracies feature debates among the principal candidates or party leaders, and some require on-air time to be provided to the parties. But most of these countries also operate government-controlled networks on which to provide such time; the United States does not.

Debates are useful for several reasons. They enable the public to see, compare, and evaluate candidates in the same setting, at the same time, and judge them on the basis of the same criteria: their knowledge of the problems, their priorities and issue positions, and their communicative skills. They allow candidates to speak in their own words uninterrupted for a specified time to which the participants have agreed (but frequently not longer than one minute). Coincidentally, certain debate formats reduce the press's role as intermediary.

debates

Not all candidates benefit equally from debates, however. Front-runners, particularly incumbents, see little advantage in debating their challengers; when they do, they are usually able to dictate the timing and format to their perceived advantage. Most candidates play it safe, anticipating their opponents' arguments and rehearsing lines in advance. Spontaneity is minimized. As the campaign progresses, candidates begin to sound like their ads.

Nor do the parties gain much from debates held during the nomination phase. Candidates usually try to distinguish themselves from one another rather than indicate what good partisans they are and with what party policy positions they concur. Moreover, nomination debates are rarely carried on the major broadcast networks, although they may be aired on local affiliates in the region or state in which the primary is to occur. The cable networks may cover some of them, but the audience is relatively small compared to the presidential debates in the general election.[54] Also the greater the number of debates (there were 47 during the 2007–2008 nomination cycle—21 Republican and 26 Democratic—and 20 among Republicans in 2011–2012), the smaller the audience tends to be although that audience is magnified by the news coverage the debate receives.

Moreover, during the early stages of the nomination quest, there are usually many candidates, particularly if an incumbent is not seeking renomination. A debate involving more than three or four people is not usually a debate but simply an opportunity for the participants to distinguish themselves, declare their positions, and try to project a presidential image. In-depth discussions are precluded by multiple candidates and limited time. Not much learning occurs unless a candidate states a position that is unpopular with that candidate's partisan supporters, such as Texas Governor Rick Perry's position on in-state tuition for children of illegal immigrants or former House Speaker Newt Gingrich's proposal for more manned exploration of the moon. At the presidential level in the general election, the audience is larger, varying in size from 36 to 90 million.

But the availability of many other entertainment shows, including competition with the baseball playoffs and World Series, reduces the size of the viewing audience and the duration of time people watch.[55] Thus, even if the debates were more easily available on television, it is likely that once their aura wore off, the principal audience would probably be composed of strong partisans who root for their candidate and inadvertent viewers who watch for a few minutes and then move on to other channels.

There are other problems with having debates as the principal vehicle through which the candidates communicate with voters. Debates reward performance skills. They benefit telegenic candidates who are well prepared, well coached, and comfortable with television—essentially those who can give quick and catchy responses to the questions of moderators, people in the audience or online, or the comments of their opponents. Those who take longer to make a point, agonize over the complexities of issues, and do not communicate easily or quickly in short sound bites may be disadvantaged. Are debate skills important for elected officials? Should they be a major factor potentially affecting the election outcome?[56] Would voters benefit from this arrangement? Would they gain and retain more objective information about the candidates, their positions, and their intellectual, communicative, and political skills? Would they be better able to make considered judgments in the voting booth?

However these questions are answered, the candidates and their handlers would not be satisfied with a debate format alone. They want time to communicate their message without interruption and criticism, and they wish to do it in a setting that enhances their image and message.[57] And the Constitution protects their right to do so, much as it protects the reporters' right to cover the election as they see fit.

Occasionally, some candidates have been given a little free time by a major cable or broadcast network. The limited time and partisan nature of the presentation normally attracts a small audience composed primarily of loyal supporters. These appearances have produced little discernible impact on public knowledge and voter decision making.[58]

Nonetheless, various free-time proposals have been advanced—from keeping the current voluntary system to requiring the networks to provide a certain amount of time to meet their public interest obligations. Naturally, the major corporations that control the communications industry oppose a free-time requirement imposed on them by government, particularly one that obligates them to provide airtime during prime time. They fear that they would lose money. They point to the large number of candidates for national office who would want to avail themselves of free time on television. Could minor party candidates be excluded? Who would decide? And how could the free time be monitored?

Although most candidates would probably use free time were it made available to them, it is unlikely that when doing so they would forgo other forms of communication, such as political advertising, or even deviate very much from the message of their ads. Would more free time then be more of the same political "propaganda," little more than advertising in another form?

SUMMARY: NEWS MEDIA DILEMMAS IN A NUTSHELL

The press is a critical link between the candidates and the electorate. Since the 1830s, the mass media—first newspapers, then radio and television, and now the Internet—have brought campaigns to the voters. Over the years, the news media have evolved from a local to a national press, from individual ownership to newspaper chains, from print to radio to television, from broadcast to cable and satellite to the Internet, and from once-a-day reporting to around-the-clock and instantaneous news. Not only have the media become diverse, but they have also become omnipresent. If these changes had contributed to a more attentive, informed, and involved electorate, then the democracy would have been well served, but, alas, there is little evidence that this is the case.

The scope, content, and format of the election news that is reported are not as informative as they need to be. A journalistic orientation toward making the election news as captivating as possible has resulted in considerable media coverage that lacks substance. The emphasis is on newness, controversy, and drama rather than on partisan and policy debates and their implications for the country's future. The coverage has become more compartmentalized, more interpretive, with an emphasis on the negative. The candidates are presented as players in an unfolding drama. The campaign story is told with sports metaphors and analogies, strewn with juicy personality tidbits and featuring contending forces, each trying to manipulate the electorate to their advantage.

Coverage affects the campaign. It forces the candidates to orchestrate their activities for the mass media with irresistible sound bites in their speeches, engaging pictures and personalities at their events, and well-known talking heads to spin their messages. It also forces them to have "war rooms" to respond quickly and decisively to any attack or allegation against them.

The public is informed primarily by this coverage. From the perspective of news sellers and distributors, it is what the audience desires, although some scholars disagree. The public, too, is critical of news coverage yet continues to consume it and claim that it has sufficient knowledge to decide on the winner. Whether that knowledge is sufficient to make enlightened voting decisions, however, remains hotly debated.

Now It's Your Turn

Discussion Questions

1. What is the connection between public interest in politics and news about politics?

2. How does journalistic bias affect the scope and content of information that people receive about election campaigns?

3. Is sufficient information available for the electorate make informed electoral judgments? If not, who is at fault: the news media, the candidates, or the public?

4. Should government exercise more control over the scope and content of campaign coverage?

5. What inducements might encourage the news media to provide more substantive policy information about contemporary election issues and more in-depth studies of the qualifications of those who seek elective office?

6. Do you think that the press currently exercises too much influence on campaigns and election outcomes?

Topics for Debate

Challenge or defend the following statements:

1. A free press cannot be a fair and objective press.

2. If voters lack the information they need to make an informed voting decision today, it is their own fault.

3. A democratic electoral process requires the electorate to be opinionated but not necessarily informed.

4. The private behavior of candidates is relevant to their public performance in office and should continue to be reported as election news.

5. The news media have an ideological bias which adversely affects their election reporting.

6. The news media have an obligation to report substantive policy debate in depth, whether or not people are interested in that debate.

Exercises

1. A major television network asks for your advice on how to improve its campaign coverage of the next election. The network would like you to prepare a memo with three goals in mind: meeting the network's public responsibility to inform voters, satisfying the interests of the viewing audience, and gaining audience ratings that are higher than its competitors' ratings. Draft the memo. In your analysis, indicate the following:

   a. the aspects of the campaign that you would cover and the proportion of coverage you would give to each,

   b. the attention to be given to third-party and independent candidates versus major party candidates, to international, national, and local coverage, and to primaries versus the general election,

   c. the ways in which the media should cover the campaign to maximize their ratings and perform their public service.

   In addition, the network would like to know whether it should:

   relax its two-source verification rule in the interest of competition;

   air rumors and allegations about personal behavior if they appear credible;

include in the candidates' personality profiles information about their physical and mental health; and

give attention to candidate misstatements, inconsistencies, and off-color remarks.

2. Review a day's election news coverage on one of the cable news network shows, one of the evening broadcast news network show, the News Hour on public television, and on one of the Web sites of a major news organization. On which did you find the most accurate coverage, the most interesting coverage, and the greatest depth of coverage? Did you detect any ideological bias? Which of these news sources do you think was the most valuable to most voters?

INTERNET RESOURCES

- Annenberg Public Policy Center: www.annenbergpublicpolicycenter.org

  Conducts studies on the media, which it makes available on this Web site; part of the Annenberg School for Communication of the University of Pennsylvania.

- Center for Media and Public Affairs: www.cmpa.com

  Evaluates the amount and spin of the major broadcast networks' coverage of the news; associated with George Mason University.

- Commission on Presidential Debates: www.debates.org

  Dedicated to the sponsorship, production, and archiving of presidential debates; nonpartisan and nonprofit organization.

- Freedom Forum: www.freedomforum.org

  Provides information on media issues, particularly as they relate to the First Amendment; sponsored by the Gannett Foundation and links to other Gannett groups, Newseum, and Press Watch, which also contain useful information on coverage of elections.

- Newspaperlinks.com: www.newspaperlinks.com

  Provides links to the online editions of local newspapers across the country through NewsVoyager site.

- Politics Online: www.politicsonline.com

  Good source for presidential campaigning on the Internet.

- Pew Research Center's Project for Excellence in Journalism: www.journalism.org

  Excellent source for an ongoing content analysis of media coverage of campaigns as well as an evaluation of that coverage

- Other media sources with campaign Web sites:

  ABC News Politics: http://abcnews.com
  Associated Press: www.ap.org/

The Daily Beast: www.thedailybeast.com
CBS News: www.cbsnews.com
CNN: http://cnn.com
C-SPAN: www.cspan.org
Fox News: http://foxnews.com
Huffington Post: www.huffingtonpost.com
Los Angeles Times: http://latimes.com
NBC News: www.msnbc.com
New York Times: www.nytimes.com
Politico: www.politico.com
Real Clear Politics: www.realclearpolitics.com
USA Today: www.usatoday.com
Washington Post: http://washingtonpost.com

SELECTED READINGS

Ansolabehere, Stephen, and Shanto Iyengar. *Going Negative: How Political Advertisements Shrink and Polarize the Electorate*. New York, NY: Free Press, 1995.

Baum, Matthew A., and Samuel Kernell. "Has Cable Ended the Golden Age of Presidential Television?" *American Political Science Review* 93 (1999): 99–111.

Denton, Robert E., Jr. *The 2012 Presidential Campaign: A Communication Perspective*. Lanham, MD: Rowman & Littlefield, 2013.

Druckman, James N. "The Power of Television Images: The First Kennedy-Nixon Debate Revisited." *Journal of Politics* 65 (2003): 559–571.

Farnsworth, Stephen J., and S. Robert Lichter. *The Nightly News Nightmare: Network News Coverage of U.S. Presidential Elections, 1988–2004*. Lanham, MD: Rowman & Littlefield, 2005.

Graber, Doris A. *Mass Media and American Politics*. Washington, DC: CQ Press, 2009.

Iyengar, Shanto, and Donald Kinder. *News that Matters: Television and American Opinion*. Chicago, IL: University of Chicago Press, 1987.

Iyengar, Shanto, Helmut Norpoth, and Kyu S. Hahn. "Consumer Demand for Election News: The Horserace Sells." *Journal of Politics* 66 (2004): 157–175.

Jamieson, Kathleen Hall. *Everything You Think You Know about Politics and Why You're Wrong*. New York, NY: Free Press, 2000.

Jamieson, Kathleen Hall, and Bruce Hardy, "What Is Civil Engaged Argument and Why Does Aspiring to It Matter?" *P S: Political Science and Politics*, 45 (July 2012): 412–415.

Kenski, Kate, Bruce W. Hardy, and Kathleen Hall Jamieson. *The Obama Victory: How Media, Money, and Message Shaped the 2008 Election*. Oxford, England: Oxford University Press, 2010.

Kerbel, Matthew R. *If It Bleeds It Leads*. Boulder, CO: Westview, 2000.

Mutz, Diana C. "How the Mass Media Divide Us." In *Red and Blue Nation? Characteristics and Causes of America's Polarized Politics*, edited by Pietro S. Nivla and David W. Brady. Washington, DC: Brookings Institution Press, 2006.

Patterson, Thomas E. *Out of Order*. New York, NY: Knopf, 1993.

Prior, Markus. *Post-Broadcast Democracy: How Media Choice Increases Inequity in Political Involvement and Polarizes Elections*. Cambridge, England: Cambridge University Press, 2009.

Sabato, Larry J. *Feeding Frenzy: Attack Journalism and American Politics*. Baltimore, MD: Lanham Publishers, 2000.

NOTES

1. To facilitate the distribution of newspapers, Congress enacted a law in 1792 to keep the postal rates for newspapers low.

2. Emily Guskin, Tom Rosenstiel, and Paul Moore, "The State of the Media: 2011," Pew Research Center's Project for Excellence in Journalism. http://stateofthemedia.org/2011/network-essay/data-page-5/

3. Statistical Abstract of the United States, "Utilization and Number of Selected Media: 2000–2010," Table 1132, www.census.gov/compendia/statab/tables/2012/tables/12s1132.pdf.

4. In style, network news was redesigned to be captivating, current, and concise to compete more effectively with the hundreds of channels that cable and satellite companies offered and with the shorter attention spans and remote control devices never far from the hands of their viewers. Thomas E. Patterson, *Doing Well and Doing Good: How Soft News and Critical Journalism Are Shrinking the News Audience and Weakening Democracy—And What News Outlets Can Do About It* (Cambridge, MA: Harvard University Press, 2000), 4.

5. "Key Findings, State of the News Media 2011," Pew Research Center's Project for Excellence in Journalism, March 14, 2011. http://stateofthemedia.org/2011/overview-2/key-findings/. In its 2012 report, the Pew Center found that cable news viewership increased by 1 percent. A much smaller percentage indicated that they get their news from Facebook and Twitter. Amy Mitchell and Tom Rosenstiel, "The State of the News Media 2012," Pew Research Center's Project for Excellent in Journalism, March 19, 2012. http://stateofthemedia.org/2012/overview-4/major-trends

6. "Trends in News Consumption, 1991–2012: In Changing News Landscape, Even Television is Vulnerable," Pew Research Center for the People and the Press, September 27, 2012. http://www.people-press.org/2012/09/27/in-changing-news-landscape-even-television-is-vulnerable

7. The 2011 and 2012 Pew surveys on the news media reported that about half of the Internet users initially turn to the Web sites of major news organizations for informing themselves about current events. Pew Research Center for the People and the Press, "Views of the News Media, 1985–2011: Press Widely Criticized, but Trusted More than Other Information Sources," September 22, 2011. http://www.people-press.org/2011/09/22/press-widely-criticized-but-trusted-more-than-other-institutions/. Amy Mitchell and Tom Rosenstiel, "The State of the News Media 2012," Pew Research Center's Project for Excellence in Journalism, March 19, 2012. http://stateofthemedia.org/2012/overview-4/major-trends

8. Tom Rosenstiel and Amy Mitchell, "The State of the News Media: 2011," Pew Research Center's Project for Excellence in Journalism. March 14, 2011. http://stateofthemedia.org/

9. The decline in news costs has facilitated the growth of specialty and ideologically oriented news sources, first in print, then radio and television, and finally, on the Internet. These sources do not need as large an audience as do mass news media.

10. The rule required journalists to confirm information they received from at least two independent sources before reporting it in a news story.

11. Pew Research Center for the People and the Press, "Public Knowledge of Public Affairs Little Changed by News and Information Revolutions," April 15, 2007. http://people-ress. org/report/319/public-knowledge-of-public-affairs-little-changed-by-news-and-information-revolutions

12. Kathleen Hall Jamieson and Bruce W. Hardy, "The Effect of Media on Public Knowledge," in *The Oxford Handbook of American Public Opinion and the Medi,* edited by Lawrence B. Jacobs and Robert Y. Shapiro (Oxford, England; Oxford University Press, 2011), 237.

13. Pew Research Center for the People and the Press, "Many Voters Unaware of Basic Facts about GOP Candidates," January 12, 2012. http://www.people-press.org/2012/01/12/many-voters-unaware-of-basic-facts-about-gop-candidates

14. Pew Research Center for the People and the Press, "What Voters Know about Campaign 2012," August 10, 2012. http://ewww.people-press.org/2012/08/10/what-voters-know-about-campaign-2012

15. Channel scanning (also called channel surfing) reduces the amount of political knowledge retained by viewers; it also increases their level of cynicism. Jonathan S. Morris and Richard Forgette, "News Grazers, Television News, Political Knowledge, and Engagement," *The International Journal of Press/Politics* 12 (Winter 2007): 91–107.

16. The 2011–2012 campaign may be part of the problem. It started slowly and received little attention fror the first nine months of the election cycle. Pew Research Center's Project for Excellence in Journalism, "How 2011 Presidential Campaign Coverage Stacks Up with 2007," December 16, 2011. http://journalism.org/numbers_report/campaign_comparison

17. "Trends A–Z: Confidence in Institutions," Gallup Poll. www.gallup.com/poll/'1597/Confidence-Institutions.aspx

18. "Trends A to Z: Media Use and Evaluation," Gallup Poll. www.gallup.com/poll/1663/Media-Use-Evaluation.aspx

19. The confidence in the news media began to decline as the cable news networks developed a partisan/ideological orientation. Republicans turned increasingly to FOX; liberals to MSNBC and National Public Radio; CNN had a slightly more diverse audience although its ratings have declined. The polarization within the American polity has reinforced and been reinforced by these patterns of news consumption.

20. "Views of the News Media, 1985–2011: Press Widely Criticized, but Trusted More than Other information Sources," Pew Research Center for the People and the Press, September 22, 2011. http://pewresearch.org/pubs/2104/news-organizations-inaccurate-trust-cable-news-press-media-coverage

21. See Diane C. Mutz, "How the Mass Media Divide Us," in *Red and Blue Nation? Consequences and Correction of America's Partisan Politics,* edited by Pietro Nivola and David W. Brady (Washington, DC: Brookings Institution, 2006); Eric Lawrence, John Sides, and Henry Farrell, "Self-Segregation or Deliberation? Blog Readership, Participation, and Polarization in American Politics," *Perspectives on Politics* 8 (March 2010): 141–157; Natalie Jomini Stroud, "Polarization and Partisan Selective Exposure," *Journal of Communication* 60 (September 2010): 556–576.

22. In its annual evaluation of the news survey, the Pew Research Center found that most people (64 percent) say that they prefer news with no political perspective; 74 percent of those who obtain news online want coverage that is nonpartisan. "Views of the News Media, 1985–2011: Press Widely Criticized, but Trusted More than Other Information Sources," Pew Research Center on the People and the Press, September 22, 2011. http://pewresearch.org/pubs/2104/news-organizations-inaccurate-trust-cable-news-press-media-coverage

23. Norman H. Nie, Darwin W. Miller, III, Saar Golde, Daniel M. Butler, and Kenneth Winneg, "The World Wide Web and the U.S. Political News Market," *American Journal of Political Science* 54 (April 2010): 428–439.

24. "Views of Press Values and Performance: 1985–2007."

25. Annenberg Public Policy Center, "Public and Press Differ about Partisan Bias, Accuracy and Press Freedom," May 24, 2005, www.annenbergpublicpolicycenter.org/NewsDetails.aspx?myId=209.

26. Kathleen Hall Jamieson and Bruce Hardy, "What Is Civilly Engaged Argument and Why Does Aspiring to It Matter?" *PS: Political Science and Politics* 45 (July 2012): 401–404.

27. Robert Y. Shapiro and Lawrence R. Jacobs, "The Democratic Paradox: The Waning of Popular Sovereignty and the Pathologies of American Politics," in *The Oxford Handbook of American Public Opinion and the Media,* edited by Lawrence B. Jacobs and Robert Y. Shapiro (Oxford, England: Oxford University Press, 2011), 721.

28. Charles S. Tabor and Milton Lodge, "Motivated Skepticism in the Evaluation of Political Beliefs," *American Journal of Political Science,* 50 (July 2006): 755–769; Charles S. Tabor, Dammon Cann, and Simona Kucsova. "The Motivated Processing of Political Arguments," *Political Behavior,* 31 (June 2009): 137–155.

29. S. Robert Lichter and his associates reported that the average campaign story on network evening news had correspondents and anchors on the air six times longer than the candidates. "Take This Campaign—Please," *Media Monitor* (September/October 1996): 2; "Campaign 2000 Final," *Media Monitor* (November/December 2000): 2.

30. The use of the talk-entertainment format has several advantages for candidates. They are treated more like celebrities than politicians. Hosts tend to be more cordial and less adversarial than news commentators and reporters. Moreover, the audience is different. Those who watch these shows tend to be less oriented toward partisan politics and thus may be more amenable to influence by the candidates who appear on them.

31. There has veen a steep decline in print journalism staffs since 2000 and increasing reliance on freelance reporting, according to the Pew Research Center's Project for Excellence in Journalism report entitled "The State of the News Media 2013," March 18, 2013. http:stateofthemedia.org.

32. Pew Research Center's Project for Excellence in Journalism, "Winning the Media Campaign, How the Press Reported the 2008 General Election," October 22, 2008. http://www.journalism.org/node/13307

33. Pew Research Center's Project for Excellence in Journalism, "The State of the News Media 2013," March 18, 2013. http://stateofthe media.org

34. "The Final Days of the Media Campaign 2012," Pew Research Center's Project for Excellence in Journalism, November 19, 2012. www.journalism.org/print/31621

35. The one exception was 2004. In that election, the major news networks' evening news gave equal coverage to policy and to the race. "Election Watch: Campaign 2008 Final: How TV News Covered the General Election Campaign," *Media Monitor* 23 (Winter 2009). www.cmpa.com/pdf/media_monitor_jan_2009.pdf

36. "Media Have Bad News for Both Parties," The Center for Media and Public Affairs, October 21, 2010. http://cmpa.com/media_room_10_20_10.html

37. "Campaign 2012 in the Media," Pew Research Center's Project on Excellence in Journalism, February 16, 2012. http://www.journalism.org/commentary_backgrounder/pejs_election_report; http://www.journalism.org/commentary_backgrounder/PEJ%27s+Election+Analysis?src=prc-headline

38. "The Final Days of 2012," Project for Excellence in Journalism, November 19, 2012. www.journalism.org/print/31621

39. "Social Media during the Closing Weeks of the Campaign," Pew Research Center's Project on Excellence in Journalism, November 19, 2012. www.journalism.org/print/31623

40. Approximately two-thirds of Americans believe the news is too negative. "Views of the News Media, 1985–2011: Press Widely Criticized, but Trusted More than Other Information Sources," Pew Research Center on the People and the Press, September 22, 2011. http://pewresearch.org/pubs/2104/news-organizations-inaccurate-trust-cable-news-press-media-coverage

41. Negativism has been particularly evident at the presidential level and has been directed against incumbents. In 1980, Jimmy Carter was treated more harshly than Ronald Reagan, and in 1984, Reagan was treated more harshly than Walter Mondale. Vice President George H. W. Bush, running for president in 1988, fared poorly as well, but so did his Democratic opponent, Michael Dukakis. Much the same pattern emerged in 1992. S. Robert Lichter and his associates at the Center for Media and Public Affairs found that 69 percent of the evaluations of George H.W. Bush—his campaign, his positions, his performance, his general desirability—were negative, compared with 63 percent for Clinton and 54 percent for Perot. Bill Clinton did better in 1996, but Robert Dole did not. Only half of Clinton's coverage on the evening news was negative; two out of three comments about Dole were negative. George W. Bush got more negative coverage than John Kerry in 2004, as indicated in Table 5.4. "Campaign 2004 Final: How TV News Covered the General Election," *Media Monitor* (November/December 2004): 5.

42. "Winning the Media Campaign, How the Press Reported the 2008 General Election."

43. Ibid.

44. Ibid.

45. See, for example, Annenberg Public Policy Center, "Voters Learned Positions on Issues since Presidential Debates; Kerry Improves Slightly on Traits, Annenberg Data Show," National Annenberg Election Survey, October 23, 2004. www.annenbergpublicpolicycenter.org/Downloads/Political_Communication/naes/2004_03_%20Voters-and-the-issues_10–23_pr.pdf

46. Thomas Patterson, *Doing Well and Doing Good: How Soft News and Critical Journalism Are Shrinking the News Audience and Weakening Democracy—And What News Outlets Can Do about it.* (Cambridge, MA: Joan Shorenstein Center on the Press, Politics and Public Policy, 2000), 5–15.

47. Ibid., 7–9.

48. Task Force on Campaign Reform, "Campaign Reform: Insights and Evidence," Report of the Task Force on Campaign Reform, Woodrow Wilson School of Public and International Affairs, Princeton University, September 1998, 23.

49. Ibid., 21–26.

50. Patterson, *Doing Well and Doing Good*, 15.

51. Ibid., 8.

52. Patterson, *Out of Order*, 207–242.

53. Ibid., 210.

54. The audience for the nomination debates is approximately one-tenth the size of the presidential, general election debates. During the 2011–2012 Republican nomination cycle, the television audience varied from a low of 3.3 million for the first debate in May 2011 to a high of 7.6

million for the debate preceding the Iowa caucus. General election debates averaged between 50 and 60 million viewers.

Brian Stelter, "Ratings Dip for Latest Primary Debate," *New York Times*, February 23, 2012. http://thecaucus.blogs.nytimes.com/2012/02/23/ratings-dip-for-latest-primary-debate/?

55. In 2004, the third debate between George W. Bush and John Kerry drew an estimated 51.2 million viewers, compared with 15.2 million who watched the baseball playoffs.

56. There are also important procedural questions that could have a major impact on the electorate. When would debates occur? Who would set the dates? Who would be invited? Would candidates have to participate? What would the format be? Which institution would determine the rules, choose the moderators, and oversee the debate? Would instant commentary by news media representatives be permitted? Such commentary may color public perceptions, as it did of the second Ford-Carter debate in 1976. That debate concerned foreign policy. Initial public reaction was favorable to President Ford; however, Ford made a misstatement in the debate, leading some to conclude that he was unaware of the Soviet Union's domination of countries in Eastern Europe. The media pointed out Ford's error in their commentary. The president's failure to correct himself for three days, combined with the media's emphasis on his mistake, changed public perceptions about the debate, its winner, and Ford's competence in foreign affairs.

57. In the 2000 Democratic nomination process, Vice President Al Gore challenged his rival Senator Bill Bradley to forgo ads and simply debate. Bradley refused, claiming that he needed to advertise because he was not as well known as Gore and did not have the vice presidential podium.

58. Christopher Adasiewicz, Douglas Rivlin, and Jeffrey Stronger, "Free Television for Presidential Candidates: The 1996 Experiment," Annenberg Public Policy Center, University of Pennsylvania, March 1997.

chapter 6

Are American Parties Still Representative?

Did you know that . . .

- the Democratic Party of the United States is the oldest political party in the world?
- in this age of telegenic candidates and carefully scripted candidate appeals, partisanship still remains the most important influence on voting behavior?
- more people claim to be independent today than vote consistently in an independent manner?
- the least and most educated voters tend to vote Democratic in presidential elections?
- no political party in the United States today commands the loyalty of a majority of the population?
- although changes in the nomination process were designed to give a larger voice to rank-and-file partisans, the process continues to allow political elites to exercise greater influence?
- a key factor that has led to a resurgence of party organizations during electoral campaigns is money and lots of it?
- no third-party or independent candidate has ever won the presidency?
- despite a plurality of people identifying themselves as independent, only two independent or third-party candidates have been elected to the Senate in the twenty-first century?
- young people tend to be more supportive of third-party and independent candidates than their elders?
- the more cohesive the parties, the less functional divided government is apt to be?
- the United States is one of the few democratic countries with a two-party system?

Is this any way to run a democratic election?

PARTIES AND AMERICAN DEMOCRACY

Political parties are considered an important part of a democratic electoral system. In fact, some scholars consider them absolutely essential.[1] They provide critical links among the electorate, the candidates, and the government.

Parties help orient, organize, and energize voters, influencing turnout and voting. They tie candidates to one another and allow them to make both generic and specific appeals clothed in partisan imagery. And they provide people with a basis for evaluating the candidates and the performance of elected officials and holding them collectively responsible for the actions or inactions of government. Responsiveness and accountability are two critical components of a representative democracy.

In a heterogeneous society like that of the United States, interests are many, varied, and often conflicting. Political parties provide a structure for aggregating these interests, packaging them, and presenting them to voters. Parties articulate interests in their platforms, their election communications, and the campaigns of their candidates. Parties also provide a mechanism for governing and for bringing together elected officials on the basis of their shared values, interests, and policy goals.

In elections, as in government, parties are likely to be the most effective coalition builders. They can unite diverse elements of the electorate as well as overcome the institutional separation of powers to facilitate the operation of government. But parties also can have the opposite effect. Divided partisan control of government reinforces the separation of powers and impedes consensus building across institutional bodies.

Each of these functions—interest aggregation, articulation, and electoral accountability—is essential to a viable democratic political system.[2] That is why parties are important.

PARTIES AND ELECTIONS

Within the populace, parties structure the electorate. They create alliances among groups and allegiances among individuals. They inform people about the issues, get them involved in the campaign, and encourage them to vote.

Parties also provide electoral choices. They enable voters to transcend the many individual public policy issue preferences they have and decisions they must make and allows them to superimpose a collective judgment that both guides and justifies their micro-level decisions. For the vast majority of voters, a major-party label conveys legitimacy, whereas a third- or minor-party label does not.

Parties anchor policy preferences. Political parties have an organizational history and a policy record that the electorate uses to evaluate how successful they have been and anticipate how successful they are likely to continue to be.

For the candidates, parties provide a collective presence and perspective, an organizational base, and the potential for enhancing their individual influence if elected. The collective entity is the party organization, its perspective, and shared values, beliefs, and positions on the issues. As organizations, parties have the resources, including money, media expertise, communications technology, and grassroots mobilizing abilities to aid candidates in their campaigns and extend their influence in government.

Party organizations have grown stronger in recent years. They have raised more money, registered and turned out more voters, and taken more consistent policy stands on a range of substantive issues. There is more party unity in Congress in the twenty-first century than there was for most of the previous one.

For candidates, partisanship provides them with a core of faithful supporters; it also gives them the opportunity to reinforce some of the ideas, beliefs, and interests they have in common with fellow partisans. The benefits that parties give to candidates have led one observer, John H. Aldrich, to theorize that parties exist because office seekers and officeholders find them useful. They contribute to the outcomes that these ambitious politicians desire.[3]

Parties also provide a framework for evaluating election results, organizing the government, and subsequently criteria for assessing their performance in office. In doing so, they convert individual victories into a combined effort, help define priorities for newly elected officials, and provide a continuing incentive—renomination and reelection—for keeping public officials sensitive to the interests and opinions of those who elected them.

Despite the importance of political parties and the role they play in democratic elections and governance, they have often become objects of criticism by scholars, journalists, and the general public.[4] The very diverse interests they represent in America, their inartful transformation of these interests into public policy proposals, the priorities they attach to these proposals and the consistency with which they adhere to them, even their public advocacy role have engendered negative academic, press, and public perceptions and commentary. (See Figure 6.1.)

If partisanship were weakened or eliminated, what would replace it and would elections (and government) be more democratic? Juxtaposed as a more idealized alternative to a partisan electorate and partisan government is the concept of independent voters and nonpartisan elected public officials. In theory, independent thinking contributes to fairer and more enlightened electoral decisions and policy judgments that would be in the public interest. In practice, it may not, however. Given the diversity of the policy issues that are debated, the variety of candidates who seek elective office, and shifts in the public mood, how could a democracy endure, much less benefit, from highly individualistic electoral and governing processes?

According to political theorist Nancy L. Rosenblum, parties are valuable because they provide inclusiveness, comprehension, and the ingredients for conciliation.[5] The major parties like to think of themselves as big tents in which everyone is welcome if they choose to enter. There are no loyalty oaths or tests for partisan identification, although a number of states do require its citizens to register with a party to participate in that party's nomination process.

The major parties take positions on a wide range of policy issues. They are broad rather than narrow, general rather than specific. They try to integrate a wide spectrum of attitudes and opinions, which are held with varying degrees of intensity. They do so through compromise, as the Democrats did with health care reform in 2010. Although partisanship facilitates compromise within parties, the highly polarized political environment impedes compromise between them.

Parties try to build and maintain an internal consensus to help persuade the electorate of the merits of their candidates and policies. Their goal is to achieve the majority or plurality necessary to win the election and transform the results into successful policy outcomes in accordance with electoral preferences.

To defend the idea of political parties within a democratic society, however, is not necessarily to defend a particular party at a particular time or a particular type of party system. Although the United States has had a two-party tradition throughout most of its history, less diverse countries have multiparty systems that seem to work reasonably well. Box 6.1 discusses the strengths and weaknesses of different types of party systems.

BOX 6.1 **Multiparty Politics: Pros and Cons**

Can two major parties adequately represent a country as large and heterogeneous as the United States? "No" say people who believe that neither of the major parties reflects or sufficiently emphasizes their most strongly held views; "no" say those who attitudes are not as ideologically consistent as the Democratic and Republican Parties today; and "no" say people who dislike political conflict and seek a more homogeneous society in which compromise is valued as a means and end.

Would a multiple-party system be better for the United States? Countries smaller and less diverse than the United States, such as France, Germany, and Spain, have such systems and have been able to maintain stable and effective governments for relatively long periods of time. Others, however, such as Italy and, to a lesser extent, Israel, have not been as successful in maintaining stability and continuity. Over the years, governments in both of these countries have had to depend on the support of minor parties to gain and sustain a parliamentary majority.

In a multiparty system, the parties combine to form governing coalitions, and compromise occurs among them. In a two-party system, if there is a majority party, then compromise may also occur within it; if the major parties share power, then compromise must occur between them.

Whether a two-party or a multiparty system is best may depend on the priorities placed on representation, accountability, and effective governance. But the question also may be academic, given the long and dominant two-party tradition in America, to which both major parties are committed, from which both derive benefit, and for which many of the laws governing the structure and operation of the system have been designed to protect.

Source: POLITICAL PARTIES AND PARTY SYSTEMS by Alan Ware (1996) Table 5.3 from p. 163. By Permission of Oxford University Press.

THE TWO-PARTY TRADITION IN THE UNITED STATES

The persistence of Democratic and Republican parties is explained in part by their flexibility over the years and their willingness to adjust and survive in light of the changes that have affected American society. The major parties have successfully weathered these changes because, until recently, they have been more pragmatic than ideological, more inclusive than exclusive, and more decentralized than centralized.

They also have not attempted to impose their beliefs and issue positions on their supporters, their candidates for office, or even their elected officials as a condition of party affiliation or electoral acceptability, although obviously they try to persuade their adherents to tow the party line.[6]

Moreover, the major parties have advantages in the political system, advantages that they have built into it and jealously guard. They are well recognized and have gained legitimacy. They have organizations in all the states, a leadership structure, and core supporters and financial benefactors. Independent candidates and especially third parties generally lack these resources as well as the perception that they can win national elections.

The major parties have systemic advantages as well. They are automatically on the ballot in all fifty states as long as they win a certain percentage of the vote. Third parties are much less likely to have won that percentage. Third-party and independent candidates usually have to collect a certain number of signatures of registered voters just to get on the state ballots. Besides, as noted in Chapter 3, the single-member district system in which the person with the most votes wins also benefits major-party candidates at the expense of minor-party candidates.

The presidential election system confers the same advantage on the major parties. The winner-take-all method of Electoral College voting used by forty-eight of the fifty states disadvantages third-party candidates, especially when their support is widely distributed across the country, as was Ross Perot's in 1992 and 1996. If the election moves into the House, the major parties also benefit. The major parties and their candidates are automatically eligible to receive federal grants during the presidential election, whereas third parties and independent candidates are not.[7] Major parties and their candidates also receive much more extensive media coverage.

Despite public opinion, which periodically looks to third parties and independent candidates when the people are dissatisfied with the major parties, third parties have had difficulty gaining acceptance and maintaining public support. The argument that they cannot win in single-member districts or the Electoral College contributes to their difficulty in winning in those electoral arenas. In addition, the reforms that were initiated at the end of the nineteenth and beginning of the twentieth century—the secret ballot for voting and primary elections for choosing party nominees—provided those with views that differed from party leaders an opportunity to pursue those views within the major parties rather than outside of them. The threat of internal challenges forces party leaders to be more flexible and sensitive to a wide range of policy positions, with the consequence that parties have often incorporated the views of those outside the party hierarchy, thereby bringing outsiders into their electoral coalition rather than encouraging them to compete with the party from the outside.

The Democratic Party at the outset of the Great Depression provides a good example of a party shifting its position to incorporate the views of people who favored a more liberal, pro-government approach for solving the nation's economic problems, an approach that neither of the major parties advocated prior to the 1930s. The Democrats' New Deal took the wind out of left-wing third parties during the Depression and after it.[8]

If third parties and independent candidacies were the only ways minority viewpoints could be heard, then the bias of the two-party system would be a serious failing in a democratic political process. But, as already noted, there are many other ways minority group interests are represented in elections and government. In fact, many believe that demographic and ideological minorities are overrepresented within the major parties and exercise disproportionate influence on them as well as on the government, much to the dismay of moderate, mainstream, rank-and-file voters. And outside of the parties, interest groups have proliferated in the form of political action committees (PACs and Super PACs) and other special interest groups within the electoral and governing arenas.

The rest of this chapter examines the principal ways in which parties help electoral democracy. We consider parties and the electorate, parties and electoral choice, and parties and electoral accountability. First, however, we offer a brief overview of the evolution of American political parties to provide a historical context for evaluating how well parties are serving the needs of electoral democracy today.

THE EVOLUTION OF U.S. POLITICAL PARTIES

Parties are not mentioned in the Constitution, nor did the framers anticipate them when they created the electoral system. They did anticipate that groups would be active within the political arena, however. Fearing domination by any one of these groups, they divided institutional spheres of authority and created separate but overlapping constituencies as a hedge against any one group, including a majority, disproportionately influencing national policy.

Implicit in this constitutional design, however, was the assumption that a lot of national policy would not be needed. With an ocean for protection, a huge frontier, and seemingly unlimited natural resources, a nation composed largely of self-sufficient farmers was thought not to need or desire a very active national government. Although economic and social needs have changed and government has grown and become more involved in the everyday life of most Americans, its constitutional structure has essentially remained intact—hence the dilemma of how to bridge the institutional divide and facilitate the functioning of government. By providing common perspectives, policy goals, and political structures, parties can unify what the Constitution separates if one party controls the principal institutions of government. However, if institutional control is divided, partisanship can reinforce the constitutional division, thereby impeding the operation of government. Over the course of American history, parties have done both.

Birth and Infancy, 1790s–1820s

Parties developed in the 1790s in support of or in opposition to the policies of the Washington administration, specifically the economic policies outlined in Alexander Hamilton's Economic Report on Manufacturers, which favored protection of manufacturers in the United States by establishing tariffs and creating a national bank for credit and commerce. Small farmers and laborers feared increased costs and decreased influence from such policies and opposed them. The party system developed along these economic divisions, with Federalists supporting the adoption of Hamilton's proposals and the Democratic-Republicans, led by Thomas Jefferson, opposing them.[9]

The creation of parties at the end of the eighteenth and beginning of the nineteenth centuries presented the political system with both a challenge and an opportunity. The challenge was to prevent a major party from dominating the system in such a way as to deny the minority its rights and disregard its interests. The opportunity was to utilize common beliefs, goals, and interests as a consensus-building mechanism within and among the institutions of government.

Thomas Jefferson's Democratic-Republican Party, which emerged as the first broad-based political party in the United States, controlled national politics and government for more than twenty-five years, beginning at the end of the eighteenth century. It was the majority faction that the framers feared, but it also bridged the gap that was developing between an expanding and more diverse electorate and the national elites who had controlled the government since its founding. By the 1820s, the Federalist Party, which supported the policies of the George Washington and John Adams administrations, had faded from the scene, and the Democratic-Republicans, the only viable party remaining, began to divide along regional lines. Two of these partisan divisions eventually evolved into broad-based parties: the Democrats who backed Andrew Jackson and the Whigs who opposed him.

Adolescence: A Growth Spurt, 1820s–1890s

Between 1828 and 1844, state party organizations loosely affiliated with the two major parties developed and subsequently changed the character of the two-party system.[10] The parties increasingly began to reflect America's federal structure. The national parties became little more than collectivities of state parties, and the state parties began to aggressively build a mass base.

Beginning in the 1840s, both major parties used their presidential campaigns to mobilize voters. During non-electoral periods, they employed their resources to provide supporters with tangible economic and social benefits. By energizing and expanding their electoral base, the parties not only extended their political influence but also began to address the country's broader economic and social needs.

In the 1850s, sectional rivalries, inflamed by the passions of slavery and westward expansion, splintered the parties and eventually led to the demise of the Whigs and the division of the Democrats into northern and southern factions.

The Republican Party emerged out of this political chaos. Organized in 1854, the Republicans appealed to former Whigs and to northern Democrats, who supported the abolition of slavery; to white laborers and small farmers who objected to its expansion; and to industrial workers who feared that the influx of new immigrants would lower their wages or cost them their jobs.

The turmoil created by the Civil War and Reconstruction led to the emergence of new partisan coalitions. Big-business tycoons who had profited from the industrial revolution gained control of the Republican Party and dominated it for more than fifty years. The Democrats remained divided into a rural southern faction, controlled by a socially conservative white elite, and a more industrialized north, influenced by banking and commercial interests.

The popular bases of both parties shrank in the second half of the nineteenth century,[11] voter turnout declined, and the partisan political environment became less competitive. Poorer farmers, blue-collar workers, and newly arrived immigrants increasingly found themselves alienated from both major parties.[12]

Adulthood: The Eras of Partisan Majorities, 1890s–1960s

A recession in 1893 during the administration of Democrat Grover Cleveland, combined with the Populist movement in the West that further splintered the Democratic Party into "free silver" supporters and opponents, resulted in the emergence of a new Republican majority. Strong in the North, popular among Protestants and older immigrant groups, buoyed by business and also increasingly by labor, and benefiting from the country's economic prosperity, the Grand Old Party (GOP), as it came to be called, dominated American politics for the next three decades. Although the Democrats were still a major party, ruling the South and even managing to gain control of both the White House and Congress from 1912 to 1918, the Republicans held onto their numerical advantage with voters until the Great Depression.[13]

A major realignment of the parties occurred during the 1930s. The Democrats, riding on the coattails of Franklin Roosevelt and his New Deal policies, broadened their coalition by appealing to those at the lower end of the socioeconomic scale, whereas the Republicans held onto the allegiances of the business community and more well-to-do members of society. The principal exception to this economically based division of the electorate was in the South, where, regardless of socioeconomic status, voters retained their Democratic loyalties.

The economic division between the parties became evident in their policy perspectives as well. The Democrats looked to government to take the lead in solving the nation's economic and social policies, whereas the Republicans viewed government involvement in the economy as a threat to the free enterprise, private ownership, individual initiative system. The Democrats supported Roosevelt's efforts to redistribute resources on the basis of individual need; the Republicans did not. The GOP continued to believe that a capitalistic system, free from government control, would provide the greatest benefit to the society as a whole.

The Democrats maintained the allegiances of a majority of voters until the end of the 1960s. As time passed, however, improvements in the economic environment following World War II, growing prosperity nationwide, an expanding middle class, and gains for organized labor all weakened the need-based foundation on which the Democrats had built their electoral and governing coalitions. New social and international issues—the civil rights movement; the Korean and Vietnam wars and the public's reaction to them; violent demonstrations on college and university campuses; deteriorating conditions in the cities, with increases in crime, drug trafficking, and racial unrest—divided the Democrats and helped unify the more socially conservative Republicans.

Transitional Politics, 1968–1970s

By the 1970s, the Democrats had lost their status as the majority party; by the 1980s, they had lost their electoral plurality; by the 1990s, the parties were operating at rough parity with each other and have continued to do so thus far in the twenty-first century.

The partisan dealignment of the American electorate and its party structure began in the late 1960s. During this period, voters became more independent, more candidate-centered, and more volatile in their voting behavior. Party leaders lost control over the nomination process (see Chapter 7); party organizations no longer ran their candidates' campaigns. Television became the principal means of electioneering, and candidates hired professionals to raise money, poll public attitudes and opinions, design campaign ads, and identify and mobilize supporters. Outside groups became more active as well during the election period, performing many of the same tasks as the candidate organizations. These changes weakened the major parties and reduced their role as the major intermediary between candidates and voters.

Moreover, the growing parity between the Republicans and Democrats combined with more split-ticket voting, ushered in an era of divided government, with control of the White House and Congress shifting between the parties.

The weakening of partisan allegiances continued into the mid-1980s. It decreased turnout and increased split-ticket voting. As partisan loyalties weakened, people looked to other factors when deciding how to vote. Television encouraged a greater candidate orientation on the part of the electorate. It also made candidates more dependent on the mass media to create a favorable image and communicate it to voters.[14] Electoral politics became more personalized with candidates tapping themselves to run, organizing their own campaigns, raising their own money, and taking their own policy positions on salient issues. In fact, their independence was often a selling point in their campaigns, allowing them to argue that they were beholden to no one but their constituents. The news media also began to emphasize personal qualities, blurring the distinction between private and public behavior.

The increasing focus on the candidate's personal qualities and behavior during the second half of the twentieth century led candidates to turn to image makers, public relations experts, and pollsters to design personal images and policy appeals that resonated with voters, as well as impugning the characters and even demonizing their opponents.[15] Sometimes, in their desire to win, they made promises and created expectations that they could not possibly fulfill, particularly in a political system that shares responsibilities and checks and balances powers. The emphasis on individuals rather than on parties undermined accountability in government.

The personalization of politics along with the decline of the Democrats' electoral majority produced another effect; it increased the probability of divided government. By voting for the person and not the party, the electorate ended up with a mixed government composed of individuals who did not share as many common, unifying priorities as did loyal partisans who had been recruited by party officials, funded by local and state party committees, and were beholden to the party organization for guiding and financing their campaigns. Instead, elected officials increasingly thought of themselves as free agents, more oriented to their constituents who had elected them than to their party. Nor did many of them develop the close-knit personal relationships with party officials and fellow officeholders that facilitated compromise. Under such circumstances, consensus building became harder to achieve, policy coalitions shifted from issue to issue, and legislative output decreased.

The Reemergence of Partisanship, 1980–Present

The growing influence of candidates and issues on the electorate's voting behavior was short-lived, however. Beginning in the 1980s, the parties began to regain strength. Strong correlations began to reappear between partisan identification and voting. Issue differences between the major parties also became clearer, as Ronald Reagan articulated an alternative conservative political philosophy to the liberal ideology that had dominated American politics since the 1930s.

The parties realigned along ideological lines. Liberals remained Democrats, but conservatives drifted to the Republican Party. As a consequence, the two parties became more internally cohesive and externally distinctive. Partisan allegiances were strengthened, while partisan cleavages within government became more pronounced. When more than one branch of government was controlled by the same party, partisanship helped unify what the constitutional system divided, thereby approaching a model of responsible party government (see Box 6.2).

The resurgence of the Republican and Democratic parties also helped the national organizations improve their fund-raising, acquire the skills and technologies of the new communications age, and increase their recruitment, training, and funding of candidates for national office. Organized outside groups supplemented the electoral activities of both major political parties.

BOX 6.2 The Responsible Party Model

The doctrine of having more responsible parties was first proposed by Professor Woodrow Wilson in his book *Congressional Government*.[1] Wilson lamented the fact that American parties were not as cohesive as those in the British parliamentary system; he urged the adoption of practices designed to make American political parties more responsible; Wilson recommended that each party propose a national program, campaign for it, and carry it out if elected.

But no matter how good the idea sounded in theory, it would have been difficult to implement in practice. Then as now, U.S. parties are more heterogeneous than their British counterparts, in large part because the United States is a larger, more diverse country than is the United Kingdom. Power is more dispersed within the American governmental system. In Britain, control of the House of Commons amounts to control of the government; in the United States, control of the House of Representatives, the people's house, is a far cry from control of the government. So is control of Congress, for that matter, if the president is of the opposite party. Besides, even when the same party has a majority in both houses, it may still be unable to dictate public policy outcomes. The committee and subcommittee systems in both houses, the unlimited-debate rule in the Senate, and the strong constituency orientation of members of Congress make it more difficult for party leaders in Congress to discipline their members than party leaders in the United Kingdom.[2]

Nonetheless, the idea of having more responsible parties has surfaced from time to time. It appealed to political scientists as their discipline developed after World War II. E. E. Schattschneider, a proponent of this view, headed a committee of the American Political Science Association that called for the Democrats and Republicans to offer clear-cut alternatives to voters, pursue those alternatives if elected, and be held accountable for their success or failure.

The period during which this idea gained currency among political scientists, however, was not one in which the major parties strove to be different. After World War II, both Republicans and Democrats accepted the need for a strong national government; both were strongly anticommunist; and both were divided internally over social issues, particularly civil rights. When the Republican Party gained control of Congress in 1946–1947 and 1952–1953, it did not try to reverse New Deal policies as much as improve their administration and moderate their effects. In 1968, when independent candidate for president George C. Wallace said "There's not a dime's worth of difference" between the major parties, he was probably more right than wrong.

Contemporary parties are more consistent with the responsible party model than were the Democrats and Republicans in the mid-twentieth century. They are more divisive along ideological lines. Party unity in government has increased. Whether these changes make elections more democratic remains a hotly debated issue. As noted earlier in this chapter, critics still complain about the parties—that they are not representative of their own rank and file, much less the country; that they do not reflect the popular will in elections; and that they have not produced a more effective and efficient government.

---

[1] Woodrow Wilson, *Congressional Government* (1885; reprint, New York, NY: Meridian Books, 1960).
[2] Morris P. Fiorina, "The Decline of Collective Responsibility in American Politics," *Daedalus* 109 (Summer 1980): 25–45.

The Contemporary Parties

Today, the electoral coalitions that comprise the Democratic and Republican parties are distinct economically, socially, and culturally. The Democrats continue to attract the allegiances of those at the lower end of the socioeconomic scale: people with lower incomes, less formal education, and fewer professional job skills. These core Democratic supporters want and claim they need more social services from government, including better public schools, more public housing, and a variety of health care and welfare services. They tend to favor government policies that redistribute resources and provide help to those less able to help themselves. The disproportionate concentration of certain minority groups, such as African Americans and Hispanics, among this economic sector of the population, has added a racial and ethnic dimension to the Democrats' base of support. Nonetheless, the party also continues to attract a liberal, well educated constituency of middle, upper-middle, and well-to-do voters for whom environmental, First Amendment, civil rights (including gender issues), and foreign and social policy issues are of paramount concern.

In contrast, the GOP gains most of its supporters from the majority racial group in the population, from people in the upper-middle and higher income brackets. Republicans tend to be more critical of a large government role within the economic sector, particularly regulations that limit the operation of the capitalistic system; similarly, they are leery of programs that extend social services. They more supportive of a stronger hand for government in maintaining law and order and protecting national security, particularly in an age of international terrorism.

Cultural factors such as religion, language, and community and family values also distinguish the major parties and their electoral bases. People who hold traditional religious beliefs and regularly participate in religious services or activities tend to be Republican; those who hold more secular views or do not attend religious services as regularly are more likely to consider themselves Democrats. The religious divide is evident on such issues as legalized abortion, separation of church and state, and government-sponsored stem-cell research, all of which Republicans are more likely to oppose than Democrats. Republicans are also more apt to back government policies on social issues, such as making English the nation's official language, allowing voluntary prayer in school, and increasing the government's policing powers. Democrats place a higher value on the exercise of political freedoms, particularly as that exercise relates to First Amendment rights. They are more supportive of social and cultural diversity and the policies that promote or permit such diversity.

The Republican base has become whiter, more conservative, and more religious. Evangelical and fundamentalist Protestants constitute core constituencies while the support of mainline Protestants has declined. With its base more homogeneous, the GOP has maintained its strong conservative orientation, which its leaders articulate in their policy pronouncements. In contrast, the

Democrats have remained more heterogeneous, attracting more diverse racial and ethnic groups to its electoral coalition, and prompting its base to maintain its liberal ideological orientation.

The makeup of each party's electoral coalition presents challenges for each of them. For the Republicans, the challenge is how to broaden their electoral base, particularly among minority groups, while maintaining the ideological beliefs of their core supporters; for the Democrats, it is how to unify such a diverse coalition around a set of acceptable public policy choices in a country which has become more economically conservative.[16]

The Republicans' problem is accentuated by demographic trends in the United States, specifically the failure of the party to attract the fastest-growing ethnic groups in America, Hispanics and Asian Americans. In addition, the party has done most poorly in recent elections among people in the lowest age cohort eligible to vote, those who are between the ages of 18 and 29. This is a problem for the Republicans because voting preferences, once established, tend to harden over time. The entrance of new voters in the 1930s helped the Democrats build and sustain their partisan advantage for more than 30 years. The Republicans also have a gender problem, particularly with unmarried women, who have consistently voted Democratic since the mid-1980s.

Attracting these and other disaffected groups will require the Republicans to become more pragmatic and less ideological. The question is, will core Republicans, who tend to be the activists within the party—the people who participate most regularly in the nomination process—be receptive to candidates whose views do not adhere to their own? The Democrats also face a similar type of dilemma: how to contend with a national populace that has become more conservative and moderate,[17] remains leery of big government despite its reliance on that government for major domestic and entitlement programs,[18] and that has become less trusting of public officials and cynical of government performance.[19] The Democrats also have a gender problem, in gaining the support of white men.

Table 6.1 illustrates the partisan allegiances of American voters since 1952.

PARTIES, ELECTORAL REPRESENTATION, AND DEMOCRATIC GOVERNANCE

Has the reemergence of partisan voting patterns, the strengthening of party organizations as campaign entities and governing coalitions, and the occasional reappearance in 2002–2006 and in 2008–2010 of unified government strengthened or weakened the democratic character of the American electoral process? Have these changes helped or hurt democratic governance?

These developments have contributed to a more responsible party system and to more accountable government. They help rectify the criticism of American parties as being too much like each other; pursuing policies that are centrist, often ambiguous, and sometimes inconsistent; and sacrificing principle for pragmatism in order to welcome all comers into their "big tent."

TABLE 6.1 Partisan Identification of the American Electorate, 1952–2008 (percentages)

Percentage within Study Year

	'52	'54	'56	'58	'60	'62	'64	'66	'68	'70	'72	'74	'76	'78	'80	'82	'84	'86	'88	'90	'92	'94	'96	'98	'00	'02	'04	'08
Strong Democrat :	23	23	22	28	21	24	27	18	20	20	15	18	15	15	18	20	17	18	18	20	18	15	18	19	19	17	17	19
Weak Democrat :	26	26	24	23	26	24	25	28	26	24	25	21	25	24	23	24	20	22	18	19	17	18	19	18	15	17	16	15
Independent Democrat :	10	9	7	7	6	8	9	9	10	10	11	13	12	14	11	11	11	10	12	12	14	13	14	14	15	16	17	17
Independent Independent:	5	8	9	8	10	8	8	12	11	13	15	18	16	16	15	13	13	14	12	12	13	11	10	12	13	7	10	11
Independent Republican :	8	6	9	5	7	6	6	7	9	8	10	9	10	10	10	8	12	11	13	12	12	12	12	11	13	13	12	12
Weak Republican :	14	15	15	17	14	17	14	15	15	15	13	14	14	13	14	14	15	15	14	15	14	15	15	16	12	16	12	13
Strong Republican :	14	13	16	12	16	13	11	10	10	9	10	8	9	8	9	10	12	11	14	10	11	15	12	10	12	15	16	13
N	1,689	1,088	1,690	1,737	1,864	1,237	1,536	1,263	1,531	1,490	2,695	2,492	2,833	2,269	1,612	1,403	2,228	2,157	2,026	1,965	2,473	1,780	1,706	1,267	1,790	1,466	1,194	2,293

Party Identification 7-Point Scale

Sources: The American National Election Studies http://electionstudies.org/nesguide/nesguide.htm

QUESTION TEXT:

"Generally speaking, do you usually think of yourself as a Republican, a Democrat, an Independent, or what?"

(IF REPUBLICAN OR DEMOCRAT) "Would you call yourself a strong (REPUBLICAN/DEMOCRAT) or a not very strong (REPUBLICAN/DEMOCRAT)?"

(IF INDEPENDENT, OTHER [1966 and later: OR NO PREFERENCE]:) "Do you think of yourself as closer to the Republican or Democratic party?"

Critics of the contemporary parties cite the rise of cynicism, decrease in trust, the increasing proportion of self-identified independents, the growing negative image of both major political parties (see Figure 6.1) as evidence that something is wrong and that the major parties should shoulder much of the responsibility for the current unhappy state of political affairs. They point to the lack of representation for moderate views and voters, the strident ideological rhetoric, and the persistent confrontations in government over financial issues as evidence.

Do Contemporary Political Parties Facilitate or Inhibit Democratic Elections?

The answer to this question depends on how satisfied people are with the candidates running and with the views they express. To the extent that the candidates are more extreme in their beliefs than the electorate as a whole, the choices they provide are less satisfactory. Then why would parties nominate candidates like these? The answer, discussed in the next chapter, focuses on reforms in the nomination process that have shifted power to activists who feel more strongly about issues and exercise disproportionate influence in the selection of their party's nominees.

The reemergence of partisanship has increased turnout and that, of course, is good from a democratic perspective. Partisanship has encouraged the parties to devote more time, effort, and money to grassroots operations, direct their appeal to their base, and emphasize traditional beliefs and policy positions to which that base subscribes. Increasing turnout, creating distinct choices, providing information on the candidates and their proposals, advocating a governing agenda, and, if elected, converting that agenda into public policy are certainly consistent with a democratic electoral process. So are soliciting contributions, hiring campaign professionals, mobilizing volunteers, and engaging in get-out-the-vote activities, all functions that political parties perform during elections. What is more problematic are activities that exaggerate claims or provide false and negative information, shape legislative districts in such a way as to make them less competitive, and adhere to policy positions that do not reflect the more moderate views of mainstream America.

The growing dissatisfaction with both major parties is also a problem. Figure 6.1 indicates this rising dissatisfaction.

Do Contemporary Parties Facilitate or Inhibit Democratic Governance?

Beginning in the 1980s, increasing ideological consensus within the major parties resulted in greater party unity in Congress. When government is divided, unity, flamed by ideology, discourages compromise and can result in a political

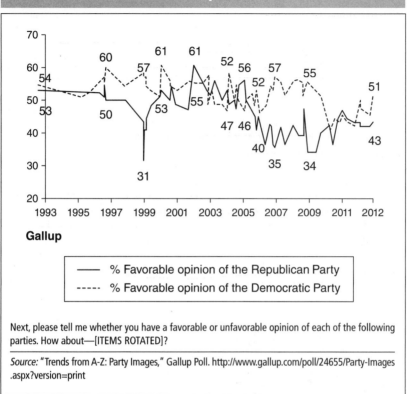

FIGURE 6.1   **Evaluations of the Major Parties, 1993–2012**

Gallup

———   % Favorable opinion of the Republican Party

- - - -   % Favorable opinion of the Democratic Party

Next, please tell me whether you have a favorable or unfavorable opinion of each of the following parties. How about—[ITEMS ROTATED]?

Source: "Trends from A-Z: Party Images," Gallup Poll. http://www.gallup.com/poll/24655/Party-Images .aspx?version=print

and institutional stalemate; when government is unified, however, it can result in the majority party achieving its legislative goals. Such conditions occurred in 2002 and were augmented by President George W. Bush's focus on national security issues in the aftermath of the September 11, 2001, terrorist attacks. They recurred in the spring of 2009 when President Obama used the economic crisis as a unifying and action-forcing mechanism in Congress to secure passage of key parts of his domestic policy agenda. He later relied on his large legislative majority to pass comprehensive health care reform.

With majority rule comes significant costs for those in the minority. They lose influence, particularly in the House of Representatives, in which the rules adopted by its members facilitate plurality voting decisions. In the Senate, rules that permit any senator to put a hold on a nomination and require the support of sixty senators for most authorization bills give the minority leverage it lacks in the House of Representatives.

Another consequence of majority rule in unified government is that the minority has to shout to be heard. Rhetoric becomes shrill, heightened by the ideological chatter of contemporary partisan debate. Civility and comity in Congress have suffered. The fact that many members of Congress do not move their families to Washington and do not socialize as much as they did in the past has also adversely affected their working relationships, camaraderie, and legislative output. (See Table 6.2.)

TABLE 6.2   **Legislation, 1989–2012**

Congress	Public laws
101st (1989–1990)	650
102nd (1991–1992)	590
103rd (1993–1994)	465
104th (1995–1996)	333
105th (1997–1998)	394
106th (1999–2000)	580
107th (2001–2002)	377
108th (2003–2004)	498
109th (2005–2006)	482
110th (2007–2008)	460
111th (2009–2010)	383
112th (2011–2012)	218

Source: "Public Laws," The Library of Congress: Thomas http://thomas.loc.gov/home/Legislative Data.php?&n=PublicLaws

---

The more ideological orientation of members of Congress and the more visible public arena in which Congress operates, as well as the decline in civility and decorum have contributed to the warring-camps' atmosphere that prevails in Congress today.

Partisan bickering, highlighted by national press coverage, has reduced public approval of Congress's job performance such that it fell to an all-time low of 10 percent in early 2012.[20] Individual members of Congress get markedly more positive assessments than does Congress as a whole.

Is Collective Accountability Possible?

Democratic governance rests on the assumption that elected officials are held accountable for their actions, primarily through elections. Since the 1970s, it has become easier to hold individual government officials accountable because of the increasingly public arena in which policy decisions are made, the greater amount of information available to people about government, the increasingly investigative bent of the news media, and the continuous scrutiny of policy-making by interested outside groups. Personal accountability has also been enhanced during elections by the amount of research that parties and candidates conduct about their opponents, as well as that offered by the news media, nonparty groups, and individuals, all of which has become more easily accessible to the electorate online.

But what about collective responsibility? Do contemporary parties contribute to that as well? The answer is that they may. Cohesive parties within a unified government provide an opportunity for the electorate to nationalize a congressional election and make a collective judgment on those in power.

Every decade or so, the conditions for such a judgment occur. In the elections of 1946 and 1952, the Democrats were repudiated by the voters. Republicans gained power only to lose it two years later in each instance. In the 1974 election, following President Richard Nixon's resignation, the opposite occurred. The Democrats substantially increased their congressional representation at a time when their proportion in the electorate was declining. Democrats lost control of the Senate in the Reagan landslide of 1980 but won it back six years later. In 1994, an electorate upset with the internal dissent and scandalous behavior of some Democrats, voted that party out of power in the political revolution that brought Republican control of the Senate and a new, more conservative leadership to the House under the direction of Newt Gingrich. In 2006 the public rebuked the Republicans for supporting the president's policy in Iraq, for their ideological rigidity, and for the scandals that beset members of that party; in 2010, it was the Democrats who were the objects of voters' displeasure, losing control of the House of Representatives and seats in the Senate.

The ability to make a collective judgment enhances democratic government. When control of Congress shifts, however, particularly in an age of highly polarized parties, the consequence may be significant shifts in policy as well.

SUMMARY: PARTISAN DILEMMAS IN A NUTSHELL

Parties are important to a democratic selection process. They provide a critical link between candidates and voters and between elected officials and the people who elected them. Without such a link, it would be more difficult to hold elected officials collectively responsible for their actions.

Parties organize ideas, people, and institutions. The allegiances they engender, the attitudes they shape, and the electoral behavior they influence provide the electorate with a frame of reference for the campaign, a motivation for participating in it, an orientation that can be used to arrive at a voting decision, and criteria for evaluating the government.

The major parties have gone through cycles in which they have gained and lost adherents; their electoral coalitions have shifted over the years. The late 1960s ushered in an era in which partisan allegiances weakened, the number of self-declared independents grew, and voters began to split their tickets, voting more for the person or issue. During this period, the candidates also became more independent in deciding whether to seek office and how to do so. They depended less on their party's organization and more on the campaign professionals they hired, experts skilled in the new survey research, grassroots organizing, and media-oriented research.

By the mid-1980s, the transition in politics had begun to run its course. Partisan ties strengthened, and partisan voting behavior increased. There was more partisan unity in government, and the parties began to rebuild their financial and grassroots bases. They also became more ideological, nominating and electing candidates with more consistent policy views. These changes polarized the electorate, and at times, immobilized the government. Partisan parity led to extended periods of divided government, beginning in the late 1960s, during which domestic policymaking became more difficult. Trust and confidence in government also declined.

Contemporary parties continue to be distinctive in their policy orientations. Civility in political discourse has declined, as has comity within Congress as well as between it and the White House. Warring partisan coalitions contest policy publicly rather than deliberate it quietly behind closed doors. Reaching compromise has become more arduous and takes longer. Serving constituency interests remains the key to reelection.

Is the current state of political affairs beneficial or harmful to a democratic electoral process? Candidates self-select but are dependent on political professionals for getting elected—more recently, including those skilled in Internet communications and other computer-based technologies. Incumbents continue to be helped by fund-raising and service advantages as well as gerrymandered districts that favor one party over the other. As a consequence, it becomes more difficult for elections to reflect the popular mood of the moment, although in 2006 and 2010, there were major shifts in the partisan composition of Congress. Nonetheless, democratic tendencies are undermined by a noncompetitive legislative election structure, especially for the House of Representatives.

Is the voice of the people being heard more clearly? Is that voice being effectively and efficiently translated into public policy? Experts are divided. Some believe responsible parties have emerged and, as a result, collective accountability has increased; others see a decrease in the representation of people with moderate views. They perceive government as being increasingly responsive to its core supporters and special interests instead of to the general public. They see it as making short-term, politically expedient decisions at the expense of longer-term policy solutions.

What should be done to enhance partisan representation and to make the parties more responsive and the government more effective? Imposing reforms on the parties is neither wise nor feasible. The parties need to reform themselves. They need to reflect the diverse character of American society more closely. But if they do so, can they still be internally cohesive, externally distinctive, and held collectively responsible?

Now It's Your Turn

Discussion Questions

1. Has the realignment of the major parties along ideological lines strength-ened or weakened their capacity to represent the American public? Has it improved or reduced their capacity to govern effectively?

2. Is it better in a democracy to vote for the best candidate regardless of par-tisan affiliation or to vote for the candidate of the party that best represents a voter's political beliefs?

3. Are political parties the key to collective responsibility in government? If not, how can government be held accountable for its public policy decisions and actions?

4. Does having only two major parties facilitate or impede the representa-tion of American voters, the conduct of elections, and the operation of government?

5. Does having two major parties make it more or less likely that public policy reflects the views and interests of the majority of people in the United States?

6. What type of electoral system most effectively represents the views of all the people? What type of electoral system results in the most effective government?

Topics for Debate
Challenge or defend the following statements:

1. All candidates who run on a party label should be required to promise that they will support the principal tenets of their party, as stated in the party platform, or be removed from the party line on the ballot.

2. Partisanship is undesirable; thus, all candidates for office should run in nonpartisan elections as independents.

3. Political parties are unnecessary and undesirable for a democratic government.

4. A two-party system is more efficient but may be less effective in represent-ing the views of society.

5. The major parties in the United States today are unrepresentative of the political views of American society.

6. A new third party should be created that speaks for the average American.

7. American political parties can reflect public opinion or they can govern effectively, but they cannot do both simultaneously.

Exercises

1. Design a strategic memorandum for a new political party that addresses the needs and desires of your generation. In your memorandum, indicate the following:

    a. the key issues and the position the new party should take on them;
    b. the campaign appeals that your party should make, not only to your generation but also to older generations;
    c. likely sources of income for the party and its nominees, and the methods you would use to raise the money;
    d. other nonparty or party groups to which you might appeal for electoral support; and
    e. the first order of business the party should take up if it were to win control of the legislative or executive branch.

2. The major parties in the United States have been criticized for catering to the views of their most active partisans and, as a result, becoming too ideological. Do you think this criticism is valid? Answer this question by comparing the major parties today on the basis of the following:

    a. their demographic and regional composition,
    b. their positions on the major issues before Congress and the president today, and
    c. their political philosophies.

INTERNET RESOURCES

-   Democratic National Committee: www.democrats.org

    Main Web site of the national Democratic Party, with links to other Democratic organizations as well as to state Democratic parties.

-   Democratic Congressional Campaign Committee: www.dccc.org

    Raises money and identifies Democratic candidates for election to the House of Representatives.

-   Democratic Senatorial Campaign Committee: www.dscc.org

    Raises money and identifies Democratic candidates for election to the Senate.

-   Republican National Committee: www.gop.com

    Main Web site of the national Republican Party, with links to other Republican organizations as well as to Republican state parties.

-   National Republican Congressional Committee: www.nrcc.org

    Raises money and identifies Republican candidates for election to the House of Representatives.

-   National Republican Senatorial Committee: www.nrsc.org

    Raises money and identifies Republican candidates for election to the Senate.

- Other political parties:

  Communist Party of the United States: www.cpusa.org
  Democratic Socialists of America: www.dsausa.org
  Green Party: www.gp.org
  Libertarian Party: www.lp.org
  Reform Party: www.reformparty.org
  Socialist Labor Party: www.slp.org
  Socialist Party: www.sp-usa.org

SELECTED READINGS

Abramowitz, Alan I. *The Disappearing Center: Engaged Citizens, Polarization, and American Democracy*. New Haven, CT: Yale University Press, 2010.

Aldrich, John H. *Why Parties? The Origin and Transformation of Political Parties in America*. Chicago, IL: University of Chicago Press, 1995.

Ansolabehere, Stephen, and James M. Synder Jr. "The Incumbency Advantage in U.S. Elections: An Analysis of State and Federal Offices, 1942–2000." *Election Law Journal* 1, no. 3 (2002): 315–338.

Bibby, John F., and Brian F. Schaffner. *Politics, Parties, and Elections in America*. 6th ed. Boston, MA: Cengage/ Wadsworth, 2008.

Black, Earl, and Merle Black. *The Rise of the Southern Republicans*. Cambridge, MA: Harvard University Press, 2002.

Brewer, Mark D. "The Evolution and Alteration of American Party Coalitions." In *The Oxford Handbook of American Political Parties and Interest Groups*, edited by L. Sandy Maisel and Jeffrey M. Berry. Oxford, England: Oxford University Press, 2010.

Bond, Jon R., and Richard Fleisher, eds. *Polarized Politics: Congress and the President in a Partisan Era*. Washington, DC: CQ Press, 2000.

Fiorina, Morris P., with Samuel J. Abrams and Jeremy C. Pope. *Culture War? The Myth of a Polarized America*. New York, NY: Pearson/Longman, 2005.

Green, Donald P., Bradley Palmquist, and Eric Schickler. *Partisan Hearts and Minds: Political Parties and the Social Identities of Voters*. New Haven, CT: Yale University Press, 2002.

Green, John C., and Daniel Coffee. *The State of Parties in America*. 6th ed. Lanham, MD: Rowman & Littlefield, 2011.

Herrnson, Paul. "The Role of Party Organizations, Party-Connected Committees, and Party Allies in Elections." *Journal of Politics* 71 (October 2009): 1207–1224.

Hetherington, Marc J., and Jonathan Weiler. *Authoritarianism and Polarization in American Politics*. Cambridge, MA: Cambridge University Press, 2009.

Hirano, Shigeo, and James M. Snyder Jr. "The Decline of Third Party Voting in the United States." *Journal of Politics*, 69 (February 2007): 1–16.

MacKuen, Michael B., and George Rabinowitz, eds. *Electoral Democracy*. Ann Arbor: University of Michigan Press, 2003.

Rosenblum, Nancy L. *On the Side of Angels: An Appreciation of Parties and Partisanship*. Princeton, NJ: Princeton University Press, 2008.

Schattschneider, E. E. *Party Government*. New York, NY: Rinehart, 1942.

Schraufnagel, Scot. *Third Party Blues*. New York, NY: Routledge, 2011.

Stonecash, Jeffrey M. *Political Parties Matter: Realignment and the Return of Partisan Voting*. Boulder, CO: Lynne Rienner, 2006.

Wattenberg, Martin P. *The Decline of American Political Parties*. 6th ed. Cambridge, MA: Harvard University Press, 1998.

White, John K. *The Values Divide: American Politics and Culture in Transition*. New York, NY: Chatham House, 2003.

NOTES

1. E. E. Schattschneider, *Party Government* (New York, NY: Rinehart, 1942), 1.
2. These party functions are presented and discussed in Samuel J. Eldersfeld, *Political Parties: A Behavioral Analysis* (Chicago, IL: Rand McNally, 1964).
3. John H. Aldrich, *Why Parties? The Origin and Transformation of Political Parties in America* (Chicago, IL: University of Chicago Press, 1995), 18–27, 277–296.
4. The image of the Republican Party has been more unfavorable than favorable since 2004, and the image of the Democrats has been more unfavorable since 2010 according to Gallup Poll data. "Trends A-Z: Party Images," Gallup Poll. http://gallup.com/poll/24655/Party-Images.aspx
5. Nancy L. Rosenblum, "A Political Theory of Partisanship and Independence," in *The State of the Parties*, edited by John C. Green and Daniel J. Coffee (Lanham, MD: Rowman & Littlefield, 2011), 298–301.
6. When David Duke, a former Nazi sympathizer and member of the Ku Klux Klan, announced that he would run for governor of Louisiana as a Republican, that party denounced his candidacy although it could not prevent him from running or claiming he was a Republican. The Democrats had similar problems with Lyndon LaRouche, who ran for the Democratic nomination for president seven times between 1976 and 2004, even from jail.
7. To be eligible for funding, third parties have to have received at least 5 percent of the vote in the previous election. If they do, they receive funding equal to their percentage of the total vote. Until they reach the 5 percent threshold, however, the funding is retroactive; they receive it after the election is over.
8. For an excellent article on this phenomenon, see Shigeo Hirano and James M. Snyder Jr., "The Decline of Third-Party Voting in the United States," *Journal of Politics* 69 (February 2007): 1–16.
9. For a history of American political parties see Wilfred E. Binkley, *American Political Parties: Their Natural History* (New York, NY: Knopf, 1959). Joel H. Sibley, "American Political Parties: History, Voters, Critical Elections, and Party Systems," in *The Oxford Handbook of American Political Parties and Interest Groups,* edited by L. Sandy Maisel and Jeffrey M. Berry (Oxford, England: Oxford University Press, 2010), 97–120.
10. Aldrich, *Why Parties?,* 118–135.
11. They did so as a consequence of new laws designed to improve the honesty and integrity of federal elections. The laws, which were enacted by the states, required citizens to register in order to vote. Some also imposed a poll tax to pay for the conduct of elections and a literacy test to ensure that voters could read and had a basic understanding of the Constitution.

12. Frances Fox Piven and Richard A. Cloward, *Why Americans Don't Vote* (New York, NY: Pantheon, 1988), 64–95.

13. The Democrats' success at the national level in the second decade of the twentieth century came as a result of a split within the Republican Party at the national level between those supporting William Howard Taft and those backing Theodore Roosevelt for the presidency in 1912.

14. For a discussion of the relationship between parties, issues, and candidate orientations, see Angus Campbell, Philip E. Converse, Warren E. Miller, and Donald E. Stokes, *The American Voter* (Chicago, IL: University of Chicago Press, 1960); Morris Fiorina, *Retrospective Voting in American National Elections* (New Haven, CT: Yale University Press, 1981); and Benjamin Highton and Cindy D. Kam, "The Long-Term Dynamics of Partisanship and Issue Orientations," *Journal of Politics,* 73 (January 2011): 202–215.

15. See Lynda Lee Kaid and Anne Johnston, "Negative versus Positive Television Advertising in U.S. Presidential Campaigns, 1960–1988," *Journal of Communication* 41 (Summer 1991): 53–64; and John G. Geer, *In Defense of Negativity: Attack Ads in Presidential Campaigns* (Chicago, IL: University of Chicago Press, 2006).

16. Lydia Saad, "Conservatives Continue to Outnumber Moderates in 2010," Gallup Poll, December 16, 2010. http://www.gallup.com/poll/145271/Conservatives-Continue-Outnumber-Moderates-2010.aspx

17. According to Gallup polls conducted in the spring of 2009, the United States is becoming more conservative. Almost twice as many people identify themselves as conservative (40 percent) than as liberal (21 percent). About 35 percent consider themselves moderate. Gallup Poll, "Special Report: Ideologically, Where Is the U.S. Moving?" July 6, 2009, www.gallup.com/poll/121403/Special-Report-Ideologically-Moving.aspx; see also Gallup Poll, "'Conservatives' Are Single Largest Ideological Group," June 15, 2009, www.gallup.com/poll/120857/Conservatives-Single-Largest-Ideological-Group.aspx. The General Social Survey of the National Opinion Center at the University of Chicago, the large national exit poll following the 2008 elections, and surveys conducted by the Pew Research Center for the People and the Press in 2008 and 2009 also found much higher percentages of self-declared moderates and conservatives than liberals.

18. Since 1992, Gallup polls have consistently indicated that more people think the government is doing too much rather than not enough. The only exception was in the first Gallup poll taken after the terrorist attacks of September 11, 2001; see Gallup Poll, "Trends from A to Z: Government," www.gallup.com/poll/27286/Government.aspx.

19. Ibid. Since the early 1970s, there have been very few instances in which a majority of people expressed a "great deal" or "quite a lot" of confidence in the major institutions of government: Congress, the presidency, and the Supreme Court.

20. Frank Newport, "Congress' Job Approval at New Low of 10%," Gallup Poll, February 8, 2012. http://www.gallup.com/poll/152528/Congress-Job-Approval-New-Low.aspx

The Nomination Process
Whose Is It Anyway?

Did you know that . . .

- the goal of improving representation at the national nominating conventions has resulted in the selection of delegates who are more representative demographically but may be less representative ideologically of mainstream partisans, much less mainstream voters?
- the changes in party rules to open the nomination process to more diverse candidates continues to favor candidates who are nationally known and well funded?
- despite the length of the nomination campaign and the extensive coverage of it by local and national news media, a majority of the electorate still does not participate in it?
- it is unclear which candidate, Barack Obama or Hillary Rodham Clinton, won the most popular votes during the 2008 Democratic nomination process?
- aspirants to a party's presidential nomination usually take more extreme policy positions in their quest for the nomination than they do in their general election campaign?
- 55.2 percent of the Republican delegates to their party's 2008 national nominating convention held at the end of August of that year were selected by the first Tuesday in February and 80 percent by the first Tuesday in March compared to only about 10.6 percent and 35.5 percent, respectively, in 2012?
- the last time a presidential nominee did not personally select his running mate was in 1956, when the Democratic convention—not nominee Adlai Stevenson—chose Estes Kefauver over John F. Kennedy as the party's vice presidential candidate?
- the amount of broadcast network television coverage of the national nominating conventions has decreased as the parties' attempts to orchestrate that coverage have increased?
- although the incumbency advantage is greater in the nomination process than in the general election, the Tea Party movement in 2010 has undermined some of that advantage for Republican members of Congress?

- the front-loading of presidential primaries works to benefit front-running candidates?
- the race for money for presidential aspirants and the Super PACs supporting them has become in effect the first test of candidate viability prior to the presidential caucuses and primaries?
- strong partisan loyalties have muted the aftereffects of divisive nominations for both major parties?

Is this any way to run a democratic election?

N o aspect of the electoral process has changed more fundamentally and more quickly since the 1970s than the way in which the major political parties choose their candidates for office. In the past, when party organizations were stronger, the leaders of those organizations shaped the process by which nominees were selected. Although the actual mechanisms varied from state to state, most nominations were controlled by party organizations, with its leadership dictating the results.

In exercising that control, the leadership had three goals in mind in addition to its primary objective of winning the general election. First, party leaders wanted to reward the faithful who had worked for their candidates in previous elections. Second, they sought to choose experienced people who had worked their way up the ladder of elective office, who understood the rules and practices, and who, above all, were willing to abide by them. Finally, party leaders desired to select partisans whose primary loyalty was to the party, its positions, its programs, and especially its leadership.

The merit of such a nomination system was that it fostered and maintained strong party organizations and loyalties. The organizations, in turn, provided continuity in programs, policies, and personnel. The loyalties gave a party a cadre of workers and voters on whom it could depend.

The main disadvantage of such a system was that it was top-down rather than bottom-up. It kept party bosses, even corrupt ones, in power. It facilitated an old-boys' network. People had to play by the rules to get ahead. Rank-and-file partisans had little influence on the selection of the nominees and the policy positions they supported. The system was neither participatory nor democratic.

FROM AN ELITE TO A MORE POPULAR NOMINATION SYSTEM

The Progressive movement began in the early years of the twentieth century as a reaction to the closed and seemingly elitist character of American political parties. Progressives wanted to reform the political system to encourage greater public involvement in the nomination and election processes. Conducting primary elections in which partisans could select the candidates they preferred for public office was one of their most touted political reforms.

The movement prospered for more than two decades. From 1900 to 1916, twenty-five states enacted laws to permit or require primary elections. After World War I, however, low turnout, higher election costs, and unhappy party leaders persuaded state officials to return to the older ways of selecting nominees.

Not until after World War II did democratizing tendencies begin to reemerge, along with a communication technology in the form of television that could bring candidates into full public view in American living rooms. The rapid expansion of television programming, the purchase of television sets by most American households, and people's addiction to this new entertainment and news medium provided incentives for candidates, particularly for those unable or unwilling to obtain positions of power within the traditional party hierarchy, to take to the airwaves to gain support necessary to win. Thus started a new era in nomination politics.

The catalyst behind the shift from a party leadership–dominated nomination system to one in which there was greater public participation were the rule changes that first occurred in the Democratic Party after its raucous 1968 presidential nominating convention. At that time, the successful nominee, Vice President Hubert H. Humphrey, won without campaigning in any of the party's primary elections. As a unifying gesture to those who had participated in the primaries and were frustrated by their failure to affect the choice of nominees, the Democratic convention approved the establishment of a commission to review and refocus its presidential nominating procedures.

In making its recommendations, the commission's primary charge was to make the selection process more open to its partisans and, in this sense, more democratic. A set of rules designed to facilitate rank-and-file involvement in the nomination process and greater diversity in the composition of convention delegates was enacted. The rules established selection criteria that state parties had to meet to ensure that their delegates to the national convention would be certified as official. Delegates not chosen in conformity with these rules could be challenged and even prevented from representing their state parties at the convention.[1]

The Democratic Party in the 1970s and early 1980s was in a strong position to impose its new rules on the states. As the plurality party, the Democrats controlled about three-quarters of the state legislatures, and they were able to convince elected officials in the states that had Democratic legislators to enact laws that put them in compliance with the new party rules.

The changes affected the Republican Party's selection process as well. Although the GOP did not initially mandate rule changes for its state parties in the presidential nomination process as the Democrats had done, many of the new laws enacted by the states were applicable to them as well, forcing their state-affiliates to conduct or giving them the option to conduct primary elections.[2] Most of them did so, not wanting to be seen as opposing popular reforms.[3]

The new system rapidly took hold. Today, all states conduct primaries for nominations for federal and state offices. More than half use them exclusively; others employ a combination of primaries, state caucuses, and conventions.

In effect, the national parties opened up their nomination process. They decentralized power that had already been decentralized by virtue of the federal system of government. Power flowed to those who participated. The parties hoped that increased participation in the nomination process would broaden their base of support, energize their electorate, enhance the representative character of nominating conventions and of the parties themselves, and make them more responsive to the interests of their partisans. It seemed like a win-win situation for the party organization and its partisans. In practice, however, it has not been.

THE DEMOCRATIZATION OF NOMINATIONS: REPRESENTATIVE OR UNREPRESENTATIVE?

The Good News

The rule changes have contributed to the democratization of the nomination processes in both parties. By opening up the nomination process, the parties have involved more people in the selection of nominees. There are more primaries, and an increasing number of delegates are being selected in them. Table 7.1 indicates the number of primaries and the percentage of delegates selected in primaries from 1952 to 2012.

A second consequence of more open nominations has been broader representation of each party's electoral coalition at its national conventions. Delegates who attend these conventions are demographically more representative of rank-and-file party voters than they were prior to the rule changes. There are more women, more minorities, and more young people.

A third result, which also has improved the democratic character of the system, has been to tie candidates closer to the desires and interests of the people who voted for them. To gain the nomination, candidates have to take positions on salient issues, and keep them if elected, because their renomination is always open to challenge.

A fourth consequence has been to increase the pool of potential candidates. The number of people vying for their party's nomination at all levels of government has increased, especially when incumbents decide not to run for reelection.[4] The range of challengers is also greater. Anyone with access to the mass media by virtue of a personal career or financial resources can mount a campaign and, in some cases, even win. George McGovern, Jimmy Carter, Michael Dukakis, Bill Clinton, and Barack Obama would not have been likely presidential nominees under the old system in which the party establishment chose the candidate. Al Gore, George W. Bush, John Kerry, John McCain, and Mitt Romney might have been, however.

TABLE 7.1 **Number of Presidential Primaries and the Percentage of Convention Delegates from Primary States, 1952–2012**

Year	Democratic		Republican	
	Number of state primaries	Percentage of delegates from primary states	Number of state primaries	Percentage of delegates from primary states
1912	12	32.9	13	41.7
1916	20	53.5	20	58.9
1920	16	44.6	20	57.8
1924	14	35.5	17	45.3
1928	16	42.2	15	44.9
1932	16	40.0	14	37.7
1936	14	36.5	12	37.5
1940	13	35.8	13	38.8
1944	14	36.7	13	38.7
1948	14	36.3	12	36.0
1952	16	38.7	13	39.0
1956	19	42.7	19	44.8
1960	16	38.3	15	38.6
1964	16	45.7	16	45.6
1968	15	40.2	15	38.1
1972	21	65.3	20	56.8
1976	27	76.0	26	71.0
1980	34	71.8	34	76.0
1984	29	52.4	25	71.0
1988	36	66.6	36	76.9
1992	39	66.9	38	83.9
1996	35	65.3	42	84.6
2000	40	64.6	43	83.8
2004	40	67.5	26a	55.5
2008	39	67.4	42	82.2
2012	38	76.7	38	78.2

Five Republican primaries with a total of 309 delegates were canceled because only George W. Bush was a candidate.

*Primaries with combined caucus delegate selection are included but not advisory primaries in which no delegates are chosen.

Source: The Green Papers. www.thegreenpapers.com/P12/ccad.phtml

Another democratic aspect of the new nomination process is that it enlarges the arena of debate by allowing candidates to use the process as a vehicle to promote their ideas—be they the liberal economic and social programs that Jesse Jackson trumpeted in his quest for the 1984 and 1988 Democratic presidential nominations; the traditional, more conservative Christian values that Pat Robertson (1988), Pat Buchanan (1992 and 2000), and Alan Keyes and Gary Bauer (1996 and 2000), and Rick Santorum (2012) advocated when they ran for the Republican presidential nomination; or the libertarian views that Ron Paul expressed (2008 and 2012). Millionaire Steve Forbes's campaign for the 1996 and 2000 Republican nominations on the promise of a flat income tax and Herman Cain's proposal for a 9 percent across-the-board tax on individual incomes, corporate profits, and capital gains in 2012 are examples. Needless to say, in the process of running for the nomination, the candidates also promote themselves, thereby fostering their own political ambitions and, at least in some cases, satisfying their own psychological needs.

The number of candidates seeking the nomination, the range of issues being debated, and the diversity of the policy appeals have sensitized the parties to their base of supporters. The parties have given economic and social groups within them a chance to be heard, to pursue their interests, and even to put forth candidates who can win nominations. All of this has put the parties more in touch with themselves. That's the good news.

The Bad News

The bad news is that the reforms and changes in the nomination process have given states which hold their contests at the beginning of the process more influence. Candidates able to mobilize the rank-and-file partisans more effectively by virtue of their national standing, financial resources, and organizational support are also advantaged. Cohesive groups within the party, partisans with strong loyalties, and more recently, well-funded Super PACs also benefit from this arrangement.

Uneven Influence of States. Although the presidential nomination process is open to all partisans, participation is uneven. It is higher at the beginning of the process and lower toward the end, especially after the nominee has effectively been determined. Partisans in states that hold their contests early receive more media attention. Candidates are encouraged to concentrate their efforts and resources in these states.

As a result of these perceived benefits, states have been moving their nomination contests earlier and earlier, thereby front-loading the schedule. In 1972, 17 percent of the delegates had been chosen by mid-April; by 1976 that percentage had increased to 33. The front-loading continued through 2008 when both parties moved the official opening of their primary calendar to the first Tuesday in February. By the end of that day, February 5, more than 60 percent of the delegates to each party's national convention had been chosen. In an attempt to reverse this trend in 2012, the major parties set back the official starting date to the first Tuesday in March. The change, however, did not stop several states from violating the new calendar by holding their contests before the designated period began.

Front-loading has very serious and undemocratic consequences for the parties and their partisans, for the candidates, and for the public at large. For the parties, it gives greater benefit to the states that hold their contests first. To the extent that partisans in these states are not representative of the party's rank and file, their electoral choices can skew the outcome.[5] The winning candidate may not be the first choice of most party voters or even the most acceptable compromise candidate.

Take Iowa and New Hampshire, for example. Both have legislation that requires them to go first—Iowa with a caucus selection process and New Hampshire with a primary. These states are certainly not representative of the country or the parties, particularly the Democrats. Together they account for less than 1.4 percent of the country's total population. Moreover, they lack ethnic and racial diversity. African Americans constitute only 2.9 percent of Iowa's population and 1.1 percent of New Hampshire's, compared to 12.6 percent for the country as a whole and between 20 to 25 percent of the total Democratic vote in recent elections; similarly, Hispanics comprise only 5.0 percent of Iowa's population and 2.8 percent of New Hampshire's, yet Hispanics make up over 16 percent of the country's population and a growing proportion of the Democratic Party's electoral coalition.[6] How fair is that?

Moreover, a front-loaded contest may be decided before all the election issues become evident, before relevant background information on the candidates becomes public, and before events occur that may influence the electorate's determination of the most relevant qualifications for the candidates to demonstrate.

From a democratic perspective, a very serious consequence of having early caucuses and primaries determine the outcome is that the nomination is decided before most people are paying attention to the election. By the time the party's electorate tunes in, many of the candidates may have dropped out. In 2000, six of the twelve Republican candidates withdrew even before the vote was cast; in 2004, two of the ten Democratic candidates did so as well; in 2008, of the nine Democrats and eleven Republicans who officially declared their candidacies, only two Democrats and three Republicans remained after the first week in February; and in 2012, of the ten major Republican candidates that began the contest, only four actively campaigned after the third week in January.

Another equality issue for the states is the delegate allocation system. Both parties allocate delegates on the basis of state size and partisan loyalty. Democrats reward loyalty on the basis of the party vote in electoral districts in the last three presidential elections; Republicans reward it on the basis of the number of elected Republican officials, with a bonus for states that voted Republican at the presidential level in the last election. The system favors the large states for the Democrats and the most partisan GOP states. Is this an equitable way to award delegates?

Unequal Opportunities for Candidates. For the candidates, front-loading moves their campaign forward into the year preceding the election, lengthening the nomination period but usually shortening its competitive phase. A front-loaded schedule forces candidates to devote more time and resources to early fund-raising since a compressed calendar leaves little time to parlay a strong showing in Iowa, New Hampshire, or one of the other early states into a successful fund-raising campaign, as George McGovern was able to do in 1972 and Jimmy Carter in 1976.

Under the current system, lesser-known candidates face a dilemma. They need to raise money to compete but have difficulty doing so because they cannot establish their electability until the caucuses and primaries are actually held. Moreover, if they are not perceived as viable by the news media, they get less coverage than the front-runners. Under the circumstances they usually raise less money, which increases their competitive disadvantage.

Nor do federal matching grants level the playing field as they did in the past. As noted in Chapter 4, the increase in campaign costs greatly exceeds the increase in spending limits that apply if candidates accept government matching funds, while the increase in the amount individuals can contribute to presidential candidates has made private funding a much more desirable option than accepting public funds, especially with the advent of Super PACs. In the 2008 and 2012 election cycles, neither of the principal candidates for their party's nomination accepted federal funds during the nominations because it would have disadvantaged them to do so. The only piece of good news for candidates unable to raise sufficient money in the year before the election is that the two candidates who had the largest war chests at the end of 2007, Mitt Romney and Hillary Clinton, did not win their party's nomination; in 2012, Romney again had the largest war chest among the Republicans and won.

Giving advantage to nationally recognized candidates is not necessarily undesirable or undemocratic. Political experience normally is considered a valuable prerequisite for higher office. However, when national recognition and political experience combine to create unequal campaign resources, then outsiders without these resources are hurt. Personal wealth alone does not suffice, as Ross Perot (1992 and 1996) and Steve Forbes (2000 and 2004) found out.

Finally, front-loading the caucuses and primaries normally creates a down period of three to five months after a winner has emerged but before the national nominating conventions are held. Naturally, public interest declines during this period, forcing the parties and candidates to engage in extensive advertising to remain in the public spotlight and to keep their base energized. McCain had trouble staying in the news as long as the Democratic contest continued in 2008. By not accepting federal matching grants, however, he was able to raise more private money and use it to gain visibility for himself, his party, and his policy positions. Similarly, Mitt Romney took advantage of his and his party's fund-raising to continue campaigning after he effectively won the Republican nomination in April 2012.

Unequal Representation of the Partisan Electorate. A front-loaded schedule is not the only problem. Winner-take-all voting, which the Republican Party did not restrict until 2012, gives those who vote for losing candidates no representation in their state's convention delegation.

Some states allow independents to vote in party primaries and caucuses, which dilutes the vote of partisans and could potentially affect the outcome of the nomination. Polls taken during the 2008 Democratic nomination contest indicated that the party's rank-and-file preferred Hillary Rodham Clinton, but independents preferred Barack Obama. The relatively early victory of McCain in the Republican nomination thus worked to Obama's advantage because it eliminated the other principal candidate who attracted the most independent votes in open state primaries. Was such a situation fair for Democratic partisans?

In 1980, the Democrats created super delegates to ensure that party and elected officials could attend the national nominating conventions, provide the decisive votes if the convention was deadlocked, and promote closer cooperation among its presidential candidate, Democratic members of Congress, and state and national party officials. Since the caucuses and primaries have been decisive, the super delegates have played no major role in the selection of the nominee, but they potentially could have done so in 2008. With the elected delegates divided, and Obama without a majority of all convention delegates until Clinton conceded in June, the super delegates held the balance of power.

Super delegates initially tend to support the front-runner, which was Clinton throughout 2007. She had contributed more money than Obama to the 2006 reelection campaigns of Democratic members of Congress, who are automatically super delegates. She was better known among the Democratic leadership and was viewed as the "inevitable" nominee by most party regulars, with the result that more party leaders and members of Congress jumped on her bandwagon early and pledged their support.

When the race got closer, with Obama in the delegate lead, increasing pressure was exerted by both campaigns on the super delegates, who constituted 19 percent of the total number of delegate votes at the Democratic convention. The possibility that the super delegates could reverse the caucus and primary results by disproportionately supporting Clinton raised the ire of Obama's supporters, who cried foul and pointed to the undemocratic consequences that such a reversal would produce for the party, its nominee, and the electorate. In the end, the super delegates proved that they were politicians sensitive to the opinion of their constituents, and most backed the judgment of the voters of their states. Nonetheless, the Democrats eliminated *unpledged* super delegates in 2012; the rule change included them as part of their state's delegate but as *pledged* delegates proportionally divided in accordance with the state's vote.

It must also be remembered, however, that the people who have participated in the nomination process over the years have not been representative of average partisan voters, much less the electorate as a whole. Primary voters and caucus participants tend to overrepresent people who are in higher income and education brackets. Older citizens that have more information, time, and incentive also tend to be more involved than the under-thirty age cohort. The less representative the people who participate in the process are, the less likely that the party's standard-bearers and its platform will reflect the wishes of its rank-and-file voters.

The reforms, intended to increase the party electorate's role in choosing nominees, have not, for the most part, achieved that objective. The current system gives party elites—composed of interest group leaders, campaign professionals, and partisan activists—people and groups that tend to be more ideological and issue oriented than average partisans—an advantage because of their activism, organizational skills, and the resources they can mobilize.

The elites control the process and usually affect the outcome. Before or during the nomination process, they usually agree on a candidate based in part on that candidate's national reputation, leadership endorsements, and performance in the early caucuses and primaries. They then join forces to help that candidate secure the nomination as soon as possible.[7] Most party leaders, including most of the elites, believe that long, divisive nominations hurt the chances of their party's nominee in the general election.

The 2008 Democratic nomination process was the exception, however. The ability of the Obama campaign to identify and get out large numbers of voters, the candidate's appeal to independents who participated in the Democratic primaries, and Obama's message of policy and political change resonated with the 2008 Democratic electorate. Further, Obama also benefited from the division of organized groups within the party's electoral coalition between Hillary Clinton and himself.

In addition to Super PACs, interest groups—such as labor unions and women's groups for the Democrats and evangelical and fundamentalist Christian groups for the Republicans—have become increasingly important during the nominations because of their capacity to commit resources to educating the public and to mobilizing their supporters. Their impact often is reinforced by their activities before and after elections in the form of public relations campaigns, lobbying, and fund-raising events that maintain the ties among these groups, the candidates, and the elected officials who are sympathetic to their cause.

By emphasizing the policy positions that these groups advocate, the candidates have become more ideological and issue-oriented themselves. They believe that belief and opinion conformity with their constituencies is necessary in order to be nominated and elected and renominated and reelected. Thus, the positions of the candidates for nomination on a range of policy issues do not usually deviate much from the well-known preferences of the party's base. And when they do, as Republicans felt differently about Ron Paul's foreign policy views and Newt Gingrich's on immigration in 2012, they are criticized and often vigorously opposed by partisan activists.

The influence of the activists in both parties is the principal reason why aspirants for the Republican nomination tend to move to the ideological right of their party and Democrats to the ideological left of theirs as they compete for their party's nomination. After they get the nomination, though, they frequently find that their initial positions alienate mainstream voters who have more moderate perspectives and more pragmatic views, so they move toward the center in the general election—although perhaps not as much as previously because of political polarization within today's electorate. The ideological influence exerted within both parties' nomination processes is also evident in the selection of convention delegates, who tend to be more ideological in their thinking and beliefs than rank-and-file party identifiers and much more so than the general public.[8]

What an irony! Parties have reformed their nomination processes to reflect more accurately the attitudes, opinions, and candidate choices of their rank-and-file supporters. They've adopted rules to tie the eventual selection of nominees more closely to the party electorate. That party electorate, however, has been disproportionately influenced by party elites, including interest group leaders who work closely with them. These elites have the incentive, the resources, and the skills to affect the nomination process and whose discernible interests and ideological beliefs distinguish them not only from the general public but also from typical supporters within their own parties. Thus, as a consequence of opening the process to achieve better representation, the parties may not represent the moderate, mainstream electorate nearly as well as they did in the pre-reform era when party leaders chose candidates primarily on the basis of their electability, not their ideological preferences or detailed issue positions.

In short, the democratization of the process has not produced the democratic outcome for which the reformers had hoped. In theory, the people have greater influence; they have the opportunity to participate in their party's nomination if they choose to do so. In practice, however, it is the elites and activists who have gained the upper hand by virtue of their greater participation and campaign resources.

And that's not all. Not only have the parties' elected officials become less representative of their rank and file, they also may be less capable of governing. Ideologues are not good compromisers.

THE IMPACT OF NOMINATIONS ON GOVERNMENT

Taking more consistent ideological stands is just the first step toward pursuing these policy positions if elected. The increasingly ideological nature of American parties has resulted in sharper partisan divisions within Congress. The old boys club that operated according to informal folkways and mores has given way to the new activist politics replete with ideological rhetoric and partisan confrontation. This partisan stridency is what closed down the government in the winter of 1995–1996 for almost a month; two years later, it led to a presidential impeachment. It has impeded the enactment of legislation during periods of divided government and resulted in periodic budget and fiscal crises, a situation that has become so common in the 112th and 113th Congresses that the ability of the U.S. government to pay its bills and function normally has been called into question by independent bond rating agencies.

The ideological gap between the two major parties has filtered down to the grassroots level. The partisan electorate has become highly polarized, creating an explosive political environment in which deliberation gives way to oratory, compromise is made more difficult, and the public has become more cynical and less trusting of those who represent them than they were two or three decades ago.

All of these factors that have contributed to sharp partisan divisions; dysfunctional government cannot be blamed on the nomination process alone. The causes are deep-seated and varied. They have taken place over a longer period of time than have nomination reforms. Moreover, they have been exacerbated by social, technological, and political change. Nonetheless, the democratization of the nomination process has had a discernible impact that many evaluate as negative.

IMPROVING THE NOMINATION PROCESS

What can be done about this representational problem and its impact on government? A return to the good old days, when party bosses controlled the selection of party candidates and influenced the policy positions they took, seems both unlikely and undesirable. There would be little public support for making the selection process more elitist and for reducing the input of rank-and-file voters, despite the fact that so many eligible voters have chosen not to take part in the process.

Nor would there be much support for taking a party's internal politics out of the public arena or limiting the news media's access to it. Some might desire the press to exercise more self-restraint, particularly when reporting and assessing the personal traits and private behavior of candidates, but there is far from unanimity on this point.

If going back to the old system is not a viable option, then what is? Perhaps the parties could level the playing field by getting a greater cross section of their partisans to participate. Because activists gain disproportionate influence from their political involvement, getting more people aware, interested, and involved in primaries could lessen this influence. Presumably, if a broader cross section of a party participated in nomination politics, the candidates would have more incentive to appeal to a wider range of interests and views. But how can more people be encouraged to get involved, given the cynicism and apathy of the electorate and the amount of media attention already devoted to nominations?

Contemporary campaigns have responded to this challenge by communicating with potential voters directly. In 2004, the Republican Party mounted a turnout campaign in which individuals were targeted, contacted personally by Republican volunteers who lived in the community, and then recontacted to get them out to vote. The party also used ballot initiatives in several key states to maximize its turnout. In 2008, both the Obama and Clinton campaigns used the Internet to activate their supporters, involve them in the campaign, and get them out to vote. The Obama campaign was particularly effective in doing so. These successful get-out-the-vote activities, combined with the closeness of the Democratic contest, generated a larger vote than usual in the Democratic nomination process.

In 2012, the Romney campaign also had a well organized ground operation; his principal opponents did not, however. Nonetheless, Romney's inability to excite his party's conservative base and to generate sustained momentum in the early stages of the nomination process provided motivation for those opposed to his candidacy to turnout despite the absence of strong field operations by the other Republican contenders. By the beginning of April, however, with Romney's delegate lead growing and his challengers out of funds, they had little choice but to suspend further campaigning. The race was over.

Are divisive nominations a problem? From the perspective of most party leaders, they are. The greater the number of candidates and the longer they campaign, the more likely the party will remain divided, the eventual winner's leadership image will be tarnished, and some supporters of the losing candidates will be harder to persuade to support the winning nominee. All of these factors decrease the odds of winning the general election, or so party leaders believe.

There are some partisans, however, who see a vigorous primary process as healthy. It tests the candidates, informs the public, and energizes partisans.[9] An extended nomination helps the winning candidate develop a more effective campaign organization, evaluate the staff who work for it, design partisan appeals, research policy positions, and build an electoral database to use in the general election.

However the process is evaluated, the parties face dilemmas. They can either encourage more candidates and voters to participate, making their nomination processes more competitive and democratic, but also possibly factionalizing themselves in the process and adversely affecting their chances in the general election, or they can discourage participation, possibly making the nominees less representative of the wishes of rank-and-file partisans. They can provide more incentives or impose more rules to make delegate selection more equitable and/or efficient, probably incurring the wrath or outright resistance of some states, or they can acknowledge the federal character of the system, possibly undermining their own organizational integrity and the conduct of a national campaign. They can continue to tinker with the procedures, responding to the latest problem or controversy such as super delegates or winner-take-all voting, or they can try to restructure the entire system with specific goals but unknown consequences. The most radical change would be to replace the various state nomination contests with a national primary.

Instituting a National Primary

Dissatisfaction with the current system has led some to recommend a national primary in which both major parties would choose their nominees in a direct popular vote. The simplicity of this suggestion, the promise of higher turnout, and the expectation that the prospective nominees would have to address national issues similar to those they would encounter in office have generated support for such a proposal, as has the fact that it would eliminate front-loading and the disproportionate influence that early states have on the current nomination process.[10]

Although proposals for a national primary vary, most advocate conducting it in the early summer, preceding the national nominating conventions. Candidates who could demonstrate their popularity and electability, perhaps by obtaining a certain number of signatures on petitions or receiving a minimum percentage of support in preprimary public opinion polls, could enter. Anyone who received a majority in the national primary would automatically become the nominee. In some plans, a plurality would be sufficient, provided it was at least 40 percent. In the event that no one received 40 percent, a runoff election between the top two finalists could be held several weeks later, or the national convention could choose the nominee from among the top vote-getters.

A national primary would be consistent with the democratic principle of one person–one vote.[11] Moreover, the attention that such an election would receive from the press and the candidates should provide greater incentives for a higher voter turnout than currently exists, particularly in states that hold their nomination contests after the apparent nominee has emerged. If more people participated, the electorate would probably be more representative than today's electorate that chooses the parties' nominees, and the winning candidate would have been tested in a national campaign. And, finally, the outcome of the vote should be clear; no longer could members of the press interpret winners and losers as they see them.

The flip side of a national primary, however, is that it would exacerbate the advantages of the front-runners, particularly Washington-based insiders and large-state governors, people who can raise the money for an expensive national campaign. Lesser-known candidates, unless they were independently wealthy or had backers who would supplement their campaign with Super PAC expenditures, would have little chance of competing on an equal scale with better-known, better-funded candidates. A national primary occurring on a single day would likely exaggerate the importance of any major event preceding that primary—whether a personal revelation or accusation, or a political, natural, or other event, where there is little time to put the matter—and responses to it—in perspective. Another potential problem is that a national primary could increase divisiveness within the parties, contribute to the emphasis on personality in politics, and weaken the organizational base of the parties. A post-primary convention could not be expected to tie the nominee to the party, although it might tie the party to the nominee, at least through the general election.

Finally, would state party leaders support a national primary in which they would probably have less influence? Would the states that benefit from the current arrangement by holding their contests early agree to schedule them later in the spring or summer and on the same day as others? Would states that have caucuses agree to a primary? And if legislation at the national level were needed, would representatives of the states that benefit from the present system vote in favor of abolishing it? Would they voluntarily give up any of their discretion to schedule and conduct elections for federal officials?

Moreover, the cumulative impact of a national primary, followed by national party conventions, followed by a general election might be too much politicking for too long a period. It might be more than people are willing or able to absorb. Imagine the same themes and appeals, statements and advertisements, debates and more debates continually echoing across the country for months, even years. Voters might tune out; they might become even more cynical and distrustful of politicians, particularly if such a long campaign produced a long list of promises that the winning candidate would be expected to fulfill and on which that candidate's presidency would be evaluated. Certainly, governing might prove to be more difficult if party leaders and members of Congress had little to do with the presidential nominee's victory and thus lacked an incentive to follow the new administration's lead.

Whether a national primary winner would be the party's strongest candidate is also open to question. With a large field of contenders, those with the most devoted supporters might do best. Candidates who do not arouse the passions of the diehards but who are more acceptable to the party's mainstream might not do as well. Everybody's second choice might not even finish second unless a system of approval or of cumulative voting were used, each of which is likely to be complex.[12] These potential negative consequences for the major parties have discouraged them from supporting such a plan, despite its general public appeal. And if there is little enthusiasm within the Democratic and Republican parties for a national primary, then it is very unlikely that Congress would ever impose it on them.

Schedule a Series of Regional or Grouped Primaries

Before the 2008 election cycle, it looked as if a regional system would evolve as a consequence of voluntary agreements among the states in the same geographic area to hold their contests on or close to the same date. The southern states were the first to enter into such agreements in 1988; some of the states in the Midwest followed in 1992. But this trend has not continued. Since the mid 1990s, the early determination of the likely nominee has encouraged front-loading rather than regionalization.

Disaffection with the party's nomination schedule, the exemptions provided certain states—Iowa, New Hampshire, Nevada, and South Carolina—and violation of calendar rules by others have prompted party leaders to explore additional options. Prior to the 2000 Republican convention, a commission recommended the implementation of a population-based nominating system in which states would be placed in one of four groups, based on their population size rather than geographic location, and then would conduct their primary election or the first stage of their caucus selection on the same day. The group containing the least-populated states would go first, and the one with the most populated states would go last, with the dates on which the four groups would hold their contests spaced approximately one month apart.[13]

Opposition to the plan quickly developed from Republican leaders and political consultants in large states who were fearful that the nominee would be effectively decided before the big states voted. Concerns were also expressed about the costs for an extended nomination contest across the country and the wear and tear it would impose on the candidates and their organizations. Not wanting the issue to divide the convention and interfere with his nomination, George W. Bush persuaded delegates pledged to him to oppose the recommendation, and it was defeated in the Republican Rules Committee.

Another proposal that has gained some backing is the so-called American Plan. It would set up a spring calendar divided into ten intervals during which nomination contests would be held. The first group holding caucuses or primaries would consist of randomly selected small states that totaled together no more than eight congressional districts—Iowa and New Hampshire combined currently have seven districts. Any state or group of states that has a combined total of eight congressional districts could schedule their caucus or primary in the first round. In subsequent rounds, state size could increase by an additional eight districts per round.

Proponents contend that such a system would be fairer than the current one. Front-loading would be prohibited; the large states could not exercise disproportionate influence. Because states within the size groupings would be chosen randomly, no one state would have a permanent advantage, such as Iowa and New Hampshire have presently. Not only would the states be treated more evenhandedly, but more candidates would have greater opportunities to compete and for longer periods of time with the need for less money up front because the states that held the early contests would be small in size.[14] Candidates with regional recognition would have greater opportunities to demonstrate their qualifications than in a national primary.

Whether Iowa and New Hampshire and the large states would agree to such an arrangement is questionable. Whether the parties could and would try to impose it on recalcitrant states is also a question, given the need for party unity to run a general election campaign, the opposition to extended nominations, and the money that such nominations would need. Moreover, such a system would require that other nomination contests within each state be held at the same time to avoid the cost of holding two separate election days to encompass all nominations. It is doubtful that incumbents and challengers for other elected offices would support such a change.[15]

Barring agreement on a new system, the current hodgepodge of primaries and caucuses, unbalanced scheduling dates amid violation of party rules, and skewed turnout and inequitable representation are likely to persist with complaints ritually voiced by journalists, academics, party leaders, and the electorate. Few seem satisfied by the current arrangement, nor is there a consensus on how the system can be improved.

NATIONAL NOMINATING CONVENTIONS: ANACHRONISM OR STILL RELEVANT?

At the presidential level, the changes in party rules have rendered national nominating conventions obsolete, at least as far as the selection of nominees is concerned. The identity of the likely candidate is known well in advance of the convention. Even the vice presidential selection is not the convention's to make. By tradition, the presidential nominee chooses a running mate, and the convention ratifies the choice because a majority of the delegates are supporters of the winning presidential nominee.

So what's left for the convention to decide? Sometimes national nominating conventions debate and resolve platform issues, but most of the time they don't. They ratify the document, which is a combination of principles and policies that a party committee, most likely controlled by the candidate who has won the primaries and caucuses, has drafted.

If disputes do emerge, they often reveal real and deep-seated differences among rank-and-file partisans, but they come to light primarily because the mass media highlight them. In other words, news coverage is an incentive for some disgruntled delegates to publicize their disagreements, taking their fight to the convention floor even though their prospects for victory are slight. It is the national visibility that makes it worthwhile. The threat of embarrassing the nominee by taking an oppositional position to the floor may be enough for the leading candidate to concede some platform points in an effort to avoid the appearance of disunity.

Why hold conventions? If the delegates are chosen in accordance with party rules and are unlikely to change the pledges they have made to support particular candidates, if the convention rules are decided in advance, if the successful candidate for the presidential nomination is preordained by the primaries and caucuses, if that candidate can choose a running mate, and if the platform is hammered out in advance, then why hold conventions at all? This is a question that the news media are asking with increasing frequency.

From the press's perspective, there's little news. In fact, correspondents and commentators often have to manufacture news by highlighting disagreements, no matter how small, by engaging in seemingly endless and often trivial commentary, and by suggesting potential conflicts, which may or may not exist or come to pass.

From the perspectives of the candidates, the parties, and the interest groups, however, the conventions remain an important political tradition that they wish to continue. The assembled delegates constitute an anointing body that legitimizes the selection of the nominees and a responsive audience that demonstrates enthusiasm for what the party has to offer. The convention provides a national podium from which the candidates can launch their campaigns and from which other leaders of the party can gain recognition.

From the party's perspective, conventions provide a unifying mechanism, one that can help heal the divisions of the nomination process. They're a reward to the delegates for their past participation and an inducement for them to continue to work in the party's political campaigns, particularly the one that is just beginning. And, finally, they are publicity for the party, its positions, its candidates, and its supporters. But there is a problem.

Naturally, the party wishes to present itself in the best possible light: unified, enthusiastic, optimistic, confident, with a clear sense of purpose, direction, and demonstrated governing abilities. Its leaders orchestrate the proceedings so they will have this desired effect. The news media, in contrast, are interested in news (naturally, as they define it—new, unexpected, dramatic, and stories of human interest). They're also concerned with their public responsibility and their profitability, with their bottom lines measured in terms of audience size and the number of readers, subscribers, listeners, and, more recently, online "hits."

The objectives of the party and the news media are in conflict. Parties need media coverage of their conventions far more than the news media need to report them, particularly if conventions are boring and predictable, as most of them have been in the last three decades. Presented with this dilemma, the parties stage their meetings; there are daily themes, scripts, films, celebrities, and politicians—all made available to live cameras and microphones. But the parties' elaborate public relations extravaganzas seem to reinforce the news media's contention that the conventions have become almost all pomp and ceremony, with little or no substance. Broadcast network coverage of the major-party conventions, which has declined substantially, may soon be eliminated entirely, with only cable news and public affairs networks covering parts of the proceedings. Nonetheless, over 30 million viewers watched the final nights of both the 2012 Republican and Democratic Conventions.[16]

Third-party conventions receive practically no live coverage on the major broadcast networks. H. Ross Perot's acceptance speech at his Reform Party convention in 1996 and Ralph Nader's at the Green Party convention in 2000 were aired only by the 24–7 cable news networks and C-SPAN. Nader held news conferences in 2004 and 2008 to announce his candidacy, and they amounted to just sound bites on the evening news.

If the major networks no longer cover convention proceedings live, then are conventions still necessary? Will they survive? The parties hope so. Beginning in 2000, they launched interactive Web sites; in 2008 they began to stream coverage of events.

If conventions were to be abolished, then how would parties unify themselves after a divisive nomination struggle? How would they decide on and approve a platform on the critical issues? How would they engage and energize the public, particularly independent voters who tend to be less interested, less informed, and less involved? When would the general election campaign officially begin, or would it be an endless campaign cycle from pre-candidacy to nomination to election and then to pre-candidacy again?

If regional or grouped primaries were to be established by voluntary agreements among states, by national rules mandated by the parties, or by an act of Congress, a national nominating convention could still serve as a potential decision maker in the event that the primaries were not decisive. It could act as a body to choose or ratify the vice presidential nominee and as a platform maker for the candidates in the general election. The cheerleader and launch-pad functions also would continue to be important for the convention.

Similarly, if a national primary were instituted and the leading candidate did not receive the required percentage of the vote, the convention could then choose the nominee from among the top candidates. It also could serve as the decisive body to approve a platform for the winning candidate.

THE INCUMBENCY ADVANTAGE

Despite all the hoopla about how open the nomination process has become, incumbents who run for reelection usually win. The deck is stacked even more against challengers in nominations than it is in general elections. Take Congress, for example. For the period from the end of World War II through the 2012 election, 238 House incumbents out of 13,515 were defeated in their quest for renomination (fewer than 2 percent), and 44 senators lost renomination out of 968 who sought it (fewer than 5 percent). At the presidential level, the last incumbent to lose a presidential nomination was Chester Arthur in 1884, although Gerald Ford came close to losing to Ronald Reagan in 1976. Two Democratic presidents, Harry Truman and Lyndon Johnson, chose not to compete for renomination in part because of the opposition and competition within their own party. Table 7.2 indicates incumbency success in renomination for Congress between 1952 and 2012.

Why do incumbents do so well? The system gives them important built-in benefits. These include greater name recognition, superior fund-raising organizations, and more campaign experience, coupled with access to more experienced campaign aides. Incumbents frequently have grassroots organizations and the ability to give help to and get help from other party leaders. These benefits translate into great odds for most incumbents seeking renomination.

The incumbency advantage is enhanced by the absence of competition. For the obvious reason that it is so difficult to defeat them, incumbents face fewer challengers than do candidates who run for open seats (seats for which an incumbent is not running); and when incumbents are challenged, it is often by candidates who cannot raise sufficient funds to mount an effective campaign against them. Besides, voters tend to be risk averse, preferring a known candidate to an unknown one, unless the known candidate allegedly engaged in immoral, unethical, or criminal activities or is out of step with public opinion.

Is the incumbency advantage good or bad for a democratic election process and for a democratic government? On the positive side, it provides the party with continuity in its candidacies. Because incumbents have an advantage in the general election, the advantage enables the party to maintain its elective positions and the constituents to keep their representative. The more senior a representative is, the greater that person's influence within the legislative body is likely to be and the more that representative is able to accomplish for constituents.

On the negative side, though, the incumbent's renomination advantage translates into more independence for an elected official. There's little a party's leaders can do to a popular incumbent who chooses to deviate from the party's position on the issues. However, outside interest groups and Super PACs can mount campaigns in support of challengers, and the threat of those campaigns tend to keep incumbents sensitive to the interests and opinions of their electoral constituents. Sometimes, however, party leaders themselves are placed in a tough position when they have to advance national legislation that conflicts with the interests of their own constituents. They are accused of losing touch with the folks back home and occasionally have been defeated.

TABLE 7.2 **Congressional Incumbents Seeking Renomination, 1952–2012**

	Senate			House of Representatives		
Year	Total seeking renomination	Number defeated	Percentage defeated	Total seeking renomination	Number defeated	Percentage defeated
1952	32	2	6	407	6	1
1956	29	0	0	411	6	1
1958	28	0	0	396	3	1
1960	29	0	0	405	5	1
1962	35	1	3	402	12	3
1964	33	1	3	397	8	2
1966	32	3	9	411	8	2
1968	28	4	14	408	4	1
1970	31	1	3	401	10	2
1972	27	2	7	392	14	1
1974	27	2	7	391	8	2
1976	25	0	0	384	3	1
1978	25	3	12	382	5	1
1980	29	4	14	398	6	2
1982	30	0	0	387	4	1
1984	29	0	0	411	3	1
1986	28	0	0	394	3	1
1988	27	0	0	409	1	—
1990	32	0	0	407	1	—
1992	28	1	4	368	19	5
1994	26	0	0	387	4	1
1996	21	1*	5	384	2	1
1998	29	0	0	402	1	—
2000	29	0	0	403	3	1
2002	28	1	4	398	8	2
2004	26	0	0	404	2	—
2006	29	1	3	404	2	—
2008	30	0	0	403	4	1
2010	25	2	1	398	4	1
2012	23	1	.4	393	13	3

*Sheila Frahm, appointed to fill Sen. Robert J. Dole's term, is counted as an incumbent seat.

Source: Harold W. Stanley and Richard G. Niemi, *Vital Statistics in American Politics, 2009–2010* (Washington, DC: CQ Press, 2011), updated by author.

SUMMARY: NOMINATION DILEMMAS IN A NUTSHELL

In theory, the movement to a nomination process in which more people have the opportunity to participate has opened the parties and theoretically expanded their base. From a democratic perspective, that's good. In practice, however, only a portion of the major parties' rank and file has gotten involved regularly and voted—the 2008 nominations, particularly the Democratic one, being the exception. From a democratic perspective, low participation is unhealthy. It contributes to the control of the process and its product—the nominee—by party elites. Front-loading, open primaries, non-proportional voting, and the automatic designation of Super delegates all detract from a democratic nomination process.

That the states holding the early caucuses and primaries are not representative of the party as a whole, that the people who do participate in the caucuses and primaries tend to have the strongest ideological orientations, and that the candidates who benefit from the current system tend to be those with the greatest name recognition, the most money, and the most organizational support all undercut the democratic character of the nomination process. This environment may also contribute to the cynicism and distrust of politicians and their parties today.

Various proposals for reforming the nomination process at the presidential level have been advanced. The goal of these proposals—democratizing the presidential selection process even more by getting more of the party's rank and file to participate—is laudable. The result, however, may be to advantage further the front-runners, particularly incumbents, to create and extend division within the parties, and to make them more subject to the influence of those who win their nominations rather than the other way around. The parties are faced with a representational dilemma. Can they simultaneously reflect the wishes of their diverse base and also provide strong, cohesive, partisan leadership? What do you think?

Now It's Your Turn

Discussion Questions

1. Why did the major political parties reform their nomination processes in the 1970s, and have their reforms achieve the desired goals?

2. From the perspectives of the parties, candidates, and partisan supporters, what are the main advantages and disadvantages of the current nomination processes for president and members of Congress?

3. How would you reform the parties' current nomination rules to minimize the disadvantages to the parties, candidates, and partisan supporters? Do you support or oppose the recent changes in party rules that instituted proportional voting for Republican delegates and eliminated unpledged super delegates for the Democrats? Do you think these changes will make much of a difference in subsequent nominations?

4. Does the advantage that incumbents have in securing renomination undercut the principle of equity in a democratic electoral system?

5. What impact, if any, does the process of nomination have on the structure of the parties and their ability to govern if elected?

Topics for Debate

Challenge or defend the following statements:

1. The reforms in the major parties' presidential nominating processes have not worked and should be abolished.

2. Congress should enact a law that establishes a national primary for selecting the major parties' presidential nominees.

3. Because Iowa and New Hampshire are not representative of the entire country, they should be prevented from automatically holding the first caucus and primary election.

4. Aspirants for their party's presidential nomination should not be allowed to campaign before the year of the election.

5. National nominating conventions are irrelevant and should be abolished.

Exercises

1. You've been asked to head a committee to reform the way your party chooses its nominees. The primary goals that the party wants you to consider when you propose your reforms are, in order of importance, to:

   a. select the strongest and most qualified candidate to run in the general election,
   b. give all partisans an opportunity to participate in some way in the nominating process,
   c. increase the likelihood that the views of the winning candidate will reflect the views of the rank and file, and
   d. have a nominating process that is open to all well-qualified candidates.

   In your plan, indicate:

   a. when and how the nominees for national office will be selected,
   b. the rules for determining who can run and who can vote,
   c. the penalties, if any, that you would impose on states that threaten to disregard party rules,
   d. the method for approving or amending your reforms, and
   e. an explanation of how and why your proposed reforms would be an improvement on the present system.

2. Critique one of the proposals mentioned in the text for changing the nomination process. Indicate whether you believe the change would positively or negatively affect the parties, the candidates, and the partisan electorate. Give examples, hypothetical or real, to support your argument.

INTERNET RESOURCES

- Campaigns and Elections: www.campaignsandelections.com

  A journal that provides an excellent source of information on campaign strategy and tactics.

- The Center for Voting and Democracy. Fair Vote: www.fairvote.com

  A Web site devoted to electoral reform. Contains debate on proposals for changing the electoral system and making it more democratic.

- The Green Papers: www.thegreenpapers.com

  A Web site that contains a wealth of information on U.S. nominations and elections since 2000.

- United States Election Assistance Commission: www.eac.gov

  Established by the Help America Vote Act of 2002; central to its role, the commission serves as a national clearinghouse and resource for information on the administration of federal elections.

SELECTED READINGS

Altschuler, Bruce. "Selecting the Presidential Nominee by National Primary: An Idea Whose Time Has Come." *The Forum* 5, no. 4 (2008): article 5.

Atkeson, Lonna Rae, and Cherie D. Maestas. "Meaningful Participation and the Evolution of the Reformed Presidential Nominating System." *PS: Political Science and Politics* 42 (2009): 59–64.

Bartels, Larry M. *Presidential Primaries and the Dynamics of Public Choice.* Princeton, NJ: Princeton University Press, 1988.

Center for Voting and Democracy. Fairvote. "Delegating Democracy: How Parties Can Make Their Presidential Nominating Contests More Democratic." 2008. http://archive.fairvote.org/?page=27&pressmode=showspecific&showarticle=201

Cohen, Marty, David Karol, Hans Noel, and John Zaller. *The Party Decides: Presidential Nominations Before and After Reform.* Chicago, IL: University of Chicago Press, 2008.

Day, Christine L., Charles D. Hadley, and Harold W. Stanley. "The Inevitable Unanticipated Consequences of Political Reform: The 2004 Presidential Nomination Process." In *A Defining Moment*, edited by William Crotty. Armonk, NY: M. E. Sharpe, 2005.

Geer, John G. *Nominating Presidents: An Evaluation of Voters and Primaries.* Westport, CT: Greenwood Press, 1989.

Kamarck, Elaine C. *Primary Politics: How Presidential Candidates Have Shaped the Modern Nominating System.* Washington, DC: Brookings Institution Press, 2009.

Mayer, William G. "Superdelegates: Reforming the Reforms Revisited." In *Reforming the Presidential Nomination Process*, edited by Steven S. Smith and Melanie J. Springer. Washington, DC: Brookings Institution, 2009.

Mayer, William G., and Andrew E. Busch, eds. *The Front-Loading Problem in Presidential Nominations.* Washington, DC: Brookings Institution Press, 2004.

Norrander, Barbara. *The Imperfect Primary.* New York, NY: Routledge, 2010.

Polsby, Nelson W. *The Consequences of Party Reform.* New York, NY: Oxford University Press, 1983.

Shafer, Byron E. *Bifurcated Politics: Evolution and Reform in the National Party Convention.* Cambridge, MA: Harvard University Press, 1988.

Smith, Larry David, and Dan Nimmo. *Cordial Concurrence: Orchestrating National Party Conventions in the Telepolitical Age.* New York, NY: Praeger, 1991.

Task Force on Campaign Reform. *Campaign Reform: Insights and Evidence.* Princeton, NJ: Princeton University Press, 1998.

Tolbert, Caroline, and Peverill Squire. "Reforming the Presidential Nomination Process." *PS: Political Science and Politics* 42 (January 2009): 27–79.

NOTES

1. The Supreme Court gave the parties this power in its 1975 landmark decision in *Cousins v. Wigoda* (419 U.S. 477). The Court held that political parties were private organizations with rights of association protected by the Constitution. Parties could compel state affiliates to abide by their rules of delegate selection for the national nominating convention unless there were compelling constitutional reasons for not doing so. The burden of proving these reasons was placed on the state that deviated from the party's rules. Although in theory the party has the power to enforce its national rules, in practice this has been difficult to do because states have the authority to conduct elections, including primary elections, for federal officials. State affiliates of the national parties are thus subject to the election laws of the state. To reject these laws and conduct their own selection process is difficult and costly.

2. Although Republicans profess the same broad goals, they initially mandated only one national rule for their state parties: that they not discriminate in the selection of delegates on the basis of race, creed, color, national origin, or gender. In other aspects of delegate selection, the GOP would enforce whatever rules a state Republican Party adopted.

3. The principal difference was that Democrats required proportional voting for the selection of delegates to their party's national convention while the Republicans did not until 2012, the first nomination campaign in which they implemented a proportional voting requirement for primaries held before April 1st.

4. There are more challengers in a nomination contest to run against an incumbent of the opposition party in the general election than there are in the incumbent's party when that incumbent is seeking renomination. The more open system, however, keeps incumbents more attuned to their constituents' interests and needs, in part because of the threat of being embarrassed—or being beaten by a challenger.

5. In 2008, the Democratic nominations were more representative than the Republicans at the beginning of the process because the larger states that held their primaries on Super Tuesday were more reflective of that party's electoral coalition than they were of the Republicans'. John McCain, a moderate Republican, benefited as a consequence.

6. United States Census Bureau, "2010 Census Results," www.2010.census.gov/2010census/data/index.php

7. John Aldrich, "The Invisible Primary and Its Effects on Democratic Choice," *PS: Political Science and Politics* 42 (January 2009): 33–38; Marty Cohen, David Carol, Hans Noel, and John Zaller, *The Party Decides: Presidential Nominations Before and After Reform* (Chicago, IL: University of Chicago Press, 2008).

8. This phenomenon was first identified by Herbert McCloskey, "Consensus and Ideology in American Politics," *American Political Science Review* 58 (1964): 361–382; see also Jeane J. Kirkpatrick, *The New Presidential Elite* (New York, NY: Russell Sage, 1976). The phenomenon appears in the surveys of delegates since then.

9. Divisive primaries, however, if they encourage turnout, can have the beneficial effect of mobilizing the party's electorate for the general election and subsequent contests. See Walter J. Stone, Lonna Rae Atkeson, and Ronald B. Rapoport, "Turning On or Turning Off? Mobilization and Demobilization Effects of Participation in Presidential Nomination Campaigns," *American Journal of Political Science* 36 (August 1992): 665–691.

10. Several surveys conducted over the years indicate public support for a direct primary nomination system. A poll by the *New York Times* and CBS News conducted in July 2007 found 72 percent favoring such a system. A Gallup poll conducted nine years earlier also found a majority in support of a national primary election. Gallup Poll, "Electoral Reforms," April 10, 1988, as reported in *The Gallup Poll: Public Opinion 1988* (Wilmington, DE: Scholarly Resources, 1989), 60–61.

11. For an extended discussion in favor of a national primary, see Bruce Altschuler, "Selecting the Presidential Nominee by National Primary: An Idea Whose Time has Come," *The Forum* 5, no. 4 (2008): article 5, www.bepress.com/forum/v015/iss4/art5

12. Approval voting allows the electorate to vote to approve or disapprove each candidate who is running. The candidate with the most approval votes is elected. In a system of cumulative voting, candidates are ordered by rank, and the ranks may be averaged to determine the winner.

13. This proposal is known as the Delaware Plan and is described by FairVote.org. http://archive.fairvote.org/?page=2064.

14. For an extended discussion of this plan, see www.fairvote.org.

15. A third proposal, "The Voter Turnout Initiative," would order state primaries based on the state's turnout in the previous presidential election with those with the highest turnout going first and being rewarded with an exclusive primary date. Held over a ten-week period, April–June, the number of states holding their contest on the same day would gradually increase. For more information about this proposal see Heather Frederick, "Reforming the Presidential Primary System: The Voter Turnout Initiative," *PS: Political Science and Politics,* 45 (January 2012): 51–57.

16. "Final Night of Republican National Convention Draws 30.3 Million Viewers," NielsenWire. http:blog.nielsen.com/nielsenwire/politics/final-night-of-republican-convention-draws-30.3-million-viewers; "Closing Night of Democratic National Convention Draws 35.7 Million Viewers," Nielsenwire. http://blog.nielsen.com/neiielsenswire/media_entertainment/closing night of democratic-national-convention-draws-35.7-million-viewers

chapter **8**

Campaign Communications
How Much Do They Matter?

Did you know that . . .

- the Republican stereotype of Democrats as big-government, liberal do-gooders and the Democratic stereotype of Republicans as big-business, mean-spirited conservatives have existed for almost eighty years?
- most people believe that personality issues are relevant and important even though they also believe that the news media place too much emphasis on them?
- political advertising in presidential elections began in 1952, and the first negative presidential ad was run in 1964?
- about 80 percent of the political commercials that were shown or heard during the competitive stage of the 2012 Republican nomination campaign were negative?
- fact checks on political advertisements reveal a consistent pattern of exaggeration, deception, and untruths?
- Romney spent more than twice as much money on advertising than did his principal Republican rivals combined during the 2012 nomination campaign; his Super PAC also spent more than the other candidates' Super PACs combined?
- incumbents use the imagery of their public office to maximize their already large reelection advantages?
- the most influential negative ads in recent presidential election campaigns—the Willie Horton ad (1988) and the Swift Boat Veterans for Truth commercials (2004)—were sponsored by outside groups, not by the official candidate and party campaign committees?
- the Internet now contains more campaign information (and also probably more unreliable information) than any other single media source?
- Barack Obama had 32 million Facebook friends and 22 million Twitter followers by election day 2012 compared to 12 million Facebook friends and 125,000 Twitter followers for Mitt Romney?
- the Obama campaign claimed that it made direct personal contact with 150 million voters during the 2011–2012 election cycle?

Is this any way to run a democratic election?

CAMPAIGN COMMUNICATIONS AND DEMOCRATIC ELECTIONS

Campaigns matter! Although they are not the only factor that determines an election's outcome, its salient issues, the turnout and voting behavior of the citizenry, and responsive government, they are a principal one that affects these aspects of electoral politics. The communications generated in election campaigns are vehicles for educating and engaging the public and encouraging them to vote. In this sense, campaign communications can and do contribute to participatory democracy.

However, campaign communications often fall short of achieving their democratic goals. Instead of clarifying the issues for the electorate, they can obscure them; instead of turning out voters, they can turn them off; and instead of providing a realistic agenda for the new government, they can create unrealistic expectations that newly elected officials may not be able to meet. And as argued in previous chapters, they also can be an instrument by which the advantaged use their superior resources (money, organization, and leadership) to maintain or extend their political influence. In short, campaign communications can strengthen or weaken the democratic character of the system, depending on how they are conducted and what impact they have.

The key question is not whether campaign communications are necessary. Of course they are. Rather, the issue explored in this chapter is how well do they meet their intended goals of informing and motivating voters? To answer this question the chapter focuses on communications from the candidates to the electorate. The discussion begins by exploring the kinds of information that should be most helpful to the electorate in making an informed voting decision, the information most people actually receive, and the extent to which it leads to an enlightened electoral judgment. Particular emphasis is placed on new communications technologies, the impact they have had on voters, and the changes they have wrought to contemporary campaigns.

The Need To Know

show issues/ solutions, convince them they can address needs

Candidates need campaigns to accomplish their principal objective of winning office. They need to learn about public concerns and to convince voters that they will address those concerns satisfactorily. The electorate needs the campaign as well: to voice its needs, espouse its interests, and gain the information necessary to follow the political debate and render an intelligent judgment.

But what information does the electorate need? At the very least the voting public must be able to identify the candidates, understand what policies they will pursue, the kinds of judgments they are likely to make, and provide an overall assessment of how successful they are likely to be in comparison with their opponents. The promises candidates make, the positions they take, and the priorities they assert should be reasonable guides to their performance in office. If they are, then voters can hold incumbents and, to a lesser extent, their fellow partisans accountable for their decisions and actions in the next election.

Knowing what the candidates have to say is only part of the information needed; learning about the candidates themselves, their experience, their qualifications, and their personal strengths and weaknesses is also essential. New issues may arise; unexpected events may occur; and the economic, social, and political environment may change in such a way that campaign proposals, once relevant, become less so. Thus, it is important to anticipate how candidates will adapt to changing conditions and unanticipated events. Character provides an insight into work style, adaptability, and the capacity to handle new challenges.[1]

In addition to knowing about the candidates, their philosophies, and their policy positions, the electorate also needs to know whether they stand a good, fair, or poor chance of winning. For many, an intelligent voting decision includes a calculation of whether the vote will affect the outcome of the election in a meaningful way, helping someone to win or preventing someone from winning. Why waste your vote?

For some, candidate viability may be less important than registering discontent by the act of voting or, sometimes, by not voting. Some people wish to use their vote as a protest. Republicans in New Hampshire in 1992 were unhappy with President George H. W. Bush. About one-third of them demonstrated their unhappiness by voting for Pat Buchanan in the Republican primary. Realistically, Buchanan had little chance of defeating the incumbent president for the Republican nomination, but angry New Hampshire voters did not care. They were more interested in registering their discontent with Bush and his policies. Similarly, in 1996, 8.4 percent of those who voted cast ballots for H. Ross Perot, even though most of them must have known that it was very unlikely Perot would be elected president of the United States. In fact, some people may have voted for Perot because he had little or no chance of winning. Thus, there would be no danger in exercising a protest vote.[2]

The Information Game

Given the importance of a debate on the issues in a democratic electoral process, how much information should candidates provide? Should they present a general map that indicates the policy directions they hope to pursue, and should they also fill in the details of what they will or will not do?

The Policy Perspective: Generalities vs. Detail. If the amount of information most people have or are interested in having is any indication of what the public desires or is capable of learning, then candidates should be more general than specific. They should talk about their philosophies, basic goals, and priorities. But being too general also can be a disadvantage if a candidate is perceived as purposefully vague. That was the case when Republican Thomas E. Dewey ran for president in 1948. Because he had a large lead in the polls and also did not want to alienate a predominantly Democratic electorate, Dewey spoke in platitudes and generalities that seemed empty and directionless when compared with President Harry S. Truman's straight talk, specific promises, and Democratic imagery. Truman energized the Democratic faithful sufficiently by the time of the election to win a surprising victory.

The same criticism—being vague and talking in generalities—was directed at George W. Bush during his 2000 nomination and election campaigns and Mitt Romney in 2012. Barack Obama was also accused by his Democratic opponent Hillary Rodham Clinton, in 2008, of being all style and no substance. Obama responded to the criticism by detailing his policy positions on his Web site and in debates he had with the other Democratic candidates.

There is another problem with being too general. Wrong impressions can be created and unrealistic expectations can result. Candidates who are relatively new on the political scene, as Ronald Reagan and Barack Obama were when they ran for president, have to contend with the "blank sheet" problem; it increases the tendency of people to see what they want and believe what they want about a candidate with whom they are less familiar. It was this perception that led Obama to try to lower expectations immediately after the news media reported that he had won the 2008 presidential election. In a victory statement that night in Grant Park in Chicago, Obama said:

> The road ahead will be long. Our climb will be steep. We may not get there *in one year or even one term* [italics mine], but America—I have never been more hopeful than I am tonight that we will get there.[3]

people assume he will do everything

The press noted Obama's expanded timeline, but public expectations remained unrealistically high.

The Republicans' Contract with America, the platform on which House Republicans ran in 1994, is another illustration of the danger of promising unattainable goals and then refusing to compromise on them. The Contract with America listed ten proposals that Republican candidates pledged to support if elected. After winning control of Congress, many of the newly elected Republicans refused to compromise on these issues, particularly those which pertained to cuts in taxes and domestic spending. Their refusal led to a confrontation with Democratic Bill Clinton and eventually to a shutdown of government in the winter of 1995–1996 that reverberated to Republicans' political detriment.

Being too optimistic can also produce the same results, unreasonable expectations, if not met, that have an adverse political impact on the evaluation of a president's performance in office. Barack Obama's "Yes we can" optimism in some respects accentuated his failure to achieve his campaign goals of reviving the economy and unifying the country mired in a stark political divide. As a consequence, his job approval declined; his political influence waned; and his leadership image suffered during his first term in office.

Providing too much detail can also backfire. It can turn off voters who do not care and alienate those who disagree with proposed changes. It can put the candidate and, if that candidate is successful, the elected official in a position from which compromise becomes more difficult, an undesirable outcome (except perhaps to true believers) in a governmental system that divides power and requires "give and take" to find common ground and build a policy consensus.

lack of interest

Many people lack an interest in politics and their level of knowledge is extremely limited.[4] Despite their own limited knowledge, or perhaps because of it, voters want candidates to be knowledgeable and have the intellectual and experiential capacity to make good policy judgments.

The generality versus specificity dilemma often places candidates in a "dammed if you do, dammed if you don't" situation. To win their party's nomination and build their electoral coalitions, they need to make specific promises to specific groups. The members of these groups are frequently the most ideologically oriented party identifiers. Then in the general election the candidates usually have to broaden their appeal; most adopt a strategy of moving toward the center of the political spectrum in order to attract independent voters and supporters of the other party. In this situation, candidates often face a difficult juggling act, made even harder by the fact that much of it is done in full public view. Promises are recorded by the news media, inconsistencies are highlighted, and exaggerations and distortions are noted. Rhetorical and behavioral deviations from past behavior are critically assessed.

The alternative strategy of maintaining policy consistency also has its limitations. This strategy placates and energizes core supporters but does not necessarily expand them into a majority of the electorate. For candidates who emphasize ideological constancy, the key to success is maximizing partisan turnout by reinforcing the attitudes and opinions of their base. The greater the number of partisans and the deeper and broader their division from their political opponents, the more likely such a strategy will produce beneficial results for the candidates who adopt it. In contrast, the greater the number of independent voters, political moderates, and people with less interest, passion, and ideological fervor, the less likely such a strategy will work to produce a winning electoral coalition.[5]

From the perspective of the electorate, information needs vary. Within their own areas of interest and expertise, people demand and digest much more information than they do in others of peripheral interest and experience. Business executives may want detailed information on tax policy, investment incentives, and labor-management issues, but they may not have much interest in or knowledge about policies that do not have a discernible economic, social, or political impact on them. The reason candidates discuss their proposals in detail, despite much of the electorate's disinterest, is that they want to demonstrate their own competence, consistency, communication skills, and, to some extent, candor. These personal traits have become increasingly important in candidate-oriented elections. In his 1972 presidential campaign, George McGovern proposed a $1,000 grant to all poor Americans, those whose annual income was less than $12,000, but he could not explain precisely how much his plan would cost. McGovern's inability to do so led many to question his understanding of budget issues. Similarly, in 2004, when replying to criticism that he opposed supplementary military appropriations for Iraq, John Kerry said, "I actually did vote for the $87 billion dollars before I voted against it." Kerry's seemingly contradictory votes reinforced Republican allegations that he was a "flip-flopper." In September 2008 when real estate prices were falling, people were defaulting on mortgages, and the credit market was in serious difficulty, John McCain said, "the American economy is basically sound,"[6] an assertion that contrasted sharply with public perceptions at that time. In what Mitt Romney thought was an off-the-record comment, he told political contributors that 47 percent of Americans did not pay federal income tax and would not vote for him, a remark that reinforced the negative image of Romney portrayed by the Obama campaign. In short, the proposals candidates make and the arguments they present provide criteria by which voters can evaluate them—their knowledge, experience, and potential for making good policy judgments in office.

The Character Issue: Public vs. Private Behavior. In recent elections, personal character has received considerable attention; in some cases it has dominated press coverage. In the 1996 presidential election, for example, only two policy issues, the economy and taxation, were mentioned more than Clinton's character.[7]

Are character issues legitimate concerns for the electorate? Most observers believe that they are, pointing to Richard Nixon's cover-up of the Watergate break-in and the other illegal behavior he ordered or condoned, Jimmy Carter's reluctance to deal with Washington insiders or even to lobby members of Congress, Ronald Reagan's penchant for delegation without adequate supervision, Bill Clinton's lack of personal integrity and candor when responding to allegations about his political dealings as governor of Arkansas and sexual improprieties, George W. Bush's unwillingness to admit mistakes about the war in and occupation of Iraq, Barack Obama's perceived aloofness and non-emotive reactions. Character is important for several reasons. It provides an indication of how candidates, if elected, may react to unforeseen events and situations, how flexible they are likely to be, how they make decisions, and how they interact with others. It tells the electorate something about leadership skills.[8]

Overemphasizing character, however, can be dangerous as well. It draws attention from policy issues. It leads people to draw inferences about behavior that may have little or nothing to do with job performance. It attributes too much influence to personality as a driving force and not enough to other factors that affect decision making. Character-based judgments also encourage flippant, often superficial, assessments by those not trained in psychological analysis and even sometimes by those who are trained.[9]

Preoccupation with personality also can lead to unrealistic expectations, both good and bad, of what a single person can do in a large, decentralized political system. Liberals feared that Ronald Reagan's strong anticommunist views and George W. Bush's antiterrorism crusade combined with their shoot-from-the-hip rhetorical styles could plunge the country into war, whereas conservatives feared that Bill Clinton's penchant to please and Barack Obama's use of government to stimulate the economy, reform health care, and rein in business excesses would undermine the American capitalistic system. That many of these fears were not realized testifies to the constitutional, institutional, and political checks that were built into and continue to operate within the American constitutional system; that some were, particularly the wars in Afghanistan and Iraq and alleged violations of personal freedoms in combating terrorism, evidences the unilateral power of the presidency, especially during crises.

Spin: Positive vs. Negative. Candidates obviously need to make their own cases. They have to articulate reasons to vote for them and against their opponents. In doing so, candidates must state their policy positions, personal qualifications, and experience, as well as somehow getting their opponents' negatives onto the public record, whether by leaking them to the news media, mentioning them in their own campaign advertising, or referring to them in speeches, press conferences, and debates.

The electorate does need to know some of this information. People have to evaluate the strengths and weaknesses of a candidate in order to make an intelligent judgment about that candidate's suitability for the office. And as we know, the candidates themselves are not candid about their own shortcomings. Most campaigns maintain an active opposition research and rapid response operations.

Campaign Imagery

Campaign appeals can distort or clarify. In articulating messages and making appeals, candidates usually use partisan imagery. They do so to rouse the faithful, stereotype their opponents, and prime and frame the issues that will resonate the most with the electorate.

Partisan Stereotyping. Sounding a partisan refrain conjures up familiar images about the parties, past and present, both positive and negative. For Democratic candidates, the positive images relate to policies that help average Americans, particularly during hard economic times. Democratic candidates emphasize bread-and-butter issues, jobs, wages, education, and social benefits for children, struggling workers, and the elderly. They contrast their empathy for the working and middle classes with Republicans' ties to the wealthy and their interests and the GOP's indifference, even hostility, toward the less fortunate.

From the Republicans' perspective, the economic images are different. Republicans see themselves as defending the free enterprise, individual–oriented capitalist system against the Democrats' penchant for big, expensive, and invasive government and for policies that redistribute economic resources, regulate business activities, and benefit disadvantaged groups.

Social images are more complex. The Democrats stress equal opportunity and political liberty, whereas the Republicans point to personal economic initiatives and to law and order within the domestic sphere. In the national security area, the stereotypes are less distinct, although Republicans have been associated with a more ideological approach that emphasizes American exceptionalism, the imposition of democratic values on nonwestern countries and cultures, and promotion of U.S. economic and political interests abroad, while the Democrats have placed greater emphasis on pragmatic, multilateral policy approaches. They see diplomacy as the principal vehicle for dealing with international, national security issues.

Partisan stereotyping can be dangerous and misleading because it puts everyone in the same box, and it exaggerates the differences between the candidates and the parties. In the 1988 election, for example, Democratic presidential candidate Michael Dukakis was characterized by his partisan opponents as a knee-jerk liberal who released hardened criminals from jail. To support this accusation, a group opposing Dukakis aired a commercial about a Massachusetts prisoner, Willie Horton, who raped, pistol-whipped, and knifed his victims while on parole. The George H.W. Bush campaign then reinforced the distinction between Bush's tough approach to criminals and Dukakis's leniency.[10]

To offset being stereotyped as a liberal in 1992, Bill Clinton called himself a "New Democrat" and took pains to differentiate his moderate policy approach from that of his liberal Democratic predecessors. Similarly, in 2000, George W. Bush emphasized his "compassionate conservatism," highlighting the human dimension of his conservative policy views. In 2008, both candidates ran against an unpopular incumbent, George W. Bush: McCain as a Republican maverick and Obama as a change-oriented Democrat. In 2012, it was more of the same with both major party candidates attempting to stereotype their opponent while distinguishing themselves as broad, empathetic, national leaders.

In addition to personal attacks, candidates also resort to "wedge issues," which they target to particular components of their electoral coalition. In 1996, Republican Robert Dole talked about border security and legal restraints to control illegal immigration to the United States; in 2004, George W. Bush reiterated his support for a constitutional amendment that defines marriage as a heterosexual relationship; in 2008 and 2012, both candidates talked about the problem of high unemployment, the partisan policies that have contributed to it, and the actions they would take to expand the economy and create more jobs.

Partisan stereotyping can get in the way of meaningful debate. It can substitute for information, and it can unfairly typecast individuals in a manner that does not accurately reflect their values, priorities, positions, or what they would do in office. Stereotyping does not educate as much as it reinforces preconceptions, dispositions, and biases.

Experience and Incumbency. "Experience is the best teacher" is a maxim that incumbents would like voters to believe. They use their "official" imagery to compare their qualifications with those of their opponents, reminding voters what they have done for them and how they can use their influence to continue to work on their constituents' behalf.

As noted previously, being an incumbent is usually an advantage. The numbers speak for themselves. Table 8.1 notes the reelection rates for members of Congress since 1952.

Although incumbent presidents have not fared as well in reelections as members of Congress because they are subject to closer and more critical press scrutiny and a more competitive electoral environment, they still have won more often than they have lost. Of the eighteen presidents who sought reelection in the twentieth century, only five (Taft in 1912, Hoover in 1932, Ford in 1976, Carter in 1980, and George H.W. Bush in 1992) were defeated, but it also should be noted that several avoided possible defeat by choosing not to run again; no incumbent president in the twenty-first century has lost reelection. In his study of the incumbency advantage for presidents, Professor David Mayhew found that the party in power kept the presidency about two-thirds of the time when it ran an incumbent but only half the time when an incumbent was not a candidate for reelection.[11]

Why do incumbents win more than they lose? A lot has to do with their name recognition and the relatively low level of public knowledge about challengers who seek political office. Name recognition conveys a "known" quality. In general, people would rather vote for someone they have heard of than for someone about whom they know little or nothing.

Incumbents tend to be disadvantaged in only two types of situations: when bad times or multiple grievances hurt those in power, and when incumbents say or do something their constituents find very objectionable.

The incumbency advantage "unlevels" the playing field. It puts the burden on the challengers to make the case for change. Unless challengers can make that case, they are unlikely to win. To defeat an incumbent requires resources, but, as previously noted, unless challengers are independently wealthy or have considerable backing from their party, or from nonparty groups supporting them, they usually are not able to raise as much money as the incumbent. This is why those who desire an elective office try to wait until a seat is open before they seek it,[12] unless they calculate that the recognition they gain by running against an incumbent (and probably losing) will put them in real contention the next time around.

TABLE 8.1 **Congressional Reelection Rates, 1952–2012**

	House of Representatives			Senate		
	Total seeking reelection who were renominated	Defeated in general election	Percentage reelected	Total seeking reelection who were renominated	Defeated in general election	Percentage reelected
1952	380	26	93.2	29	9	69.0
1954	401	22	94.5	30	6	80.0
1956	405	16	96.0	29	4	86.2
1958	393	37	90.6	28	10	64.3
1960	399	25	93.7	29	1	96.6
1962	390	22	94.4	34	5	85.3
1964	389	45	88.4	32	4	87.5
1966	403	41	89.8	29	1	96.6
1968	404	9	97.8	24	4	83.3
1970	391	12	96.9	30	6	80.0
1972	378	13	96.6	25	5	80.0
1974	383	40	89.6	25	2	92.0
1976	381	13	96.6	25	9	64.0
1978	377	19	95.0	22	7	68.2
1980	392	31	92.1	25	9	64.0
1982	383	29	92.4	30	2	93.3
1984	408	16	96.1	29	3	89.7
1986	391	6	98.5	28	7	75.0
1988	408	6	98.5	27	4	85.2
1990	406	15	96.3	32	1	96.9
1992	349	24	93.1	27	4	85.2
1994	383	34	91.2	26	2	92.3
1996	382	21	94.5	20	1	95.0
1998	401	6	98.5	29	3	89.7
2000	400	6	98.5	29	6	79.3
2002	390	8	98.0	27	3	88.9
2004	402	7	98.3	26	1	96.2
2006	402	22	94.5	29*	6	79.3
2008	399	19	95.2	30	5	83.3
2010	398	54	86.4	25	4	84
2012	380	26	93	22	1	95.5

*Includes Joseph Lieberman, who was not renominated by the Democrats but ran as an Independent and won.

Source: Harold W. Stanley and Richard G. Niemi, *Vital Statistics on American Politics, 2009–2010*. Washington, DC: CQ Press, 2010. Updated by author.

Political Advertising

Political advertising on radio, television, and, more recently, the Internet has become the primary means of projecting images and conveying information about the candidates. The ads are a big part of the distortion problem.

Candidates and their political consultants believe they need to advertise to reach voters. They may be right, although the emphasis on personal contact and grassroots organizing has reduced the influence of generic political commercials. Technological devises, such as remote controls, TiVo and DVR, DVDs, and direct-dial movie channels, have also had an impact because they allow people to silence or avoid advertising when they watch or record their favorite programs.

Nonetheless, candidates for national office still spend the bulk of their money on political advertising, and 2012 was no exception. More than $21.1 million was spent by Republican candidates on advertising during the competitive phase of the GOP presidential nominations and another $41.2 by Super PACs supporting them during this period.[13] According the *Washington Post's* "Ad Tracker," $404 million was spent on ads supporting Obama during the entire presidential campaign ($333 million by the candidate and the rest by party and nonparty groups) on 562,664 ads; Romney and his supporters spent $492 million ($147 million by the candidate and the rest by party and nonparty groups) on 223,584 ads.[14]

Why do candidates and their consultants believe that advertising is so important and spend so much on it? The answer is that advertisements provide critical information that people need and may not get through their normal sources for news. Ads are repeated frequently, whereas news stories are not.[15] Moreover, political advertisements can be dramatic, startling, and even funny in contrast to the news that is supposed to be seriously presented, in a matter-of-fact, albeit attention-grabbing manner. Studies have shown that people actually obtain and recall more substantive information about the candidates and their policy stands from advertisements than they do from news reports.[16]

There are several reasons why ads are more effective than news reports in their informational impact on voters. They can prime the electorate by drawing attention to issues or candidate traits and behavior, frame the voting decision by providing criteria by which candidates and their parties can be evaluated, and persuade voters by their argumentation, testimonials, and emotive content. Almost all advertising scripts have been pretested to find out which words and pictures best evoke the desired response. And ads target their audience more than broadcast journalists can target theirs. Most ads have a simple message. There is often little subtlety in the ads, and the point is usually hammered home again and again. They usually use emotion to reinforce the message.

The effects of advertising are often heightened by referring to stories already in the news. In fact, one feature of the 2012 presidential ads was their use of news reports by well known television anchors prominently featured in the ad. In the 2012 Republican nomination contest, Mitt Romney ran a commercial that included Tom Brokaw's report from January 21, 1997, that the House of Representatives voted overwhelmingly to sanction Speaker Newt Gingrich for ethics violations. This particular Romney ad was shown 2,225 times in the 5 days leading up to the Florida primary, a primary in which Romney defeated Gingrich by 14 percent.

News reports add credibility and objectivity. They also can leave the impression that the reporter concurs in the message of the ad and may even endorse the candidate that sponsored it. Not only do political commercials contain news items, but the ads themselves can become newsworthy if they are controversial. Negative ads fit this category more than positive ones. Political scientist John G. Geer contends that the increased attention given to negative advertising in contemporary presidential campaigns is a primary reason why the proportion of negative political commercials has gotten larger. He cites the anti-Kerry ads sponsored by the Swift Boat Veterans for Truth as an illustration. Less than 1 percent of the public actually saw these ads on the few media markets on which they were aired but 80 percent of Americans said that they had heard about the ads within one month of their showing, most from news stories.[17]

And the negativity has continued, with a big spike in 2008 and another in 2012. In the 2008 presidential nominations, political scientist Darrell M. West found that " . . . 61 percent of the . . . Democratic ads were negative, compared with 43 percent of the Republican ads";[18] in 2012, the *Washington Post* reported that over two-thirds of the advertising during the Republican nomination process was negative.[19]

In the general election it was more of the same, only worse. Eighty-two percent of the ads supporting Obama and 91 percent of those supporting Romney were negative.[20]

The public also perceives that the ads have become increasingly confrontational (as indicated in Table 8.2) and has penalized some candidates for being too negative. When Robert Dole raised character issues about President Bill Clinton in his 1996 election advertising, Dole's poll ratings actually declined, as did Richard Gephardt's and Howard Dean's after a series of negative ads they aired against each other prior to the 2004 Iowa caucuses. Sensitive to an adverse public reaction, Mitt Romney withdrew negative ads in Pennsylvania against Rick Santorum after his opponent's daughter was hospitalized and Santorum stopped campaigning to be with her.

The increase in negativity prompted campaign reformers to include a "stand by your ad" provision in the 2002 Bipartisan Campaign Reform Act that requires candidates to take responsibility for the ads their campaign sponsored. The framers of the law assumed that the provision would result in fewer false and vicious claims made in the ads, but it has not done so. In fact, the legalization of Super PACs has not only contributed to the increased negativity, but it has also allowed candidates who benefit from it to avoid taking responsibility.[21]

TABLE 8.2	**Public Perceptions of Negativity in Presidential Elections, 1996–2012**

Question: Compared to past presidential elections, would you say there was MORE mudslinging or negative campaigning in this campaign or LESS mudslinging or negative campaigning in this campaign?

	1996	2000	2004	2008	2012
More	49	34	72	54	68
Less	36	46	14	27	19
Same (volunteered response)	12	16	12	16	11
Don't know/refused	3	4	2	3	2

Source: Pew Research Center for the People and the Press, "Low Marks for the 2012 Election," November 15, 2012. http://www.people-press.org/2012/11/15/low-marks-for-the-2012-election/ ; Pew Research Center for the People and the Press, "High Marks for the Campaign; A High Bar for Obama," November 13, 2008, http://people-press.org/report/471/high-bar-for-obama.

Political professionals, however, believe negative ads work. They generally subscribe to the view that the more negatives a candidates has, the less likely that the candidate will be elected.[22] Most political scientists agree. Although a study based on experimental research indicated that negative messages can turn off voters, thereby decreasing turnout and increasing cynicism,[23] most students of political advertising think these ads attract attention, provide information, and energize voters, specifically strong partisans who are energized by the criticism of their opponents.[24] The polarized political environment has undoubtedly contributed as well.

The effect of the ads, both positive and negative, is short-lived, however. Although ads can have a strong impact on voter preferences, their content fades quickly from viewers' and listeners' memories, a reason that advertisers use repetition and reinforcement to extend the life and influence of their messages.[25]

Not surprisingly, the public claims that advertising, pro or con, does not help them make their voting decisions. In polls taken by the Pew Research Center for the People and the Press following presidential elections since 1992, more than two-thirds of the respondents said that candidate commercials were not too helpful or helpful at all in deciding how to vote.[26]

Everyone seems to agree that false, inaccurate, and deceptive ads, positive or negative, are not helpful. They confuse and misinform voters.

COMMUNICATION DISTORTION

If advertisements mislead the public, which many scholars claim that they do, should they be monitored and, if so, by whom? Some countries do not allow political advertising. Whether such a prohibition is good or bad is probably

[handwritten: can't violate constitutional rights]

immaterial in the United States because the First Amendment to the U.S. Constitution protects a candidate's right to free speech. But it does not necessarily follow that candidates should be free to say or claim anything they want under the banner of constitutionally protected speech. Just as obscenity is not protected by the First Amendment, neither is libel nor slander. However, the Supreme Court has also made it extremely difficult for public officials to demonstrate that they have been libeled or slandered by the news media. Falsehood alone is a necessary but not sufficient condition. In addition, malice also has to be proven.[27]

Short of suing for libel and slander, what else can be done to promote and police truth in political advertising? Perhaps the regulations for commercial advertising, which make advertisers liable for the false claims of their products and give an independent regulatory body, the Federal Trade Commission, authority to prescribe penalties, could be applied to politics. However, it might be very difficult to prove an ad false if it presents only one side of the story.

What about the private sector? Should the news media monitor the ads *[handwritten: they have no reason to]* from which they profit? They are not exactly the most expert or impartial judges. Nonetheless, some of the major news sources have begun to pay attention to the content of the ads with fact checks of their own. The problem, however, is that they treat these checks as a single news item while the ads continue to appear and reappear. Besides, people tend to remember the point of the ad more than they do the criticism of its factual content.[28]

"Fact checks" are still important, however, because they call attention to false claims and charges and help to correct perceptions that the public may develop about candidates and their issue positions. They may also encourage ad designers to be more careful about what they say, although there is not a lot of hard evidence that they have accomplished this objective.[29] The Annenberg Public Policy Center (APPC) at the University of Pennsylvania operates two Web sites that evaluate the accuracy and veracity of political advertising, www .factcheck.org and www.flackcheck.org. The latter contains text and videos of misleading ads as well as parodies of commercials on historic presidential elections. *[handwritten: not as influential as the ads though]*

In 2012, the Annenberg Public Policy Center reported that in the first three months of the Republican nomination campaign, more than half the ads sponsored by candidate-oriented Super PACs (costing $23.3 million) contained deception or misleading claims of one type or another, with the Restore Our Future, a Super PAC supporting Mitt Romney's candidacy, airing and spending the most.[30] Throughout the 2012 campaign, APPC's Web site, factcheck.org, highlighted misleading ads by the major party candidates as well as party and nonparty groups, along with misleading and incorrect statements by the candidates in their speeches and debates.[31]

Checks on advertising also come from opposition candidates as well as private citizens. Nancy Reagan strongly objected to a 1996 Bill Clinton ad on gun control that contained footage from the assassination attempt on her husband.

The Clinton campaign removed the objectionable footage from the ad, but not before it had aired the commercial many times. In 2004, when an ad for George W. Bush contained two seconds of footage from Ground Zero at New York City's World Trade Center in which fire personnel were seen carrying a stretcher, presumably which held human remains draped in an American flag, families of the victims protested and subsequent Bush commercials omitted the scene, but continued to show Ground Zero and the president's actions after the tragedy.[32]

THE NEW COMMUNICATIONS TECHNOLOGY

Messaging and Targeting

One of the major changes in political campaigns today has been their increasing professionalization. Political consultants, many of whom operate profit-making businesses, have replaced party pros and their precinct captains as the new message makers and marketers. Practically every aspect of modern campaigning from the public opinion polling to the focus group reactions to the pretested speeches, to staging events and ensuring responsive audiences at them is now planned and orchestrated by experts in political communication.

The bookends of the campaign are public opinion polls. Surveys are used to find out what is on the public's mind; the initial perceptions of the candidates, parties, and issues; and the salient issues for groups within and outside the party's electoral coalition. Armed with this knowledge, campaign planners design their basic message strategy, replete with issue appeals and candidate imagery, tailored for and targeted to specific electoral constituencies.

The basic rule of thumb is to be careful. Spontaneity is discouraged. Major ideas and policy proposals are pretested in focus groups to gauge reactions and see which words and phrases have the greatest impact, both positive and negative. After the message is designed and tested, it is directed toward people who fit into the intended group. There used to be four principal targeting mechanisms: telephone solicitation, direct mail, radio, and broadcast, cable, and local television. Now, with the Internet and apps, there are more.

The targeting mechanism is used in conjunction with large databases that the parties, consultants, and candidates have assembled. Without knowing it, people become part of these data sets when they make a contribution, write a letter, respond to a query, subscribe to a politically oriented publication or Web site, or provide their cell phone number or e-mail address to a candidate, party, or nonparty group. Armed with those data, the campaign compartmentalizes and targets its messages to those who will find them most salient and appealing.

Targeting reduces scope of information about the candidates that people receive. Campaign handlers justify their narrowing of issue appeals and sometimes even candidate imagery on the grounds that people in the targeted group would be less interested in other information, become confused by it, or, worst yet, object to it. Voters may not realize the limited breadth of information they receive.

Nor does the press bring a lot of attention to consistent messaging, focusing instead on new candidate positions, inconsistent statements and stands, and faux pas. The more routine and expected the communication, the less newsworthy it is considered to be. The more circumscribed the campaign debate, the less it meets the democratic criteria of an informed electorate for making an enlightened judgment.

The Internet

The use of the Internet as a communication vehicle began in the 1990s. The Clinton-Gore campaign communicated internally via e-mail, keeping its staff informed on policy and political matters. In 1993, the White House launched its first Web site, as did the Congress. By 1994 some candidates running in the midterm elections and most major news outlets had Web sites on which they presented videos of the campaign, poll data, as well as news and other items. In the ensuing years, using the Internet evolved from occasional outreach efforts designed to gain attention and reach a relatively small number of people to a major communications technology to get the message out, maintain continuous contact, solicit donations, recruit volunteers, build crowds for campaign events, energize supporters, and turn out voters.

The increase in campaign-related information online has paralleled the growth of Internet users. The Pew Internet and American Life Project reported that in 2002 only 7 percent of all adults used the Internet as a major source of campaign news; that percentage has steadily increased. During the 2010 midterm elections, about one-quarter of the population said that they turned to the Internet for their principal source of campaign news; in 2012, 47 percent cited it as the major source for election news.[33]

Not only do more people go online, but they do so in a more proactive way. Pew reported that about 22 percent of online users accessed a social networking site for political purposes to see how their friends were voting, to get information about the candidates and their campaigns, or to post political content of their own.[34]

Age, education, and, to a lesser extent, gender differentiate social network users, with the youngest and better-educated using them more. Men also tend to frequent such sites more than women. Ethnicity, income level, and partisanship do not distinguish Internet users as much.[35]

BOX 8.1   A Brief History of Online Presidential Campaigning

John McCain was the first candidate for a major party's presidential nomination to solicit contributions on the Internet. In 2000, he raised $5 million from his Web site, most of it following his surprise victory over George W. Bush in the New Hampshire primary.[36] But McCain's effort paled in comparison to Democrat Howard Dean's four years later. Joe Trippi, Dean's campaign manager, created a campaign blog, which thousands accessed and on which he and other campaign staff, including the candidate himself, regularly communicated. Dean raised $27 million online, much of it in the form of small contributions.[37] The press took notice. More than 500,000 people signed up on Dean's Web site, but his campaign's failure to turn out these online backers in Iowa and New Hampshire cast doubts on how effective the Internet could be as a strategic link between the campaign organization and the electorate. In 2008, the Obama campaign eliminated those doubts.

Obama's Web operation began even before his official declaration of candidacy. Moved by his keynote address to the 2004 Democratic National Convention, several college students had already set up Obama blogs to pass the word about him and drum up support for a potential presidential run. Obama's Internet advisers took advantage of these blogs, encouraged others to start their own, and eventually incorporated the most successful ones into the campaign's Web operation.

Headed by Chris Hughes, one of the cofounders of Facebook, Joe Rospars, an Internet consultant who had worked on Howard Dean's campaign in 2004, and several others with experience in online technology, the Obama campaign hired programmers, statisticians, and bloggers, set up a multipurposed, user-friendly site, and encouraged those who accessed it to start their own online discussion groups, network with their friends, contribute money, and disseminate information.

The campaign acquired a large database of e-mail and snail mail addresses, cell phone numbers, and other information which was not only used by campaign staff but made available to volunteers to spread the word online, solicit funds, and expand the pool of potential supporters. The Obama team also took advantage of the Web site You Tube for what amounted to free video advertising on which repeated showings of the candidate's speeches, interviews, and public events could be seen. Obama's speech on race, for example, given after the incendiary remarks of his Chicago pastor, Rev. Jeremiah Wright, was viewed by 4 million on television but 6.7 million on You Tube.[38]

Obama's reelection campaign designed and staffed an even more sophisticated Internet operation. The president's announcement that he was running for reelection was posted on Twitter, e-mailed to online electoral supporters, and seen, heard, or reported on all the major news media networks and Web sites. A new group called Technology for Obama, co-chaired by the founders of Facebook, Napster, LinkedIn, Yelp, and Craigslist was created to raise money, identify, and corral Internet experts to collect, assemble, and consolidate data, develop codes for using the data, and design an innovative marketing system to reach out to a broad electoral base. Facebook "friends" of Obama were encouraged to visit his Web site, barackobama.com, through Facebook, a site that had quadrupled in users since the 2008 election, thereby giving the campaign access to the personal information they stored on their Facebook page as well as information about their friends. The Obama campaign Web site was also redesigned to make it more adaptable for mobile use.

The campaign proceeded to assemble a huge data bank with the new Facebook information, as well as data from Vote Builder, a source that contained the voting history of millions of people, their partisan allegiances and registration information, plus information from the campaign's previous canvassing, turnout, and Internet operations. The data were consolidated and used to personalize campaign appeals and direct them to targeted groups of voters. The campaign also used the new mobile technology to send messages directly to cell phones, smartphones, and other mobile devices.

The scope of the operation and the reach of the campaign were impressive. By election day 2012, Obama had over 32 million "friends" on Facebook compared to about 2 million four years earlier. He had 22 million followers on Twitter and 2 million on Google. The campaign had over 350,000 events organized online via one of its Web site interactive tools, Dashboard. It raised more than $500 million online from 4.4 million individual donors.[39]

Cognizant of the Democrats' lead in Internet communications, the GOP had launched its own updated Web operation following the 2008 elections. By 2010, Republicans were also using social networking, including Facebook, Twitter, and You Tube, to extend their partisan appeal. Mitt Romney spent about 10 percent of his 2012 nomination budget on Internet-related activities including advertising, but his general election operation paled by comparison to Obama's. Romney had 12 million Facebook friends, 125,000 Twitter followers, and 1 million on Google.[40]

From the perspective of the electoral process, the reach of the new technology, the Internet and its interactive potential and text messaging, has contributed to the democratic character of elections by informing and energizing the electorate. The Internet extends political debate to more people, especially to younger generations who had not been as heavily involved in national politics as their elders.

The Internet facilitates participation in various ways, from soliciting contributions, to volunteering time and expertise, to personal communication with friends and associates. It has increased the amount of information that is easily accessible to online users. Campaigns maintain Web sites which contain biographical information, issue positions, speeches and ads, favorable news commentary, responses to criticism, campaign schedules and events, as well as data and instructional material that can be used for canvassing, on-the-ground organizing, and registration and voter turnout efforts. The Internet has been a vehicle for internal communications among staffers and volunteers, for spreading the word and debating policy issues, and for conveying appeals to specific groups of voters. It has encouraged participation in the electoral process.[41] That's good!

The Internet has the potential to reverse some of the previous distortions of campaign communication. The accessibility and variety of news outlets as well as the interaction it encourages on a personal level allows the online public to be as knowledgeable as it desires to be, to gain information from impartial as well as partisan sources. But it also has the potential to create greater distortions. Rumors spread rapidly, as does misinformation, which can circulate on the Web for years, increasing the difficulty of correcting these misperceptions and false claims and allegations. If people choose to maintain their beliefs despite evidence that those beliefs are incorrect, there is little a campaign can do. Finally, although the Internet has become increasingly available to people across the country, it is estimated that 22 percent of Americans still do not use it.[42] There are, of course, other problems. Security can be breached, and campaign sites have been invaded. In 2008, the FBI informed both the McCain and Obama campaigns that their Web sites had been hacked by a foreign source and information from their database may have been compromised. With the help of government experts and private companies specializing in computer security, both campaigns added protection to their Web sites and their data sets.

Nonetheless, if the Internet facilitates communication; if it better informs the electorate; if it brings more people into the campaign and turns out more voters; and if it provides additional opportunities for candidates, parties, and nonparty groups to discuss the issues at greater length and depth, then the democracy is being well served and the election process has been improved.

SUMMARY: CAMPAIGN COMMUNICATION DILEMMAS IN A NUTSHELL

Political campaigns are part and parcel of a democratic electoral process. They are important for several reasons. They enable candidates to interact with the electorate, hear people's concerns, and respond to them. They also give candidates a podium from which to express their views, demonstrate their knowledge, articulate their policy decisions, and appeal to voters. For political parties and nonparty groups, campaign communications provide them with opportunities to present their case, educate and energize their base, and persuade the electorate. For the citizenry, campaigns are an important source of information; they provide voters with a frame of reference and criteria for evaluating the candidates, parties, and policy positions, all essential for making enlightened voting judgments.

The communications dilemmas stem from conflicting candidate and voter needs and goals. A candidate's goal to win, a party's need to defend its nominees and policy positions, and nonparty groups' promotion of their own special interests naturally shape the scope, content, and spin of the information they provide. What the candidates and their supporters consider their most effective issues are not necessarily the country's most salient problems or those with which government can deal effectively. Partial perspectives, not comprehensive ones, are presented. The voters are left with an incomplete, sometimes inaccurate, and occasionally irrelevant picture, and one in which the negatives often outweigh the positives. Is it any wonder that people are suspicious of politicians, parties, and special interest groups and the influence they exercise over government and public policy?

Campaigns distort information. Partisan appeals conjure up familiar stereotypes by which individuals and parties are categorized, sometimes unfairly, and almost always too simplistically. Incumbent imagery is used to buttress the resources and recognition that already give those in office an immense advantage when they run for reelection. Symbols, code words, and sound bites often substitute for argument and debate. Messages are more effectively targeted and increasingly personalized with modern computer-based marketing techniques to rally the faithful, convince the undecided, and try to inform less attentive, interested, and knowledgeable voters.

Personality traits and wedge issues receive disproportionate attention, even though those traits and issues may not be essential or relevant for job performance or public policy decision making. For those who see election to high public office as a position of trust, respect, and great moral and ethical responsibility, having the proper virtues and leading the exemplary life are essential qualifications. For those who have a results-oriented view of public service and who are more interested in policymaking than personal modeling, rhetorical, and leadership skills are critical.

All of the hype and hoopla and all of the promises and images can create unrealistic expectations that, if not met, can contribute to mistrust of politicians, apathy toward the elective process, and cynicism about government. Nonetheless, there have been some hopeful developments. Campaign communications are being increasingly evaluated for their truthfulness by partisan and nonpartisan groups and the news media. Candidates have to acknowledge that they approve their campaign's ads, but not those of Super PACs and other groups that support them. Candidates are using the Internet to reach a broader electorate. Newer, quicker, cheaper, and more direct communications have the potential to make elections more democratic by improving the amount and accessibility of information available to voters. That's the good news. The bad news is that there continues to be exaggeration and deception, emotionally-charged speech and argumentation, and increasing negativity.

Nonetheless, the electorate continues to believe that it has sufficient knowledge about the candidates, parties, and issues to make an informed judgment. If this belief accords with reality, then campaigns are serving their principal functions to inform, energize, and mobilize voters, as well as guide government officials in the agendas they pursue and the decisions they make after the election. If voters lack the information they need, or if that information is inaccurate, incomplete, or irrelevant, then the democracy is not being well served.

There is another problem. It relates to the electorate's processing of information. If the voters' judgments are superficial, if they are driven more by emotion than reason, if they are made on the basis of beliefs that are maintained despite reliable information to the contrary, then citizens are not meeting **their** obligations to make enlightened voting decisions. A close relationship between knowledge and judgment is a vital ingredient for a successful democratic election.

[handwritten note: citizens not fulfilling duty as responsible voters]

Now It's Your Turn

Discussion Questions

1. Is information about personal behavior outside of public office a relevant consideration for election to public office?

2. Does partisan stereotyping add to or detract from an informed voting decision, particularly for voters who are less attentive to the candidates, their parties, and their policy positions?

3. Have the growth of issue advocacy and the activities of nonparty groups, especially Super PACs, in political campaigns resulted in a more informed electorate or one that is more subject to manipulation by political professionals?

4. Should the federal government regulate truth in political advertising as it does in commercial advertising?

5. Is the incumbency advantage undemocratic? Does it facilitate or impede the operation of government?

6. Has the Internet on balance had a positive or negative affect on electioneering, the electorate, and election outcomes?

Topics for Debate

Challenge or defend the following statements:

- Candidates should be required to be truthful in their political advertisements, on their Web sites, in their speeches, statements, and interviews, and be disqualified if they are not.
- The government should establish a nonpartisan, independent agency to monitor and evaluate campaign communications on the basis of their accuracy, veracity, and relevance.
- Candidates who are the object of negative ads should be allowed to respond to the charges in those ads at the expense of the candidate, party, or group who sponsored them.
- All polling should be conducted online so everyone has a better opportunity to participate.
- The incumbent advantage is harmful to a democratic electoral process and should be modified by term limits or in some other way.

Exercises

1. A new federal agency has been established to monitor, and, if need be, regulate political communications. You have been asked to develop a mission statement for this agency. In your statement indicate the principal goals of the agency, the methods you suggest for monitoring communications, and the kinds of activities that should be regulated.

2. Assume that you have just been assigned by your local newspaper, television station, or news Web site to be its campaign monitor. Over the course of the election, describe the scope and content of the advertising of the major party candidates vying for the same position. Which of their advertisements were most effective and why? Did the ads seem to make a difference in the outcome of the vote?

3. You have just been appointed Internet coordinator for your candidate's campaign. Write a memo to your candidate indicating the various ways in which the Internet could be used to benefit the campaign, and also warn the candidate of its potential dangers and how to reduce or eliminate them.

INTERNET RESOURCES

Most of the sites for Chapter 7 are applicable for campaign communications as well. In addition, the offices of incumbents running for reelection should be useful for monitoring their campaign activities or linking to their campaign Web sites. For federal officials, begin with their institution:

- House of Representatives: www.house.gov
- Senate: www.senate.gov
- White House: www.whitehouse.gov

  All candidates and their campaigns should be accessible through their parties.

  Listed below are a few additional sites on the media:

- Accuracy in Media: www.aim.org

  Conservative organization that monitors liberal bias in the press.

- Center for Media and Public Affairs: www.cmpa.com

  The best single source for evaluating the content and spin of news stories on the three major broadcast networks.

- Factcheck: www.factcheck.org

  Monitors campaign statements and advertisements; site run by the Annenberg Public Policy Center at the University of Pennsylvania.

- Flackcheck.org. wwwflackcheck.org

  A site that shows deceptions, exaggerations, and false claims of political advertising through parody and humor. Also operated by the Annenberg Public Policy Center at the University of Pennsylvania.

- Pew Internet and American Life Project: pewinternet.org

  A site run by the Pew Research Center that examines Internet usage.

- Pew Research Center for the People and the Press: http://people-press.org/

  Independent opinion research group that surveys attitudes toward the press, politics, and public policy issues.

- Project for Excellent in Journalism: www.journalism.org

  Analyzes campaign coverage from print and electronic sources and evaluates that coverage on the basis of its content, themes, spin, and strengths and weaknesses; part of the Pew Research Center.

SELECTED READINGS

Brader, Ted. "Striking a Responsive Cord: How Political Ads Motivate and Persuade Voters by Appealing to Emotions." *American Journal of Political Science* 49 (April 2005): 388–405.

Coleman, Stephen, and Jay G. Blumler. *The Internet and Democratic Citizenship: Theory, Practice, and Policy*. Cambridge, England: Cambridge University Press, 2009.

Denton, Robert E., ed. *The 2012 Presidential Campaign: A Communication Perspective*. Lanham, MD: Rowman & Littlefield, 2013.

Franz, Michael M., Paul B. Freedman, Kenneth M. Goldstein, and Travis N. Ridout. *Campaign Advertising and American Democracy*. Philadelphia, PA: Temple University Press, 2008.

Geer, John G. *In Defense of Negativity: Attack Ads in Presidential Campaigns*. Chicago, IL: University of Chicago Press, 2006.

—. "The News Media and the Rise of Negativity in Presidential Campaigns." *PS: Political Science and Politics* 45 (July 2012): 422–427.

Haynes, Audrey A., and Brian Pitts. "Making an Impression: New Media in 2008 Presidential Nomination Campaigns." *PS: Political Science and Politics* 42 (January 2009): 53–58.

Huber, Gregory, and Kevin Arceneaux. "Uncovering the Persuasive Effects of Presidential Advertising." *American Journal of Political Science* 51 (October 2007): 957–977.

Issenberg, Sasha. *The Victory Lab: The Secret Science of Winning Campaigns*. New York, NY: Random House, 2013.

Jamieson, Kathleen Hall. *Dirty Politics: Deception, Distraction, and Democracy*. New York, NY: Oxford University Press, 1996.

—. *Packaging the Presidency: A History and Criticism of Presidential Campaign Advertising*. New York, NY: Oxford University Press, 1996.

Lau, Richard R., and David P. Redlawski. *How Voters Decide: Information Processing during Election Campaigns*. New York, NY: Cambridge University Press, 2006.

Lawson-Borders, Gracie, and Rita Kirk. "Blogs in Campaign Communication." *American Behavioral Scientist* 49 (2005): 548–559.

Lupia, Arthur, and Matthew McCubbins. *The Democratic Dilemma: Can Citizens Learn What They Need to Know?* New York, NY: Cambridge University Press, 1998.

Miller, Claire Cain. "How Obama's Internet Campaign Changed Politics." *New York Times*, November 7, 2008. http://bits.blogs.nytimes.com/2008/11/07/how-obamas-internet-campaign-changed-politics.

Smith, Aaron. "The Internet's Role in Campaign 2008." Pew Internet and American Life Project, April 15, 2009. http://pewresearch.org/pubs/1192/internet-politics-campaign-2008.

Troy, Gil. *See How They Ran: The Changing Role of the Presidential Candidate.* New York, NY: Free Press, 1991.

West, Darrell M. *Air Wars: Television Advertsing and Social Media in Election Campaigns 1952–2012.* 6th ed. Los Angeles, CA: Sage/CQ Press, 2013.

—. "A Report on the 2008 Presidential Nomination Ads: Ads More Negative than Previous Years." Brookings Institution, October 18, 2009. www.brookings.edu/papers/2008/0630_campaignads_west.aspx

NOTES

1. There is no one right way to adapt to change. From the perspective of those who hold certain policy positions paramount, the candidates' consistency and determination to pursue their policy goals despite situational changes may be critical criteria in their evaluation. George W. Bush's conservative views and his antiterrorism policies, especially the war in Iraq, were seen by those of a similar political persuasion as strength. Others less happy with Bush's policies and his unwillingness to change them despite the human and material costs of the war saw his actions as weakness, an inflexibility to adjust to changing circumstances and information. In contrast, Bill Clinton's and Barack Obama's adaptability, their willingness to compromise in the light of opposition to many of their domestic policy proposals, was seen as a strength by those who wanted results—the half-a-loaf is better than no-loaf crowd—but a weakness by those who didn't know where they stood, what they believed, and what they would do next. These critics found them unprincipled, and they found that unnerving.

2. In many nomination processes, unhappiness with a front-runner contributes to voting for an opponent even though that person has little chance of winning.

3. "President-elect Obama's Grant Park speech," *Chicago Sun-Times,* November 5, 2008. http://blogs.suntimes.com/sweet/2008/11/obamas_grant_park_speech.html

4. A recent survey by the Annenberg Public Policy Center on the Constitution found that only 38 percent could identify all three branches of government; a third could not correctly name any of them. "New Annenberg Survey Asks: How Well Do Americans Understand the Constitution?" The Annenberg Public Policy Center, September 16, 2011. www.annenberg-publicpolicycenter.org

5. More voters identify themselves as independents than vote independently. In 2012, about 40 percent of the people indicated that they were independents but analysts who advised the campaigns believed that most of them leaned in a partisan direction. As a consequence, both Republican and Democratic presidential candidates adopted a get-out-the-base strategy in which they magnified their partisan appeal.

6. "Our economy, I think, still, the fundamentals of our economy are strong." John McCain, speech in Jacksonville, Florida, September 15, 2008 as quoted in Sam Stein, "McCain On 'Black Monday': Fundamentals of Our Economy Are Still Strong," *Huffington Post,* September 15, 2008. http://www.huffingtonpost.com/2008/09/15/mccain-fundamentals-of-th_n_126445.html

7. "Campaign '96 Final: How TV News Covered the General Election," *Media Monitor* 10 (November/December 1996): 3.

8. Which of these traits is most relevant to the voting decision varies, however. Some are endemic to the job, whereas others are important because of the times or the frailties of the previous president.

9. Perhaps the most flagrant so-called personality analysis of a candidate occurred during the 1964 presidential election. *FACT* magazine sent a letter and survey to the more than twelve thousand members of the American Psychiatric Association, asking them whether Republican Barry Goldwater was psychologically fit to serve as president. Approximately 19 percent of the psychiatrists responded, with two out of three saying "no." The magazine not only cited the psychiatrists' responses as evidence of Goldwater's unfitness for the presidency, but it also published parts of their comments, editing out some of the qualifying statements that the psychiatrists had included in their responses. Groups such as the American Medical Association and journals such as the *American Journal of Psychiatry* quickly criticized the study as bogus medical science. Warren Boroson, "What Psychiatrists Say about Goldwater," *FACT* 4 (September/October 1964): 24–64.

10. The most potent of the George H. W. Bush crime ads, entitled "Revolving Door," pictured prisoners walking through a revolving door while an announcer said: "As governor, Michael Dukakis vetoed mandatory sentences for drug dealers. He vetoed the death penalty. His revolving-door policy gave weekend furloughs to first-degree murderers not eligible for parole. While out, many committed other crimes like kidnapping and rape. And many are still at large. Now Michael Dukakis says he wants to do for America what he's done for Massachusetts. America can't afford the risk." L. Patrick Devlin, "Contrasts in Presidential Campaign Commercials of 1988," *American Behavioral Scientist* 32 (March/April 1989): 389.

11. David R. Mayhew, "Incumbency Advantage in U.S. Presidential Elections: The Historical Record," *Political Science Quarterly* 123 (Summer 2008): 201–228.

12. One principal reason that many prominent partisans choose not to seek their party's nomination is the challenge they would face in running against an incumbent. In 2012, Republicans Haley Barbour, Chris Christie, Mitch Daniels, James DeMint, Mike Huckabee, Sarah Palin, David Petraeus, Marco Rubio, and John Thune all decided not to seek their party's nomination even though the principal frontrunner, Mitt Romney was viewed as vulnerable.

13. "Mad Money: TV Ads in the 2012 Campaign," *Washington Post.* http://www.washingtonpost.com/wp-srv/special/politics/track-presidential-campaign-ads-2012/?tid=rr_mod

14. Ibid.

15. The principal exceptions are the 24–7 news stations and channels that inevitably repeat their top stories but not as frequently as paid advertising.

16. Thomas E. Patterson and Robert McClure, *The Unseeing Eye* (New York, NY: Putnam, 1976), 58; and Craig Leonard Brians and Martin P. Wattenberg, "Comparing Issue Knowledge and Salience: Comparing Reception from TV Commercials, TV News, and Newspapers," *American Journal of Political Science,* 40 (February 1996): 172–193.

17. John G. Geer, "The News Media and the Rise of Negativity in Presidential Campaigns," *PS: Political Science and Politics,* 45 (July 2012): 422–427.

18. During the 2007–2008 election cycle, only 31 percent of ads by Democratic presidential aspirants and 36 of Republican ones were negative. Darrell M. West, "A Report on the 2008 Presidential Nomination Ads: Ads More Negative than Previous Years," Brookings Institution, July 2, 2008. www.brookings.edu/papers/2008/0630_campaigns_west.aspx

19. "Mad Money: TV Ads in the 2012 Presidential Campaign," *Washington Post.* http://www.washingtonpost.com/wp-srv/special/politics/track-presidential-campaign-ads-2012/

20. Ibid.

21. Super PACs cannot spend money "in concert or cooperation with, or at the request or suggestion of, a candidate, the candidate's campaign or a political party"; a candidate cannot accept responsibility for it.

22. The proposition that the greater the negatives about a candidate, the less likely that candidate is to win was advanced by Republican strategist Lee Atwater, who directed the George H. W. Bush campaign in 1988; see Thomas B. Edsall, "Why Bush Accentuates the Negative," *Washington Post,* October 2, 1988, sec. C.

23. Stephen Ansolabehere and Shanto Iyengar, *Going Negative: How Political Advertisements Shrink and Polarize the Electorate* (New York, NY: Free Press, 1995), 141–142.

24. Brians and Wattenberg, "Comparing Issue Knowledge and Salience." See also Stephen Ansolabehere, Shanto Iyengar, and Adam Simon, "Replicating Experiments Using Aggregate and Survey Data: The Case of Negative Advertising and Turnout," *American Political Science Review* 93 (December 1999): 901–909.

25. Alan S. Gerber, James G. Gimpel, Donald P. Green, and Daron R. Shaw, "How Large and Long-lasting Are the Persuasive Effects of Television Campaign Ads? Results from a Randomized Field Experiment," *American Political Science Review,* 105 (February 2011): 135–150.

26. Pew Research Center for the People and the Press, "Low Marks for the 2012 Election," November 15, 2012. http://www.people-press.org/2012/11/15/low-marks-for-the-2012-election/ 2012.); "High Marks for the Campaign, a High Bar for Obama," Pew Research Center for the People and the Press, November 13, 2008. http://www.people-press.org/2008/11/13/section-3-a-new-political-landscape

27. To demonstrate libel or slander, government officials and others deemed public figures must not only prove that the news item or advertising was false but also that it was published with malicious intent. The latter is very difficult to prove. See *New York Times Co. v. Sullivan,* 376 U.S. 254 (1964).

28. Stephen Ansolabehere and Shanto Iyengar, *Going Negative: How Campaign Ads Shrink and Polarize the Electorate* (New York, NY: Free Press, 1996).

29. Of the political consultants surveyed, 56 percent indicated that they believed ad watches (that is, fact checking by journalists) have made campaigns more careful about the content of their ads. Pew Research Center for the People and the Press, "Don't Blame Us," June 17, 1998, question 17, http://people-press.org/report/86/.

30. "APPC calculates dollars spent by four highest spending third party groups on deceptive TV ads attacking or supporting Republican presidential contenders," Annenberg Public Policy Center, Press Release, April 27, 2012. http://www.annenbergpublicpolicycenter.org/NewsFilter .aspx?mySubType=PressRelease&

31. For false claims and accusation in the 2012 presidential campaign, see "Whoppers of 2012, Final Edition," factcheck.org. www.factcheck.org/2012/10/whoppers-of-2012-final-edition

32. Devlin, "Contrasts in Presidential Campaign Commercials of 2004," 282.

33. "Low Marks for the 2012 Election," Pew Research Center for the People and the Press, November 15, 2012, http://www.people-press.org/2012/11/15/low-marks-for-the-2012-election;"The Internet and Campaign 2010," Pew Internet and American Life Project, May 17, 2011. www.pewinternet.org/Reports/2011/The-Internet-and-Campaign-2010

34. "Post-election Survey," Pew Internet and American Life Project, November–December 2008. www.perinternet.org/PPF/r/272/report_display.asp

35. "The Internet and Campaign 2010," Pew Internet and American Life Project, May 17, 2011. www.pewinternet.org/Reports/2011/The-Internet-and-Campaign-2010.

36. Anthony Corrado, "Financing the 2000 Elections," in *The Election of 2000,* edited by Gerald Pomper et al. (New York, NY: Chatham House, 2001), 102.

37. Joshua Green, "The Amazing Money Machine," TheAtlantic.com, June 2008. www.theatlantic.com/doc/200806/obama-finance.

38. Claire Cain Miller, "How Obama's Internet Campaign Changed Politics," *New York Times,* November 7, 2008. http://bits.blogs.nytimes.com/2008/11/07/how-obamas-internet-campaign-changed-politics

39. Michal L. Sifry, "Presidential Campaign 2012, By the Numbers," Techpresident.com. http://techpresident.com/news/23178/presidentail-campaign-2012-numbers

40. Ibid.

41. Aaron Smith, Kay Lehman Schlozman, Sidney Verba, and Henry Brady, "The Internet and Civil Engagement," Pew Internet and American Life Project, September 1, 2009. pewinternet.org/ . . . /2009/15—The-Internet-and-Civic-Engagement.asp

42. Kathryn Zickuhr and Aaron Smith, "Digital Differences," Pew Internet & American Life Project, April 13, 2012. www.pewinternet.org/Reports/2012/Digital-differences/Overview.aspx

chapter 9

Elections and Government
A Tenuous Connection

Did you know that . . .

- divided partisan control of the national government has been the rule, not the exception, since 1968?
- in approximately one-third of the states, the governor's party does not control both houses of the state legislature?
- during the 2010 election, there were a total of 159 ballot propositions in 36 states on which voters could register their policy preferences, and in 2012, there were 174 in 38 states?
- since 1992, Americans believe that the government is trying to do too many things that should be left to individuals and businesses, but they also oppose cutting government spending for Social Security, Medicare, education, the environment, health, the arts, aid to farmers, antipoverty programs, and national defense?
- it is difficult to convert an electoral coalition into a governing coalition and keep that governing coalition together for an extended period of time?
- the distinctions between campaigning and governing have become blurred in recent years as elected officials engage in constant campaigning to maintain their job approval and political popularity?
- election mandates rarely occur, even when one party dominates the outcome of elections, as in 1994, 2006, 2008, and 2010?
- exit polls taken after people vote explain more about the public opinion on election day than do the actual votes themselves?

Is this any way to run a democratic election?

Who governs, and how prepared are they to do so? What priorities and policy positions should newly elected officials pursue, and which party and candidates are more likely to be successful? How can those in power be simultaneously attuned to popular sentiment, responsive to public needs, and make good governing decisions?

We hold elections to answer these questions. Elections determine the personnel and provide direction for government. They help forge and reinforce the coalitions that enable a government of shared powers and divided authority to make and implement public policy. Elections are also the principal enforcement mechanism by which citizens keep those in power responsive to their needs and interests, as well as accountable for their collective and individual behavior.

This chapter explores how well American elections serve these purposes. Do they make governing easier or harder? Do they provide guidance and legitimacy for the public policies that ensue, or do they present mixed signals, undefined mandates, and conflicting claims upon those in power? Do they tie government decisions and actions more closely to the popular will, or do they usually reveal the absence of such a will? Do they encourage responsiveness in government or provide a nearly blank check for public officials?

The discussion begins by looking at the link between who wins, who governs, and how they govern. Then it moves to the policy mandate—what the election means and how that meaning affects the policy decisions of newly elected officials. From the mandate and its impact, we next turn to the tie between electoral and governing coalitions, the transference or maintenance of power by groups within the American polity. Finally, the chapter ends by completing the circle from public choice to government responsiveness, examining the extent to which elections hold public officials accountable.

WHO GOVERNS?

The Compatibility of the Winners

The election determines the winners, but those winners are not always compatible with one another. They may not know one another, may disagree on the priorities and issues, and may have different perceptions of how to do their job, yet they all come with an electoral mandate to represent their constituency and act in its interests. One issue that directly affects government's ability to function efficiently is how to enhance the compatibility of newly elected officials in an electoral system designed to mirror the diversity of the population and the character of the federal system more than reflect a national consensus or even mood.

The compatibility problem is largely systemic, the product of a constitutional framework designed to check rather than promote the dominant opinions of the moment by creating differing but overlapping electoral constituencies and terms of office. It also is rooted in the political environment, in the self-selection process of running for office, in the unequal resources that the candidates and their backers have at their disposal, and in the decentralized party structure. Given the systemic problem, achieving compatibility in outlook, goals, and policy priorities requires a strong cohesive national party, an overriding national threat, or some issue that unifies the population and helps produce a consensus for action, such as the terrorist attacks of September 2001 or the economic crisis of 2008–2009.

A related issue pertains to the compatibility of those elected with those already in office—other elected officials, those who serve for fixed terms or at the pleasure of the top executive officials, and civil servants. Rarely do the personnel of an entire governmental body change. And even though a complete turnover is theoretically possible in the House of Representatives and in many state legislatures, in practice, turnover tends to be very limited because of incumbency advantages and the lack of competitive legislative districts. The absence of turnover limits the impact of those who wanted and voted for change.

From the perspective of a participatory democracy, muting the latest expression of the popular will is an unfortunate consequence of overlapping terms of office. The trade-off is more experience, savvy, and continuity in government—all of which may produce better public policy over the long run and more legislative independence from the president. With the limited knowledge that the public has on most issues, constraininging the emotion of the moment may result in a more considered judgment later on, as "cooler heads" prevail and more information becomes available to more people who begin to understand the complexities of the issue and the consequences of various policy options in a more sophisticated manner.

Obtaining a considered judgment in the public interest but not becoming prisoner to the passion of the moment was part of the original rationale for dividing powers and for overlapping constituencies and terms of office. Leery of an aroused majority, particularly if that majority tried to deny minorities their rights, the framers of the U.S. Constitution wanted to place hurdles on the road to public policymaking. Their system of internal checks and balances requires sustained support over time, across electoral constituencies, and within and among institutions of government to formulate new public policy.

That system, artfully designed in 1787, remains alive and well today; however, public expectations of the role of government have increased enormously. These expectations have been fueled in large part by the needs of an industrial and, later, technological society; by governmental responses to those needs, such as the New Deal and Great Society programs; and by politicians' promises made in their quest for elective office. How to overcome what the Constitution separates is the political challenge public officials face today, a challenge made more difficult by the autonomy of federal elections; competing policy agendas within and between the major parties and their elected officials; and, more often than not, divided partisan control of government.

Voting for the best person regardless of party reinforces the separation of powers. Add to this Americans' distrust of big and distant government and their more contemporary fear of ideologically driven partisans imposing their beliefs on the country, and one quickly arrives at a justification for split-ticket voting and divided government.

The point here is that the current electoral system, with its propensity to focus on the candidates and their distinctive policy positions, can result in a government of virtual strangers whose ties to their electoral constituency are stronger than their ties to one another.[1] To repeat this chapter's theme, contemporary elections mirror America's diversity more than they reflect a national consensus, a consensus that could serve as a guide for policy, a foundation on which a governing coalition could be built, and legitimacy for government actions.

The Qualifications of New Hires

Not only does an election determine those who will serve, it also influences those who will help them in office. Except for professional campaign consultants, who continue to provide elected officials with for-profit services, such as polling, media consulting, event organizing, Internet communications, and grassroots operations. The people most likely to accompany the newly elected into public service are those who worked long and hard on their campaigns. They are unified by their loyalty to the winning candidate, but they may lack the analytical skills and substantive knowledge necessary for a top staff position in government. Many of these aides also lack governing experience, magnifying the initial adjustment problem for the newly elected.

There are several reasons why newly elected officials turn to their campaign aides when choosing their advisory and support staffs. They owe them a lot, and undoubtedly some of the aides have ambitions of their own, which may include moving to the capital and working with the person they helped elect. Moreover, campaign workers have demonstrated their loyalty and industry, two important qualifications for good staffing. That they are not part of the previous team, which might have been rejected at the polls, is also seen as an asset by the winners. And, finally, those who have just won election to a new office do not usually have the contacts and acquaintances that incumbents possess. On the other hand, candidates who are first elected are familiar with their campaign staff. They know what they can do. So why not hire them?

Actually, there are plenty of reasons for not doing so. The principal ones are that campaigning differs from governing, and the skills and attitudes required for each also differ, although there is some overlap between campaigning and the public relations dimension of government.[2]

THE RELATIONSHIP BETWEEN CAMPAIGNING AND GOVERNING

Do contemporary campaigns facilitate or impede governing? Do they provide the skills necessary for elected officials to perform representative and policy-making functions, or do they divert their focus, harden their positions, and convert governing into constant campaigning? In truth, they do both.

Similarities: The Constant Campaign

Governing is becoming more campaign oriented than ever before. Increasingly, it is conducted in the public arena and is poll driven, with mass-marketing techniques used to gain support and promote policy positions. A principal motivation for elected officials making public policy decisions is how those decisions will affect their own reelection or quest for higher office.

In campaigns, candidates and their entourages have to sell themselves and their policies to the electorate. They continue doing so once elected. Executive and legislative leaders, in particular, have to build public pressure for their proposals outside of government in order to gain the enactment of their policy priorities within government. They also must be concerned with their own popularity because it contributes to their political influence and subsequent policy successes or failures.

Although both candidates and government officials appeal to the public, they do so in slightly different ways. In campaigns, the candidates try to lead the media, respond quickly to their opponents' charges and to press allegations, and continuously spin campaign-related issues to persuade voters to support them. In government, elected officials announce their plans, explain how those plans should work to remedy major policy problems, and use the prestige of their office to enhance the credibility of their remarks and the success of their policymaking efforts. As public officials responsible for the formulation and execution of policy, they have to respond to critical media, who tend to highlight disagreement more than consensus and focus on the potential or actual negative consequences that follow from governmental decisions. Moreover, they also have to contend with investigative journalists and their political opponents. Candidates may be moving targets for those observing and critiquing the political process, but elected officials are sitting ducks, especially when term limits stop them from running for reelection.

In both campaigns and government, the press imputes the political motives of the people they cover. During the campaign, having a political motive is expected; political motives are what campaigns are all about. Not so in government; in that arena, political motives are viewed as self-interested, petty, partisan, even personal. Government officials have to defend the reasons for and merits of their actions and do so in terms of the public interest. Thus, candidate Bill Clinton could criticize Bob Dole's policy positions during the 1996 campaign even though his motive was political, but the congressional Republicans' focus on Clinton's behavior in office and the impeachment trial that followed were seen by many as blatant partisan politics. The 2011 debate over budget deficits and the debt ceiling was perceived to be a partisan-ideological clash, one that persisted through the 2012 elections and thereafter.

Once elected, incumbents keep their eyes on the next election and do their best to ready themselves for it by raising money, performing services, staying in the news, and taking positions that will help them with the voters.

The representative role—servicing constituency needs, representing constituency views, and satisfying constituency interests in the short run—has become more important, less difficult, and much less expensive. In contrast, legislating longer-term national policy has become less important but more difficult for individual legislators. Executive oversight has received more emphasis, particularly during periods of divided government. It contributes to partisan posturing for the next election and spotlights the watchdog activities of members of Congress.

That more and more governing functions are subject to media scrutiny and take place within the public arena has both positive and negative consequences for democratic government. It benefits democracy in that elected officials are motivated to stay closely tied to their electoral bases and responsive to their constituency's needs. The cost of maintaining such ties, however, has been a growing public perception, fueled by the press, that elected officials follow, not lead, and do what is best for themselves and their parties, and not necessarily what is best for the country.

A second problem that stems from the campaign-oriented environment in government is the hardening of policy positions. If candidates for office are increasingly defined by and held accountable for the promises they made and the positions they took during the campaign, it will be harder for them as elected officials to adjust to new conditions and make the compromises neces-sary to govern, particularly if those compromises have to be negotiated in full public view. Strong ideological beliefs magnify this problem today.

The difficulties that a campaign-style atmosphere creates for government suggest that there are fundamental differences between campaigning and governing. Unless and until these differences are understood, the constant campaigning will continue to impede rather than facilitate the operation of democratic government.

Differences: Pace, Mentality, Orientation, and Experience

Pace—Hectic vs. Deliberative. A campaign has to keep up with events and presumably stay ahead of them or face defeat on election day. It is frantic almost by definition. In a competitive electoral environment, a campaign exists in a state of perpetual motion; often, a crisis atmosphere prevails, and most have "war rooms" to deal with them. But all of this motion and activity ends on a certain day, the same day that most of the campaign's personnel are out of jobs and are jockeying for positions in government if their candidate wins.

Not so with government. It cannot operate in a perpetual crisis for extended periods without sacrificing the deliberation and cooperation needed to reach policy solutions on pending issues. Elected officials of the opposing parties still have to interact with one another after a major vote has occurred or executive policy decision has been made. Whereas campaigns are a single battle with a definable end, government is a multiple set of political skirmishes fought before and after elections among many of the same combatants. It is ongoing. The relationships within government and the problems with which it deals persist over time, across institutions, and over the course of several administrations.

Mentality—Win at All Costs vs. Give and Take. A campaign is what political scientists like to call a zero-sum game. If one candidate wins, the other loses, and the game is over. The winners no longer have to consider the losers, who may fade quickly from the scene. Government is not a zero-sum game. For one thing, the losers on a particular issue do not disappear after a battle has been lost. They stay to fight the next battle. The history of the clashes between environmental and economic interests, between secular and sectarian groups, labor and management, and producers and consumers are good examples of continuous conflicts that occur and recur within the political arena.

Campaigns need to be run efficiently. Their organization and operation are geared to one primary goal: winning the election. In government, although efficiency is desirable, prioritizing democratic values are equally important. A legislative body has to deliberate on the issues. In doing so, it must conduct hearings to become familiar with the points-of-view of outside groups, forge compromise among the contending individuals and parties, and then oversee the executive branch's execution of the law. All of this takes time and involves different people with different views from different constituencies in different parts of the government. The legislative process may not be efficient, but it must be representative and should be deliberative.

Similarly, there is also tension between efficiency and effectiveness within the executive branch. The Clinton administration tried to reduce the costs of government by downsizing the number of federal employees, whereas the administration of George W. Bush focused on competition between public and private sectors, known as "competitive sourcing," to improve the operation of government and make it more efficient. The Obama administration emphasized new economic and social policy initiatives in its first two years in office; after that, it reacted to the problems of individual departments and agencies that were highlighted by the news media.

Orientation—Consistency vs. Compromise. Candidates are judged by their potential for office. In demonstrating their qualifications, particularly if they are not incumbents, they need to show that they have a grasp of the issues, have good ideas, and will keep their promises if elected. More often than not, keeping promises means adhering to the policy priorities and positions they articulated during the campaign.

Government officials are judged by their performance as well as by conditions that are alleged to be a consequence of that performance. They need to show results or at least be in a position to claim achievements. Strictly adhering to policy positions and not compromising on them can create perceptions of intransigence and lead to a stalemate in government. It can also tie public officials to outside pressures trying to influence their decision making.

Not only are campaigning and governing different, so is the permanency of the coalitions on which candidates and public officials depend. Electoral coalitions usually stay together for the duration of a political campaign. Governing alliances shift more with the issues. Today's opponent on one public policy issue may be tomorrow's opponents on another. Unlike those in campaigns, the losers and winners in government cannot afford to become permanent enemies.

Experience—Outsiders vs. Insiders. The distinction between running and governing has been exacerbated of late by two developments: the changes within the electoral process that have provided greater opportunities for those with limited experience to run for office and the public's mistrust of those in power and its desire for new faces not connected to the "mess in Washington." In an increasing number of elections, lack of experience, in particular the absence of a connection to the political establishment in government, is regarded as a virtue, not a liability. This was evident in 2006, when Democratic challengers defeated 22 Republican incumbents in the House and 6 in the Senate to gain control of Congress; in 2008, when a candidate in national office for fewer than four years defeated several senior senators and a former first lady for the Democratic nomination and a well-known senior senator and war hero for the presidency; and in 2010, when 63 congressional incumbents running for renomination and relelection lost.

Not only are many challengers who win election neophytes to governing, but their campaign staffs most likely are neophytes as well. In the past, the political pros who ran the campaigns had experience in electioneering and governing. Today, the political pros have been largely replaced by professional campaign technocrats—pollsters, media consultants, political strategists, fundraisers, Internet and computer geeks, and grassroots organizers who sell their skills to the highest bidders, some even without regard for partisanship.[3] These campaign technocrats usually have little if any governing experience and little desire to work **in** government; they do want to work **for** government, though, content to sell their wares and services to those in power, especially to incumbents getting ready to run again.

The others working on campaigns are the trusted soldiers and partisans, both paid and volunteer, who perform the day-to-day, nitty-gritty grunt work of staging events, writing speeches, doing research, dealing with the press, setting up phone banks, responding to critics, and blogging with supporters. They work long and hard for low salaries or for free; many are young, in or recently out of college, with little government experience. They may be involved because they believe in the candidate, enjoy the excitement of the campaign, or want a job once the campaign is over. They may even be doing it for social reasons, such as meeting like-minded people.[4] Whatever their motivation, they are not likely to have the inside information that a newly elected public official needs the most: knowing how things work and which people have the skills and power to get things done.

The presidential transitions of Jimmy Carter and Bill Clinton suffered from many of these staffing inadequacies. The people they appointed to their White House staffs came from their campaigns and had little or no experience in Washington politics or in dealing with the national press corps, the congressional leadership, and, in Clinton's case, the military establishment. Moreover, these newly appointed aides suffered from another malady that frequently afflicts the newly elected and their staffs: they came to power with chips on their shoulders. They assumed, probably correctly, that they had won because people had grievances against those who ran the government. Because Carter and Clinton were outsiders, even within their own party, they were suspicious of those in the establishment, Democrats and Republicans alike. Initially, they tried to have as little to do with them as possible—with disastrous results.[5] Their legislative initiatives failed, their White Houses became embroiled in controversy, and they lacked a consistent policy message. By the time they got on their feet, they had lost much of the enthusiasm that accompanies a new administration into office and the political capital that it brings.

George W. Bush in 2000 and Barack Obama in 2008 ran against the strident partisan tone of Washington politics, promising to return civility to political discourse and a bipartisan dimension to governing. Although both lacked much direct Washington experience, Bush's knowledge of his father's presidency (1989–1993) and administration and Obama's four years as U.S. Senator from Illinois (2004–2008) were such that both understood the importance of surrounding themselves with experienced Washington hands. Most importantly, their top aides cooperated with one another in the transition from one administration to the other. As a consequence, they got off to better starts than did the administrations of Carter and Clinton.

Running against the establishment may be an effective campaign strategy, particularly if the public is unhappy with the way it perceives the national or state government to be working, but it is not an effective governing strategy, especially if the goal is to bridge institutional and political divides in order to make and implement new public policy. Understanding how government functions and its limits is a prerequisite for getting it to work.

The Impact of Campaigning on Governing

Contemporary campaigning has made contemporary governing more difficult. Campaigns raise public expectations about public policy and public officials at the same time that they feed into distrust of politicians and the politics in which they engage. They emphasize personal accomplishments in a system designed to curb the exercise of institutional and political power. They harden policy positions in a governmental structure that depends on compromise. They have increasingly brought partisan and ideological rhetoric into the policymaking arena, whereas a more pragmatic approach and more quiet diplomacy may often be needed to get things done. And the candidates have developed a public persona that they continue to project once in office, a persona that can get in the way of behind-the-scenes compromises on major issues on which they have articulated public policy positions.

A second impact of campaigning on governing, especially since the 1970s, has been the increasing number of winning candidates who have not come up through the ranks and lack governing experience. These candidates may overestimate their ability to make a difference, emphasize and adhere to their campaign promises, and underestimate the views and legitimacy of others who are part of the governing establishment. "Reinventing the wheel" wastes time and energy and increases the start-up costs of government.

To make matters worse, candidates who are not incumbents usually do not have regular access to the information and expertise that government officials have. They do have access, however, to poll results that indicate political attitudes, salient issues, and public opinions. Armed with this information, it is relatively easy to craft a position popular with a specific group. Campaigning by public opinion polls is just a short step away from governing by public opinion polls. An increasing number of public officials seem to have taken this step, but as we have noted, opinion is often divided, held with varying degrees of intensity, and based on limited information, much less understanding of the issue.

Directions for Reforms

If contemporary campaigning has contributed to the difficulty of governing, what changes might reverse this pattern and make governing easier? More control by party leaders over the electoral process might reduce the number of free agents elected to government and impose more discipline on those who are elected. But how can this be accomplished in light of the reforms to the nomination process? Those who regularly participate in primaries and caucuses are not likely to voluntarily give up their right to participate in the choice of their party's nominees.

If terms of office were longer, voters more nationally focused, and people in general less interested in the short-term impact, then elected officials would have more opportunities to make decisions in what they believed were the country's long-term interests rather than their constituency's short-term interests. But then the ties between government and the governed also would be looser, responsiveness might suffer, and incumbents might be even more advantaged than they are today. Term limits could reduce this advantage, forcing greater turnover in office, but term limits also would result in the election of less experienced and knowledgeable people who would need time to acquire expertise or would be more dependent on civil servants and professional legislative staff for support. Besides, the Supreme Court has held term limits for members of Congress is unconstitutional.[6]

THE ELECTION AND PUBLIC POLICY

In addition to choosing who governs—which candidates, parties, and staffs—elections should provide policy guidance for government: what issues to address, what approaches to take, and even what specific proposals to make. Except for policy initiatives, which appear on state ballots, elections refract rather than reflect public opinion on most issues. The reason they do so is because they are primarily designed to choose people, not policies.

The Movement toward Policy Initiatives

Voting on state constitutional amendments, policy initiatives, and other substantive measures has become an increasingly popular vehicle for individuals and, especially, for organized groups to pursue their policy agendas when they are unable to do so successfully through the legislative process. A majority of the states, primarily those in the West and Midwest, provide for voting on substantive policy issues. These votes illustrate direct democracy at work.[7]

But changing public policy in this manner usually requires substantial resources. The signatures of a certain percentage of the state's eligible voters have to be obtained within a specified period of time just to get the policy initiative on the ballot. The higher the number of signatures needed and the shorter the time frame for obtaining them, the more difficult and expensive ballot access becomes. If an organization lacks enough of its own volunteers, including the foot soldiers who gather these signatures, it will have to engage an outside firm to collect them and pay several dollars per name. The total cost can run into the millions, and that is just the first step.

A public relations campaign for the initiative also must be waged during the election period. If successful, it still may be challenged in the courts, as were propositions approved by the voters to oppose same-sex marriage and to deny education and health benefits to illegal aliens and their families.[8] The legal charges can be substantial.

Interest groups have become adept at using the ballot initiative process to their own economic, ideological, or political advantage. The gambling industry; sports promoters; the Humane Society; and groups who want to impose legislative term limits, make English the official U.S. language, legalize the sale of marijuana, permit doctor-assisted suicides, issue school vouchers, increase taxes for education, and (as noted above) permit or prevent same-sex marriage all have used the initiative process to circumvent or pressure recalcitrant state legislatures.

State executive and legislative leaders have also used referendums to avoid making tough, unpopular decisions, but they have not always been successful in doing so. Take the case of former governor Arnold Schwarzenegger of California. Faced with a huge budget deficit in 2008 and not wanting to raise taxes or cut spending, the governor and state legislative leaders agreed to put six budget-related measures on the ballot. Voters rejected five of them, however, forcing the governor and legislature to do the cutting themselves and accept the political consequences.[9]

A few wealthy, public-interested individuals also have tried to use this process to achieve what they consider to be desirable public policy. Billionaire financier George Soros has spent millions in support of initiatives that would legalize the medical use of marijuana and provide the forfeiture of assets and rehabilitation rather than lengthy jail terms for convicted drug offenders. Paul Allen, the cofounder of Microsoft, contributed $3 million to a group that was supporting an initiative to establish charter schools in the state of Washington. Businessman Tim Draper spent $23 million of his own money on an initiative to provide school vouchers to children in California. The list goes on.[10]

The amount of money that it takes to mount a successful initiative drive and the fact that much of it may come from outside the state have led some states to try to limit the number of ballot initiatives and the influence of outside groups and people who do not live in that state. Colorado enacted legislation that permitted only its registered voters to circulate initiative petitions. It required those who circulate petitions to wear badges identifying themselves and their affiliation and that the cost of initiative drives be made part of the public record. In 1999, however, the U.S. Supreme Court found that these restrictions violated the First Amendment by inhibiting communications with voters.[11]

In addition to the financial issue, there are other problems with the widespread use of these public referenda. Some are extremely complicated and difficult to understand, much less evaluating their costs and consequences. Just reading these ballot initiatives can take a considerable amount of time, which holds up voting for others. (In the 2012 election, Florida Republicans were even accused of allowing numerous initiatives on the ballot as a means of slowing, and thereby suppressing, the vote.) Moreover, initiatives circumvent the legislative process, thereby diminishing the role of those whose job it is to consider public policy issues and also presumably have more time, knowledge, and skills to consider them than the average person or voter.

According to the Initiative and Referendum Institute of the University of Southern California, there have been almost 2,400 state ballot initiatives since 1904, when the first one was placed on the ballot in Oregon. Of these initiatives, approximately 41 percent have been approved by voters. In 2012, two states, Colorado and Washington, approved the legalization of marijuana, three states voted in favor of same sex marriage, and Californians refused to abolish the death penalty.[12] Table 9.1 lists the number of policy initiatives on state ballots since 2000.

Issue Voting in a Candidate-Oriented Environment

With the exception of voting on policy issues, most elections are imperfect mechanisms for determining public policy. People vote for a variety of

TABLE 9.1 **State Ballot Initiatives, 2000–2012**		
Year	Number of Initiatives	Percentage approved
2000	76	33
2001	4	3
2002	51	21
2003	7	3
2004	64	35
2005	18	2
2006	79	32
2007	2	1
2008	68	26
2009	5	2
2010	46	20
2011	10	5
2012	42	41

Source: Initiative and Referendum Institute, University of Southern California. www.iandrinstitute .org.

candidates for lots of reasons. Partisan affiliation, candidate qualifications, and issue positions are some of the factors that affect voting behavior. Of these, substantive policy issues are least likely to be the primary focus for most voters.[13]

People also may be voting against candidates because they are unhappy with the job they have done, the conditions that occurred while they were in power, their behavior while in office, or even their personal traits or policy preferences that are revealed during the campaign. Such a negative vote, if discernible, may indicate what the electorate does not want but not what it does want, except perhaps by inference.

Another factor contributing to the difficulty of understanding the meaning of elections is that there are many candidates and many issues at many levels of government. People have different reasons for casting different votes. They may split their ballots, voting for candidates from different parties. This type of voting behavior often produces mixed results from which a clear message is not always or easily discernible, despite political pundits' and exit pollsters' explanations to the contrary.

If a voting pattern were to emerge, if one party were to win or maintain control of the legislative and executive branches, then there might be some reason for believing that voters were sending a message—although the substance of the message would not necessarily be clear. At the national level, however, such a pattern has been the exception, not the rule since 1968. During this forty-five-year period, the same party controlled the White House and both houses of Congress for a total of twelve years.[14] Under these circumstances, with mixed results in overlapping constituencies, what can the election returns tell us about the policy direction that newly elected officials should take? The answer is, usually, not very much.

The Absence of Policy Mandates

The national electoral system is not structured in a way that facilitates policy voting. It has encouraged partisan voting, but the declining use of the party-column ballot, the candidate orientation of many voters, and diverse results, stemming from partisan parity since the 1990s, make it more difficult to achieve clear mandates today. Some do claim that the 1980 and 1984 presidential elections and the 1994 and 2010 midterm elections produced such mandates for the Republicans, and the presidential elections of 1932, 1964, and 2008 and the midterms of 1974 and 2006 did so for the Democrats.

To have a mandate for governing, a party's candidates must take discernible and compatible policy positions that are distinguishable from the opposition's, and the electorate must vote for them primarily because of those positions. Most elections do not meet these criteria. Candidates usually take a range of policy positions, waffle on a few highly divisive and emotionally charged ones, and may differ from their party and its other candidates for national office in their priorities and their stands on others.

House Republican candidates did take consistent policy positions in 1994; all pledged to support the goals and proposals in their Contract with America. Other Republican candidates, however, did not take such a pledge. Nonetheless, the results of the 1994 election, in which every Republican incumbent for Congress and governor won and the Republicans gained seats in most state legislatures, were interpreted as a partisan victory. What did such a victory mean? What policy goals did it imply?

Newly elected Speaker of the House Newt Gingrich chose to interpret the vote as an affirmation of the ten basic goals and legislative proposals in the House Republicans' Contract with America. Such an interpretation provided Gingrich with a legislative agenda to pursue and promote in the House of Representatives. But his interpretation also created performance expectations that the Republicans were unable to meet outside of the House.

Moreover, it was probably an incorrect interpretation. The vote in 1994 was a repudiation of the Clinton administration and the Democratic-controlled Congress; it was also a rejection of big government, big deficits, and big social programs such as universal health care for all Americans. Indirectly, it could be interpreted as a vote for less government, lower taxes, and a smaller deficit. It was not a vote for the Republicans' Contract with America. How do we know? Exit polls indicated that only 25 percent of the voters and 20 percent of the population had ever heard of the Contract with America, much less knew what was in it. How, then, could the 1994 election be a mandate for the policy proposals in that contract if such a small proportion of the population was aware of that contract, much less the proposals in it?

Similarly, the Tea Party's success in the 2010 Republican nominations and the general election was interpreted by some to mean that the electorate wanted decreased government spending, lower budget deficits, and a reduction of the national debt, but there was no consensus on how to achieve these goals. Disagreement among elected officials almost immobilized government following that election and has led to persistent partisan confrontations since then. In contrast, the presidential elections of 1984, 1996, 2004, and 2012 also were seen as referendums in support of the administration in power. Presidents who are reelected have received a vote of confidence for their past leadership; they have support to continue the policy actions that they initiated, but not necessarily to start something new. Beyond that, gleaning much meaning and guidance from an incumbent's reelection is problematic at best. Nonetheless, most presidents claim public support for their second-term goals and promises, some of which they articulated during the reelection campaign.[15]

The defeat of an incumbent, however, such as Jimmy Carter in 1980 and George H. W. Bush in 1992, indicates that the electorate is dissatisfied with the conditions in the election year and the leadership (or lack thereof) that contributed to those conditions. Under the circumstances, the safest plan for candidates who defeat incumbents is to try to fulfill their campaign promises and thereby maintain their credibility.

Exit Polls and the Meaning of the Vote

The results of elections may not explain very much, other than who wins and who loses, but election day surveys that probe voters' opinions and preferences to discern why they voted as they did provide more useful information. Such surveys enable analysts to correlate the demographic and attitudinal characteristics of voters and their opinions and preferences with self-reported voting behavior. In this way, it is possible to interpret the meaning of the election.

Election day exit polls interview people after they have cast ballots at randomly selected voting precincts across the country.[16] A large number of people are surveyed. In 2012, 26,565 voters participated in the exit poll plus another 4,408 early voters who were interviewed via telephone.[17]

Exit polls are usually very accurate because of their large size (compared with about 1,000–1,200 for other national surveys) and because they are conducted at many different voting precincts across the country over the course of the day. The principal limitation of the exit poll, however, is that it provides only a snapshot of how voters think, feel, and remember how and why they voted on one particular day. Exit polls do not measure opinion shift over the course of the campaign. To do that, the same respondents have to be queried more than once over a period of time. Surveys conducted by the Annenberg Public Policy Center at the University of Pennsylvania and those for a consortium of universities led by researchers from the universities of Michigan and Stanford, known as the American National Election Studies (ANES) do so. Data from both these surveys are subsequently made available to election analysts.

There is another problem with election surveys. Most of them contain close-ended responses. They encourage respondents to choose an answer that best reflects their opinion, but whether the responses accurately mirror that opinion is another issue.

Although exit polls are not necessary to know who wins, they do reveal patterns of voting behavior. (See Table 9.2.) The principal factor is partisanship. Since the end of the twentieth century, the major parties have been at near parity with one another. Partisans tend to vote overwhelmingly for their party's nominees. Core groups within each party's traditional electoral base also vote along party lines, with African Americans, Hispanics, and organized labor for the Democratic candidates and the Christian Coalition and other religious groups for Republicans. Since the truly independent vote has been of limited size and usually closely divided, the key is maximizing the base vote.

The election of 2008 was different. It produced a larger-than-usual vote for the winning candidate, Barack Obama, the first Democrat since Jimmy Carter to receive a majority of the popular vote. Obama also redrew the Electoral College map, winning states in the South, Southwest, and Midwest that had previously voted Republican at the presidential level. His effective grassroots operation also turned out record numbers of voters. Obama won traditional Democratic groups by large margins: African Americans (91 percent), Hispanics (more than 2 to 1)), and labor union households by more than 20 percent of the vote. He increased the sizes of the gender and age gaps that favor the Democrats. Although the country had become more conservative since the 1980s, Obama countered the conservative trends by gaining more support from moderate voters.

Similar voter patterns emerged in 2012, although Obama's overall support declined slightly. A deep partisan divide remained within the American polity, with over 90 percent of party identifiers voting for their party's presidential and vice presidential candidates. Gender, racial, and ethnic differences continued with greater numbers of women and minorities supporting Obama and greater numbers of men and the white majority backing Romney. Obama also received the overwhelming support of gay voters. The ability of the Obama organization to turn out its base, particularly in the battleground states, cemented his victory. The changing demographics of the U.S. population, including its increasing multi-ethnicity, was evident in the changing demographics of the electorate because the Obama campaign was able to turn out young and minority voters at a slightly higher level than in the past. Age, income, and religious trends also persisted. People in the older and higher income groups gave proportionately more support to Romney, as did voters who were more active within their religious communities. However, the proportion of the religious cohort within the electorate declined slightly while the percentage of individuals identifying themselves as secular or nonregular churchgoers has increased.

In the end, Obama's vote reflected his job approval rating, which was 53 percent, the same percent that approved George W. Bush's performance as president when he was reelected in 2004.

TABLE 9.2 **Portrait of the American Electorate, 2000–2012 (percentages of the total vote)**

Percentage of Total in 2012	Year / Candidates	2000		2004		2008		2012	
		Bush	Gore	Bush	Kerry	Obama	McCain	Obama	Romney
	Total Vote^	48	48	50	49	53	46	51	48
	Proportion of Group in The Electorate								
47	Men	53	42	54	45	49	48	45	52
53	Women	43	54	47	52	56	43	55	44
72	White	54	42	57	42	43	55	39	59
13	Black	9	90	11	89	95	4	93	6
10	Hispanic	35	62	42	55	67	32	71	27
3	Asian	41	55	41	59	62	35	73	26
60	Married	53	44	56	43	47	52	42	56
41	Unmarried	38	57	40	59	65	33	62	35
19	18–29	46	48	44	54	66	32	60	36
27	30–44	49	48	51	47	52	46	52	45
38	45–64	49	48	50	49	50	49	47	52
16	65 & older	47	51	53	46	45	53	44	56
3	Not high school	38	59	49	50	63	35	64	35
21	High school graduate	49	48	51	48	52	46	51	48
29	Some college	51	45	53	46	51	47	49	48
29	College graduate	51	45	51	47	50	48	47	51
18	Postgraduate	44	52	43	55	58	40	55	42
53	Protestant/Other Christian	56	42	58	41	45	54	42	57
25	Catholic	47	50	51	48	54	45	50	48
2	Jewish	19	79	24	76	78	21	69	30
26	Born Again/Fundamentalists	80	18	77	22	24	74	21	78

(continued on next page)

TABLE 9.2 **Portrait of the American Electorate, 2000–2012 (percentages of the total vote)** *(continued)*

Percentage of Total in 2012	Year Candidates	2000 Bush	Gore	2004 Bush	Kerry	2008 Obama	McCain	2012 Obama	Romney
18	**Union household**	37	59	39	60	59	39	58	40
	under $15,000	37	57	36	63	73	25		
20	**$15,000–$29,999***	41	54	41	58	60	37	63	35
21	**$30,000–$49,999**	48	49	48	51	55	43	56	42
31	**$50,000–$74,999**	51	46	55	44	48	49		
	$75,000–$99,999*	52	45	53	46	51	48	46	52
	$100,000–$149,999	54	43	56	43	48	51		
21	**$150,000–$199,999***	-	-	-	-	48	50	44	54
7	**$200,000 (& over)***	-	-	-	-	52	46	44	54
25	**Better today**	36	61	79	20	37	60	84	15
41	**Same today**	60	35	48	50	45	53	58	40
33	**Worse today**	63	33	19	80	71	28	18	80
32	**Republican**	91	8	93	7	9	90	6	93
29	**Independent**	47	45	47	50	52	44	45	50
38	**Democrat**	11	86	10	89	89	10	92	7
25	**Liberal**	13	80	13	86	89	10	86	11
41	**Moderate**	44	52	44	55	60	39	56	41
35	**Conservative**	81	17	83	16	20	78	17	82
60	**Work full time**	48	49	52	46	55	44	49	49
40	**Do not work full time**	48	47	49	50	50	48	53	45
53	**Approve incumbent's performance**	20	77	90	9	10	89	89	9

^ Indicates proportion of total vote.

*Income breakdown in 2012 was as follows: Under $30,000; $30,000–$49,999; $50,000–$99,000; $100,000–$199,999; $200,000–$249,999; $250,000 and over.

+Question in 2008 was: Do you work full time?

Source: The major exit polls reported by principal news sources (and can be found on their Web sites) are conducted for them by Edison Research.

In summary, the results of an election indicate who won but not much else: not the reasons people voted as they did and not the mandate the winners usually claim. Elected officials who act as if they had a mandate usually are doing so to gain support within the government for the policy initiatives they wish to pursue. It is also important to understand that the more time that elapses after the election, the less important the election is as a guide to policy and an influence on those who make it.

POLICY AND PERFORMANCE: RESPONSIVENESS AND ACCOUNTABILITY

Government is based on the consent of the governed. That's the reason why public officials are so concerned about the meaning of the election and why they frequently claim it is a mandate from the voters. That meaning or claim ties elections to government in three ways:

- Elections provide direction for public officials.
- Elections help generate popular support for achieving election-based goals and specific campaign promises.
- Elections reaffirm the legitimacy of the actions of government

Providing Direction

Campaigns are full of promises, both substantive and stylistic. They provide a broad blueprint for those in power. They also create a climate of performance expectations. These expectations are often hyped by the emphasis the candidates and their campaigns place on certain character traits they claim to possess and promise to exercise if elected: strong and decisive leadership, high moral and ethical standards, and excellent policymaking and management skills. Successful presidential candidates have pledged to "never tell a lie," create "a kinder and gentler America," exercise "compassionate conservatism," initiate "policy and political change," and "protect the middle class." But candidates have to be careful not to promise too much. If they set too high a bar for themselves, they may not be able to clear it, with the likely result that their job approval and probably the public's confidence in them will decline, as it did for President Obama during his first term.

Normally, multiple campaign pledges and policy initiatives, low levels of information among voters, and people's preoccupation with the conditions that concern them the most give public officials considerable leverage in designing policy, as long as they stay within the broad parameters of acceptability and the policy produces a beneficial short-term result. In this sense and on a collective level, the electoral process provides both opportunities and flexibility for those in power. What it often does not provide is the consensus necessary to govern. The Obama administration's drive to reform health care is a case in point.

BOX 9.1   **ObamaCare: Winning the Congressional Vote and Losing the Public Debate**

During the 2008 campaign, Barack Obama promised to reform the nation's health care system, reducing costs and providing opportunities for everyone to get coverage. Although the economy was the major issue in the 2008 campaign, only 9 percent of the people said health care was the most important problem (see Table 9.2). As the economy worsened and people lost their jobs, the number of Americans without health insurance grew. After the enactment of the American Recovery and Reinvestment Act and the president's budget, the Obama administration turned its attention to health care.

Initially, the plan was to let the Democratic Congress take the lead in formulating the legislation. With large majorities in both houses and the public desiring reform, according to public opinion polls (see figure 9.1), the administration hoped that Obama's health care reform would receive broad support and that Congress could reach agreement on the matter. Several different committees in the House and Senate debated and drafted proposals, while the administration made deals with various groups in the health care community to gain their support. These deals, however, did not stop the industry from spending millions of dollars to lobby Congress for a bill that did not adversely affect its multitude of interests.

Meanwhile public support was shifting, a consequence of Republican criticism of Democratic proposals, the large budget deficit, and general suspicion that a government-run plan would be inefficient, increase costs, reduce options, and dig the government deeper into debt. A gap was developing between the concept of helping the uninsured get adequate health care coverage, which the public supported, and the specific proposals for legislation on which there was disagreement.

Fearful that a divided Congress would not reach a consensus on the legislation, the White House planned to launch a public relations campaign. But in the spring of 2009, Republican members of Congress mounted a "PR" campaign, holding town meetings around the country at which angry protests about the legislation, especially the fact that it would be mandatory, were heard. There were even allegations that government "death panels" would decide whether medical treatments would even be available to some. The protests fueled extensive news media coverage. They put the president on the defensive. He lost control of the debate.

With so many other problems demanding his attention, the president found it difficult to stay focused on health care, much less frame the legislative issue to his political advantage. And by delegating the drafting of the legislation to Congress, Obama left himself open to accepting a bill that he may not have liked.

The debate influenced public opinion. In November 2008, when Obama was elected, 64 percent of the public believed that it was the responsibility of the federal government to make sure all Americans had health care coverage; 33 percent did not think it was a government responsibility. One year later, support had dropped by 10 percent and opposition increased by almost that amount. Two years later, more people said that health care coverage was not a federal responsibility than said it was. (See Figure 9.1.) Opposition continued, and the country remained closely divided.

But the president remained convinced that health care reform was necessary for economic and social reasons. The House of Representatives had enacted a health care bill in November 2009 and the Senate in December, right before Christmas. But the bills were different and had to be reconciled for new public policy to become law.

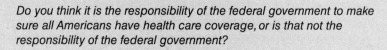

FIGURE 9.1 **The Government's Responsibility for Health Care Coverage**

Do you think it is the responsibility of the federal government to make sure all Americans have health care coverage, or is that not the responsibility of the federal government?

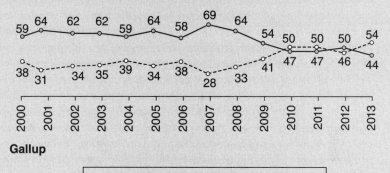

Gallup

——— % Yes, government responsibility

----- % No, not government responsibility

Source: Topics A-Z: Healthcare System, Gallup Poll. http://www.gallup.com/poll/4708/Healthcare-System.aspx

Although opinion was split deeply along partisan lines, the president remained adamant. He wanted comprehensive reform, not incremental change. In January 2010, he told his cabinet during the football playoffs that he was on the two-yard line and did not want to settle for a field goal. The issue had become personal for him. The president saw the enactment of health care legislation as connected to his political capital and policy agenda, to the Democrats' ability to survive the midterm elections, to his presidential legacy, and most important, to a principal reason that he ran for president: to help those who needed help the most. The uninsured fit into this category.

To the exclusion of almost everything else, the president focused on getting the House of Representatives to accept the Senate bill and then a bill that reconciled differences in the legislation. He and Speaker of the House Nancy Pelosi identified sixty-eight Democratic members of the House of Representatives whose vote on the final package was uncertain. During a two-week period in March 2010, they met or spoke with each of them.

In the end the president and Speaker were successful. They got the House to support the Senate bill and a reconciliation package that reformed the system. Public opinion, however, remained divided.[18] The president won the legislative battle but lost the public opinion war. Did his actions conform to the tenets of a democratic political process? Should he have led or followed? The electorate voted against his party in the 2010 midterm elections, although the extent to which the health care legislation figured in the evaluation of congressional Democrats, particularly in the House, is unclear.

(continued on next page)

Nonetheless, the health care debate and the legislative outcome illustrate the tenuous relationship between elections and governance. Elections influence governance but they do so indirectly. They obviously and directly affect who wins and loses. They affect political judgments, especially those who have just been elected, but not everyone involved in the governing process has just been elected. They condition relationships inside and outside of government, but for how long and under what circumstances? As time passes, the last election becomes less important and the next one more important.

In short, elections are critical to a democratic political process. They legitimize that process and its products, but they do not dictate public policy outcomes.

Getting Results

The public's foci shift after the election. People become disappointed when their expectations go unmet. Constituencies clash within as well as between parties. Well-financed interest groups continue to exercise power and spend millions lobbying those in power to achieve or at least shape their policy goals. The result may be that the election determines the policymakers. What it does not usually provide is the coalition across institutions of government that is necessary to get results. The principal task for elected leaders is to build that coalition and do so as quickly as possible by using their victory and the goodwill that ritually follows an election outcome to enhance their base of support.

Having a partisan majority helps, but it does not guarantee success, as George W. Bush found out at the beginning of his second term. To get results, constant campaigning is necessary, priority by priority. Pollsters are used to determine policy parameters, and focus groups are employed to refine the language of messages and target each to the appropriate group or groups. Partisan and nonpartisan appeals are made, depending on the issue and the political configuration of public opinion. Interest group coalitions, organized by the White House, political parties, or outside groups, are used to promote the policy and mobilize support for it.

Ensuring Accountability: Individual and Collective

As a check on those in government, the electorate holds a trump card: rejection at the polls the next time around. The card is not played often, however, for several reasons. The practical advantages of incumbency usually outweigh the theoretical option of voting someone out of office. With the exception of the president and other chief executives, it is difficult to assign individual responsibility for institutional action or inaction. It is even hard to assign individual responsibility for economic and social conditions, although chief executives (the president, state governors, and mayors) do tend to receive more credit and blame than they usually deserve for these conditions.

Another reason it is difficult to assess responsibility for what government does is that people generally are not well informed about the actions of government, much less about the specifics of the programs. They don't become better informed until the news media focus on a particular problem for a sustained period. Assigning collective responsibility is even more difficult than holding individuals accountable. When control of the government is divided, credit and blame are shared. Which institution and political party were to blame for the huge increase in the national debt that occurred during the Reagan and George H. W. Bush administrations? Were Republicans or Democrats, president or Congress, neither or both responsible for the government bailout of Wall Street investment and other too-big-to-fail firms during the 2007–2009 financial crisis? Was the bailout of too-big-to-fail firms fair or unfair, wise or unwise? One of the most negative consequences of divided government is the inability to hold one party collectively accountable for public policy outcomes.

For individual behavior, however, responsibility can be pinpointed, even though it does not necessarily result in electoral defeat. There are some exceptions to the nonrejection rule. Outrageous personal behavior in office is one of them. Illegal acts, such as the theft of government property, acceptance of bribes, lying under oath, failure to pay income taxes or child support would probably produce sufficient negative media and public concern to force an official to resign from office or face the strong possibility of defeat in the next nomination or election. Similarly, immoral or unethical behavior, such as sexual improprieties, the flagrant misuse of public property, or making false claims about one's military service or educational qualifications, would endanger an official's reelection prospects, if only to encourage a quality challenger.

Accountability in government is enhanced by transparency. In the public arena of government, under the eye of an investigative press, and with the public relations campaigns that one's partisan or ideological opponents can wage, public officials have incentives to behave as if they were in the spotlight most of the time. As a result, responsiveness and accountability are fostered by the increasing availability of information.

SUMMARY: ELECTIONS AND GOVERNMENT DILEMMAS IN A NUTSHELL

Elections provide a critical link between the people and their government. That link is the most important reason for having elections: to choose the people who will make the major public policy decisions, to provide them with policy direction and political support, to give their decisions legitimacy, and to hold them accountable for their behavior in office.

Elections satisfy these democratic goals, but they do so imperfectly. They determine the winners, but the winners are not always compatible with each other, much less with those already in power. Elections choose the most popular candidates (with the obvious exception of the 2000 presidential contest), but popularity and governing ability are not synonymous and, in some cases, may not even be closely related.

Elections for different offices at different levels of government over different time periods more often than not yield mixed results. Governing becomes more difficult when the differences among elected officials outweigh their commonalities. Adding to the problem is the public's perception that successful candidates are and will continue to be primarily beholden to their supporters, contributors, and constituents, but not necessarily to the president, some larger public interest, or even their own best, nonpartisan judgment.

Doing what makes political sense for the folks back home becomes a primary motivation and guide to legislative decision making. As a consequence, the electoral process seems to mirror the country's diversity much more effectively than it reflects majority sentiment. This parochialism is a problem for governing at the national level, a problem that can be magnified by electing inexperienced candidates who in turn select inexperienced staff who lack adequate knowledge. To a limited extent, public opinion polls that reflect national popular sentiment counter the constituency orientation of legislative bodies, but not a lot.

The differences between campaigning and governing remain significant. Campaigns have definite winners and losers; government does not. Campaigns are replete with political and ideological rhetoric. Such rhetoric is an impediment to compromise in government. Campaigns generate a harsh, spirited, partisan debate that is not conducive to the deliberation and adjustments that must accompany sound policymaking among diverse public officials. Because governing is being conducted more and more in the public arena, however, the campaigning skills of going public—that is, of tailoring and targeting messages to special groups to build support and achieve a favorable impression—are becoming an increasingly important instrument of governing.

Elections are supposed to guide public officials in what they do and in when and how they do it, but their outcomes often present mixed verdicts and messages. Unless the electorate is voting directly on a policy issue, such as a state initiative, it is difficult to discern the meaning of an election, much less translate that meaning into a policy agenda for government. Exit polls and other national surveys provide some guidance about voters' attitudes, opinions, and the most salient issues, but they are not exact measures, and certainly not blueprints, for governing. And they are time bound. Conditions change as do opinions. As a consequence, public officials usually have considerable discretion when making policy judgments, as long as they do so within the broad parameters of mainstream thought, and for the most part, partisan politics.

The potential for election defeat, combined with negative publicity and a "thin skin" for criticism, keep elected officials responsive to their constituencies, more so on an individual than a collective basis. Accountability is enhanced by transparency in government, by an attentive media, and by those who wish to gain political advantage from the decisions and actions of their partisan opponents.

Elections are also important for converting promises into performance. The key here is not only the composition of the majority, but also the ability of its elected leadership to convert a winning electoral coalition into a successful governing plurality. To be effective, that plurality has to cross constituency, institutional, and sometimes even partisan lines, a reason why the composition of coalitions shift, issue by issue.

Do elections serve government? Yes, they do. They renew and reinforce the link between the elected and the electorate. They contribute to policy direction, coalition building, and legitimacy for and accountability in government. But they do so imperfectly and often indirectly, and they sometimes impede rather than enhance the compromises and consensus building necessary for governing effectively.

Now It's Your Turn

Discussion Questions

1. Is the election of candidates who are more ideologically and politically polarized a good or bad development for American democracy? Explain why or why not.

2. How would federal elections have to be changed if the electorate were given the opportunity to vote on national issues rather than just on the candidates running for office? Would the meaning of elections be clearer and governing made easier by issue referenda?

3. Can representative government and collective responsibility be strengthened at the same time?

4. How do elections affect the permanent government: the bureaucracy and the federal judiciary?

5. Now that you have completed this book, how would you answer the question, "Is this any way to run a democratic election?" What are the principal strengths and weaknesses of the U.S. electoral system from a democratic perspective?

Topics for Debate
Challenge or defend the following statements:

1. To enhance responsiveness and accountability in government, all elected public officials should stand for reelection at the same time.

2. The electorate should be given the opportunity to express its opinion on the ten most salient issues when voting in national elections.

3. No president shall be removed from office except by a special election of the American people.

4. All candidates for the presidency should be required to announce their choices for their cabinet and senior White House aides at least one month before the election.

5. All new public officials should be required to take a course on the structure and operations of the institution to which they were elected or appointed.

6. All voters should be required to know the basic positions of the major candidates for office.

Exercises

1. Upset by the gap between democratic theory and practice, a presidential commission has been studying ways to make American elections more compatible with the goals of a democratic political system. The commission has identified three objectives that it hopes any new electoral process will achieve:

   a. increase voter knowledge about the candidates and the issues;
   b. increase candidate knowledge of the opinions of their constituents;
   c. increase citizen participation in the electoral process.

   Recommend changes to the American electoral system that would make it more compatible with these democratic goals.

2. List the major campaign promises that the Democratic and Republican presidential candidates made in the most recent election. You can find these promises on their Web sites as well as those of most major news organizations.

   Determine, if you can,

   a. how the candidates prioritized these promises,
   b. which of them the election winner has tried to achieve in office, and
   c. how successful that president has been in fulfilling campaign promises.

   (Hint: Check the Web site Politifact.com, www.politifact.com/truth-o-meter/promises, for data that will help you with your analysis.)

INTERNET RESOURCES

Most major media sources report the large election exit poll in detail. The Gallup Organization (www.gallup.com) as well as the Pew Research Center for the People and the Press (www.people-press.org) conduct preelection and postelection surveys and make the results available on their Web sites. For a longitudinal analysis, the preelection and postelection surveys from the American National Election Studies (www.electionstudies.org) are the principal data source on which most political scientists depend when analyzing elections.

SELECTED READINGS

Abramson, Paul R., John H. Aldrich, and David W. Rohde. *Change and Continuity in the 2008 and 2010 Elections*. Washington, DC: CQ Press, 2012.

Cohen, Jeffrey E. "The 2008 Presidential Election, Parts I and II." *Presidential Studies Quarterly* 40 (June and September 2010): 230–309, 387–514.

Conley, Patricia Heidotting. *Presidential Mandates: How Elections Shape the National Agenda*. Chicago, IL: University of Chicago Press, 2001.

Dahl, Robert A. "Myth of the Presidential Mandate." *Political Science Quarterly* 105 (1990): 355–372.

Fishel, Jeff. *Presidents and Promises*. Washington, DC: CQ Books, 1985.

Ginsberg, Benjamin, and Alan Stone, eds. *Do Elections Matter?* Armonk, NY: M. E. Sharpe, 1996.

Jacobson, Gary C. "Polarized Politics and the 2004 Congressional and Presidential Elections." *Political Science Quarterly* 120 (2005): 199–218.

—. "The 2008 Presidential and Congressional Elections: Anti-Bush Referendum and Prospects for the Democratic Majority." *Political Science Quarterly* 124 (Spring 2009): 1–30.

Miller, Arthur H., and Martin P. Wattenberg. "Throwing the Rascals Out: Policy and Performance Evaluations of Presidential Candidates, 1952–1980." *American Political Science Review* 79 (1985): 359–372.

Nelsen, Michael E., ed. *The Elections of 2012*. Los Angeles, CA: Sage/CQ Press, 2013.

Popkin, Samuel L. *The Reasoning Voter*. Chicago, IL: University of Chicago Press, 1991.

Wattenberg, Martin, ed. "2004 Presidential Election." *Presidential Studies Quarterly* 36 (2006): 141–296.

Wayne, Stephen J. *The Road to the White House 2012*. Boston, MA: Wadsworth/Cengage Learning, 2013.

NOTES

1. The term "a government of strangers" was first suggested by Hugh Heclo in his book *A Government of Strangers* (Washington, DC: Brookings Institution, 1977).

2. For an excellent discussion of the differences between campaigning for and governing in the presidency, see Charles O. Jones, *Passages to the Presidency* (Washington, DC: Brookings Institution, 1998).

3. A good example of the latter is Dick Morris, who came to President Clinton's aid after the Democrats' defeat in the 1994 midterm elections. Morris, who engineered Clinton's reelection victory, had previously worked as a political consultant for Clinton in his third campaign for the Arkansas governorship, as well as for such conservative Republicans as Trent Lott, the Senate Republican leader, and Jesse Helms, a senator from North Carolina.

4. Like the candidate they supported, they also may have little executive experience and be unfamiliar with the formal and informal procedures of the institution to which their candidate has been elected and with the people who work there.

5. Although senior members of the Reagan administration did not fall into this morass with the political establishment, they did do so with civil servants who staffed the federal bureaucracy. Reagan and his supporters distrusted the federal government, particularly the bureaucracy, and they tried to circumvent it when putting their priority proposals in place. The problem was that Reagan's newly appointed department heads and their aides lacked the expertise to get things done. Over time, most of Reagan's political appointees grew to depend on and respect the civil servants who worked for them.

6. *U.S. Term Limits, Inc. v. Thornton,* 514 U.S. 779 (1995).

7. In addition to policy initiatives placed on the ballot by citizen petition, some states also have a procedure known as a referendum, which allows a state legislature to put questions and previously enacted legislation directly on the ballot for a vote.

8. Federal courts in California found both initiatives unconstitutional.

9. The one measure that was approved prohibited certain state officials from getting salary increases when the budget was in deficit.

10. Others have turned to initiatives to change policy, gain recognition, and even make money. Bill Sizemore has used the initiative process in Oregon probably more than any other state resident. He placed numerous initiatives on election ballots. Sizemore runs a business that collects signatures for ballot initiatives, so he makes money and tries to affect public policy at the same time. He also used his visibility in the state to run for governor in 1998, but he was defeated. Richard J. Ellis, "The States: Direct Democracy," in *The Elections of 2000,* edited by Michael Nelson (Washington, DC: CQ Press, 2001), 143–145.

11. *Buckley v. American Constitutional Law Foundation,* 97 U.S. 930 (1999).

12. Initiative and Referendum Institute, University of Southern California. wwwlandrinstitute. org/IRI%20Intitiative%20Use%20(2012–1).pdf

13. For issues to be an important influence on voting behavior, voters must have an opinion about them, perceive differences in the candidates' positions, and then vote on the basis of these differences and in the direction of their own policy preferences.

14. There was one-party control at the beginning of George W. Bush's administration, but it lasted for only five months until July 2001, when Senator James Jeffords, in a series of disputes with the Bush administration, defected from the Republican Party.

15. Take George W. Bush following his 2004 election victory. Bush believed that his reelection ended Iraq as a political issue and gave him political capital to pursue his second-term domestic policy priorities: a national energy policy, the partial privatization of Social Security, tax reform, a new immigration policy, and an extension of his first-term tax cuts. Exit polls, however, offered little evidence that these priorities were on voters' minds on election day, much less were the primary reasons that Bush won reelection. Had the president not misread the meaning of the election, he might have saved himself the political embarrassment of failing to achieve most of these policy goals.

16. The random selection is made within states in such a way that principal geographic units (cities, suburbs, and rural areas) and a precinct's size and past voting record are taken into account. Approximately 1,200 representatives of the polling organization administer the poll to voters who are chosen in a systematic way (for example, every fourth or fifth person) as they leave the voting booths. Voters are asked to complete a questionnaire (thirty to forty items) designed to elicit information on voting choices, political attitudes, candidate evaluations and feelings about candidates, and the demographic characteristics of those who voted. Several times over the course of the day, the questionnaires are collected and tabulated, and the results are sent to a central computer bank. After most or all of the election polls in a state have closed, the findings of the exit poll are made public. Over the course of the evening, they are adjusted to reflect the actual results as they are tabulated.

17. "The Building Blocks of Re-election," *New York Times,* November 11, 2012, p. SR 7. http:// elections.nytimes.com/2008/results/president/exit-polls.html.

18. "Trends A-Z: Healthcare System," Gallup Poll. http://www.gallup.com/poll/4708/Healthcare-System.aspx

INDEX

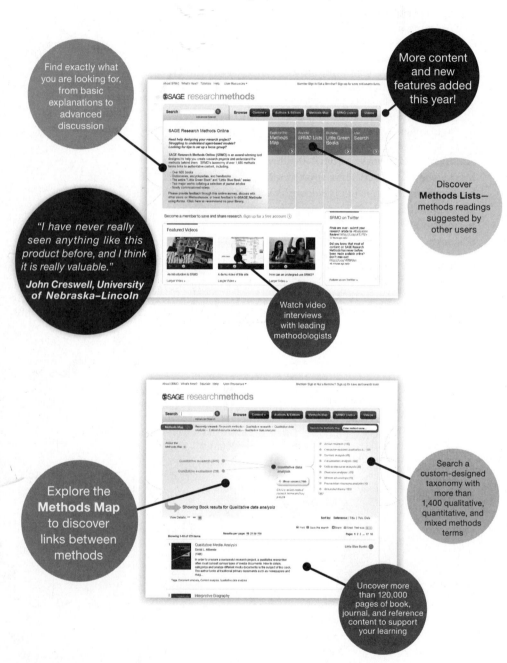